Terrible Beauty

ELEPHANT – HUMAN – IVORY

Terrible **Beauty**

ELEPHANT – HUMAN – IVORY

HIRMER

Contents

Ivory and Its Elephant

HARTMUT DORGERLOH AND LAURA GOLDENBAUM

"When wood breaks it can be repaired, but an ivory break is for good."
(Yoruba adage, West Africa)

A group of white elephants. They are pacing in single file, close behind one another and graduated in size, proudly holding their heads and trunks high (Fig. 1). This fragile and delightfully lifelike carving was recently offered on an art and antiquities website. The price: 5,000 euros.[1] While the movement of these elephants is lively, the origin of the material from which they are made remains unfathomable— what you don't see: that the column of eight animals roughly 70 centimeters (27.5 in) long was carved from a single elephant tusk. This is evident in the slight curve of the base the elephants stand on and in their graduated sizes.

The use of ivory as a material necessarily involves the slaughter of an elephant. It is the substance of its powerful tusk, which it does not surrender voluntarily and without a fight. The website fails to tell us when the elephant was killed, or when and by whom the carving was made. All that is certain is that, like an incredible number of elephants before it, this one had to lose its life, and, like all the others, survives as a mere vestige of itself in this artfully worked and extremely durable material. Human hands have transformed its tooth into exquisite beauty, into a moving, especially sumptuous image with an increasing monetary value.

---

*When "ivory" is mentioned in the captions of this book and not more closely defined, then the reference is always to "elephant ivory."

1 Elephant herd (eight elephants), ivory*, ca. 70 × 9 cm.

Why does this material, one of the earliest to have been employed in the fine arts, have such an attraction—a fascination nearly as old as human culture itself? Possibly because in no other material aside from bone are the grandeur and power of a living creature reflected in the lifeless object; and because the preciousness of the unique biological life, a creature as much as four meters (13 feet) high, seven meters (23 feet) from trunk to tail, and weighing up to six tons, further heightens the value of the unique artistic form. Also, each piece of this organic material from its tusk, which can weigh on average up to 45 kilos (100 lb), is unique. It has its own creation story.

But on the seller's website we read: "As a material, ivory is not of any particular worth. It is mainly the artistry in ivory carvings that determines their value."[2] But is it not far more than that?

This question suggests itself not only when we look at the row of carved elephants. It is already raised by a delicate Stone Age mammoth figure only 3.7 centimeters (1.5 in) long (see Fig. 5, p. 27) that is included in the Humboldt Forum's exhibition *Terrible Beauty: Elephant–Human–Ivory*, and it is the question that prompted this book. Ivory and the millennia-old art of carving it are here viewed from a number of different perspectives: Why is precisely this material so highly valued? What links humans to elephants? And what has changed in this relationship over the course of time? What does this mean for the people who live with elephants, and how does the poaching of ivory threaten the very existence of the species?

Consideration of the elephant–human–ivory relationship leads to a recognition of the long history of the use of ivory—and of the exploitation of elephants as a disposable resource in the value system of colonialism during the Industrial Age and the height of imperialism. This brings us to our present-day globalized world and points out the production of dependencies and inequalities here as well. This book also directs our gaze to the structures of colonized, commercialized territories, in addition to the relationship between people and animals. Fundamentally, it is this relationship that lies at the bottom of the fateful simultaneity of appropriation and loss with which the dynamic of appreciation and depreciation is connected. In this way, the captivating beauty of ivory art confronts us with the injustice, with the suppression and violence, that are directly associated with the "extraction" of the material and the trade in it, as well as with the works of art made from it.

The study of ivory objects therefore goes far beyond simple admiration for and fascination with these virtuosic creations. It raises fundamental questions and touches on manifold issues—our treatment of nature; the archaeology of human cultures; the spiritual, intellectual, symbolic, material, aesthetic, and artistic values and qualities of this unique organic raw material and supposed medium; the effects of craftwork and mass-production; the pressing and increasingly demanding challenges of species protection and nature preservation using the example of the relationship between humans and elephants; and the animal's symbolism and usefulness, as well as its relevance for the ecosystem.

On the one hand, the high esteem in which ivory has been held is directly based on fear of these massive, powerful animals and on the mystical notions people have associated with their huge tusks. Ivory came to stand for concentrated energy. Thus implicit in the artistic carving of ivory is the conquest of wild nature, the taming and appropriation of the inexhaustible energy of this strange species, the elephant. On the other hand, ivory has been valued as a raw material that is especially durable yet soft and fine-textured. Even the tiniest, filigree details can be created in it using blades, drills, and graving tools. Like virtually no other material, it has stimulated virtuosity in craftwork and provided enhanced aesthetic delight. In it, forms and backgrounds can be artfully combined, faces rendered with the most fleeting expressions. Figures in ivory, as opposed to ponderous, brittle, and large-grained stone, can be supported by the slenderest of load-bearing elements, so that they appear to be light as a feather, as though standing on tiptoe. Its warm, milky color, its especially soft surface, and its netlike, organic markings make it particularly well suited for depictions of human figures. Ivory can be polished to such a mirrorlike smoothness that fine-limbed, shimmering bodies can even appear to be perspiring.

Whether Stone Age artifact, cosmetic jar, or furniture ornament from Mesopotamia, whether colossal deity statue from ancient Greece, consular diptych from ancient Rome, reliquary shrine or pax from the Christian Middle Ages, chessmen from the Viking era, royal gong from Benin, hunting horn from Sierra Leone, Mithuna figure from Srirangam, miracle sphere, ornamental vessel, or portrait bust from the European Baroque, netsuke figurine from Japan, or Baule mask from the Côte d'Ivoire—artistically carved ivory objects have an altogether special radiance.

There appears to be something hyperphysical, transcendental inherent in such objects, something that assures protection and strength, healing, special powers and good fortune to those who come to possess them.

Just as humans have associated manifold meanings with ivory, so they have ascribed the most varied functions and roles to the elephant itself: it is both exotic marvel and monster, entertainer and artist, slave and servant, competitor for food, enemy, weapon in warfare, worker, hunting trophy and quarry, mount, power symbol, political issue, faithful companion, temple guard, and god.

As a mythical beast and object of religious worship, in South and South East Asia especially, the elephant is not only an important working animal. In Hindu cosmology, the entire weight of the world rests on the backs of the eight "world elephants", called *Dikpalas*, among them Airavata, the first elephant created and the sacred white mount of the creator god Indra. Airavata is a symbol of good fortune and bringer of rain, depicted with three heads and four tusks.

2 Will Burrard-Lucas, *Elephant Queen*, Elephant cow tusker F_MU1, died 2017, photo 2017, from the book *Land of Giants* (2019).

In Buddhism, the elephant is a symbolic figure especially worthy of veneration, for the Buddha himself lived seven previous lives as an elephant. It is the embodiment of unlimited power, its strength infused with the wisdom with which it effortlessly overcomes obstacles. It stands for a noble gentleness, a rest on one's journey, and spiritual strength. A white elephant protects against all manner of evils, and even played a role in the Buddha's conception: his mother Mayadevi dreamt of a white elephant with lotus blossoms as tusks, which encircled her three times and pierced through her right side. When Mayadevi awoke, she was pregnant.

One of the best known and most beloved Hindu dieties is the potbellied Ganesh. He is equally venerated by Hindus, Jains, and Buddhists. As a composite creature half man, half elephant, he is credited with special divine powers—the god of good fortune, master of obstacles and of all beginnings. Seeing how friendly and contented he appears to be, who could think of the dead elephant that brought him back to life and whose severed head he has worn since his youth?

The cynical ignorance that limits the elephant to its "usefulness" as a provider of raw material for art has today nearly caused its extinction. Even its name is derived from the material: ἐλέφας in Greek means "ivory". Bertolt Brecht takes this to the extreme when he has his Mr Keuner describe his favorite animal: "When Mr. K. was asked which animal he esteemed above all others, he named the elephant and justified his choice as follows: […] He has a thick skin, knives snap in it; but he has a gentle disposition. He can become sad. He can become angry. […] He dies in a thicket. […] He is gray and conspicuous because of his bulk. He is not edible. He can work hard. […] He does his bit for art: he supplies ivory."[3]

More ivory – Fewer elephants

The history of the largest land mammal and only living proboscidian reaches much farther back than that of humans—but it could end in only a few decades if the mass killing and displacement of wild elephants from their habitat is not stopped. The elephant originated in Africa, probably as early as the Miocene, some seven million years ago, as did the much younger *Homo sapiens* roughly 315,000 years ago. The mammoth, some 20 million years old, an ancestor of the elephant, reached western and northern Eurasia and North America. It is now hard to imagine that the European forest elephant, a hairy giant some four meters (13 feet) tall, once roamed through Europe—from the Mediterranean to Great Britain—even before *Homo sapiens* reached the Atlantic coast of the Iberian Peninsula.

The Humboldt Forum's two namesakes, Wilhelm and Alexander von Humboldt, may never have seen an elephant in the wild, but they were surely familiar with ivory. Their thirst for knowledge and their curiosity about the world-famous giant did not stop them. In Philadelphia in 1804, Alexander von Humboldt saw the skeleton of the famous "Peale's Mastodon", and supported the nascent American archaeology, which had excavated the elephant fossil on the bank of the Hudson River in 1801, in its contention that American fauna was by no means degenerate, as Europeans, in their superiority, had formerly maintained. The discovery of the huge bones proved otherwise, and was for President Thomas Jefferson an event of national importance.

The only three species still living in the wild, the African savannah elephant, the African forest elephant, and the Asian elephant, have lost huge tracts of their original distribution. The Asian elephant was at home on nine million square kilometers, all of Asia from west to east. Until the Middle Ages, the African elephant ranged across the entire African continent up to the Mediterranean coast.

Along with a globalized traffic in human slaves in Africa, ivory became a commodity exported in great quantities. The name Côte d'Ivoire (Ivory Coast), formerly called the Zahnküste (Tusk Coast) in German, refers to what was for a long time, beginning in the 15th century, the country's most important export and the main transshipment point for ivory. The Côte d'Ivoire was one of West Africa's most important export centers, along with Benin and the coast from Camaroon to Angola—primarily in trade with Portugal. Beginning in the 17th century, this market was dominated by France. In 1893, the Côte d'Ivoire became a French colony, and in 1895 part of French West Africa; it gained its independence as the Republic of Côte d'Ivoire in 1960.

By the end of the 19th century, the elephant was a common exotic in Europe, exhibited in zoos and ethnological shows, and moreover, as the composer Johannes Brahms ironically noted, was "a dangerous animal, for piano keys are made from its tusks". At that time, colonial exploitation of Africa was at its height, and with it the demand for ivory. Colonial dominance found its confirmation in the subjugation of species and ethnicities, in transnational supply chains, in the exhibition of exotic animals, and in massive imports of their body parts as raw materials. In parallel with the slave trade, ivory, or "white gold", became a colonial trophy, a status symbol.

With the ban on the transatlantic slave trade, the colonial powers, in their hunger for profits, switched to the import of rubber and ivory, which showed enormous growth rates in Europe. By the end of the 19th century, an average of 850 tons of ivory were shipped to Europe and America each year—for broad outlets and the mass production of

such everyday objects as knife and cutlery handles, combs, piano keys, billiard balls, cosmetic jars, glove stretchers, and doorknobs. Of this immense quantity, "only" six tons of raw material were transformed by ivory carvers into art objects, for example in "the ivory city Erbach" in the Odenwald, Germany. It is estimated that the 19th-century ivory craze cost some 20 million African elephants their lives.

It was only about 50 years ago that people around the world began to rethink this issue and to reverse this historical and highly dubious understanding of value between the poles of availability and shortage occasioned by the almost inexorable disappearance of the gray giants in Africa and Asia, the alarming "decimation of the resource elephant"— blamed on climate change and the increasing scarcity of water, on loss of habitat, and on global trade in ivory worth billions. Whereas at the beginning of the 20th century some three to five million elephants still roamed the savannahs and forests of Africa, today there are only some 400,000 left, limited to the territories south of the Sahara in southern and eastern Africa. Between 1970 and 1989 alone, 700,000 animals, half the population at the time, were killed. In that same period, as many as 62,000 elephants died from poaching in East Africa each year. More than 80 percent of the trade in ivory was concentrated on the Far East. Yet nature is responding to the centuries-long hunt for ivory with its own evasive shrewdness: it is noted that in Africa increasing numbers of elephants are born, owing to their exploitation by humans, with only rudimentary tusks or no tusks at all.

Especially old elephants, of majestic size and with powerful tusks reaching down to the ground and weighing as much as 55 kilos (120 lb), called "big tuskers", are now rarities in Africa. It is said that only some 30 to 40 individuals have escaped the greed for tusks. One of them, the 60-year-old elephant cow named F_MU1, "the Elephant Queen", was pictured by the British photographer Will Burrard-Lucas shortly before her natural death at a waterhole—an impressive colossus that, with great self-assurance, completely fills the center of the picture, commanding distance and respect, a majestic vision scarred by life (Fig. 2).[4]

Since only the bulls of Asian elephants develop tusks, and these are much smaller, the existence of animals living in the wild in South and South East Asia, including the Malay Islands, is threatened not so much by ivory hunters as by diminishing habitat, the result of an explosive consumption of space and resources, whether through deforestation or ongoing settlement. Several of the countries in which the Asian elephant is endemic are among the poorest in the world. Raging conflicts with these large animals directly impact people in need.[5]

In nearly all Asian countries, shrinking elephant populations point to the demise of the species. Laos once called itself Lane Xang, the "Land of the Million Elephants"; today it has around 850 animals, only 400 of them living in the wild. 15,000 elephants live in captivity on the Asian continent, while the number of wild elephants varies between 25,000 and 35,000, half of them in India. Even with such depressing figures, these regions are among the remaining core areas on the Earth in which the elephant species has been able to survive, in which it is tolerated and protected as a wild animal going about its own business.

Since 1973, Asian and African elephants have been considered endangered species threatened with extinction. All international commercial trade in live elephants and their body parts has been officially banned.[6] Within the framework of the CITES treaty, trade in ivory has been strictly banned since 1990. In 2018, the United Kingdom passed its own restrictive legislation, prohibiting the sale or purchase of ivory objects regardless of age and origin. Since the law went into effect in 2019, there have been heated debates: regarding protection of the nation's cultural heritage and the issue of dealing responsibly with relics of the colonial period in European museum collections, as well as the protection of the animal and plant worlds and the expansion of animal rights. In addition, there is the uncomfortable question of whether nature conservation financed with "White money" is not a continuation of colonial practices, just like the related safari tourism.

Given these facts, the ivory carving of a row of elephants described above stands for both "beauty" and the "terrible". As an artwork it is moving, yet it is nonetheless offensive in its evocation of destructive as well as constructive forces.

Displaying ivory at the Humboldt Forum?

From this brief overview of the manifold uses of ivory, it is clear why the Humboldt Forum is devoting one of its first major exhibitions to it.

As a new cultural center with global collections, exhibitions, and interests, it hopes to provide orientation in a complex, increasingly confusing time, to promote different perspectives, to bridge cultural differences, and, without bias, to create room for thought and action. Specific issues and assumptions, especially when they illuminate the diversity and complexity of our history and our present day and age, contribute to these efforts, though we can approach them only piecemeal, and imperfectly.

Thus in its first year the Humboldt Forum is examining a highly complex triangular relationship: elephant–human–ivory. It is a challenge that engages all the possibilities and core concerns of this new space for culture and science, dialogue and debate. And, ultimately, it raises the sensitive question of whether it is appropriate for a museum to display ivory objects nowadays at all.[7]

Any ivory object evokes any number of pressing, even painful, issues that trouble our globalized present, that lead into the past, and that provide a glimpse of a conceivable future. Exhibitions should do far more than simply display historical objects; they should stimulate discussion. The collections of the Staatliche Museen zu Berlin, the Ethnologisches Museum, and the Museum für Asiatische Kunst, all of which are moving into the Humboldt Forum at the end of 2021, furnish the materials with which, in collaboration with all the Humboldt Forum's participating institutions, and drawing on their expertise and perspectives, we hope to promote continuing engagement with these problematic issues. With them, we attempt to provide examples of the art connoisseur's limited view of ivory objects and to counter it, to point to "the elephant in the room", as it were. This delightful metaphor for the touchy subject one prefers to overlook, whether out of fear or complacency, is here particularly apt.[8] The exhibition *Terrible Beauty: Elephant–Human–Ivory* and the present book trace the carved ivory object through the centuries and back to the elephant.

No one provides a closer look at the animal's massive body than Asher Jay in her photo series *Half Remembered Past*. Its leathery skin, laced with a network of deep fissures, resembles a whole landscape well worth exploring. In eye contact with the beast, the viewer begins to sense what it could be like being an elephant.

Nicholas J. Conard takes us back to the beginnings, to the inception of art, music, and religion, and focuses on mammoth-ivory artifacts more than 40,000 years old. Kathy Curnow's essay traces the history of elephants, ivory carving, and trade in ivory in Benin back into the 15th century. Harald Floss and Sibylle Wolf add a further facet to the definition of the *conditio humana*: using the example of the use of ivory, they discuss the violent introduction of an exploitative mentality in *Homo sapiens*

3 Dying elephant, stage sculpture, length ca. 10 m, for Giuseppe Verdi's opera *Otello*, Festspielhaus Baden-Baden, 2019 (staging: Robert Wilson, stage sculpture: Ralf Schira).

in the Late Paleolithic, some 40,000 years ago. Sarah M. Guérin's text deals with ivory's changing symbolism and iconography from the beginning up into the late Middle Ages. Interviews with the Chinese artist Ai Weiwei, Robert Kless from the International Fund for Animal Welfare (IFAW), and Khyne U Mar, a veterinarian and activist from Myanmar, consider what it is that makes ivory so attractive, how to imagine future coexistence between people and elephants if a given habitat has to be shared by both species, and whether socially responsible museums should exhibit ivory objects at all. Lydia Kitungulu writes about the ivory collection in the National Museum of Kenya and the role of post-colonial museums, while Lars-Christian Koch explains how ivory has been used throughout history in the making of musical instruments of all kinds.

With its varied program, the Humboldt Forum hopes to appeal to a broad public, especially young people. In its efforts to inform and to educate, it places great importance on working with children. Two contributions reflect this desire to let children and young people take part in the planning of an exhibition and to incorporate their perspectives. For "An Ivory ABC", pupils from a Berlin elementary school near the Humboldt Forum provided texts and drawings on subjects from the "Asian Elephant" to "Zaire". David McKee, the British creator of the children's book *Elmer the Patchwork Elephant*, which has been translated into more than 50 languages, talks about how even in small ways

we can make this world more just and livable for both humans and animals.

Along with ivory's unique composition, one has to consider its tactile qualities. There is something about the feel of ivory that closely links it to the human body, the consequences of which are shown by Alberto Saviello. Nanette Snoep emphasizes the urgent need to consider the problems posed by ivory artifacts so as to renegotiate and define how museum should deal with them. In doing so, she relates the history of ethnographic displays produced in a time of colonial expansion and intended to confront Europeans and Americans with supposed "others". Stephanie Marek Muller points out the direct connection between the exploitation of humans and animals in the interests of colonialism, which involves racism and speciesism. She challenges us to deal with exhibited ivory objects sensitively and critically, and to engage in an emancipatory process of decolonization that takes into account both people and animals. Katharina Trump, in turn, focuses on the elephant itself, a complex social being whose very existence is greatly threatened. Fritz Vollrath writes about how people and elephants can live together as free of conflict as possible, namely with the help of judiciously introduced colonies of bees. Finally, Dorothee Wenner considers the elephant's appearance in films, reviewing the involuntary career of a non-human-species that illustrates how little we know about this animal deprived of its rights.

4 Bharti Kher, *The Skin Speaks a Language Not Its Own*, 2006, a life-size elephant made of fiberglass, 148 × 432 × 183 cm.

5 Bharti Kher, *The Skin Speaks a Language Not Its Own* (detail).

Elephant and ivory in contemporary art

In today's politicized art, the tragic figure and haunting protest image of the dying elephant is taking the place of its tusks, in the form of the artfully shaped ivory object, in exhibition spaces. Ivory carving belongs to the past. Like the writing on the wall, for some years now the suffering of the fallen giant has become a universal symbol of a sick world, a profound, worldwide unease that the French writer Romain Gary tried to capture in 1967 in his "Letter to an African Elephant": "In my eyes, dear Elephant, sir, you represent to perfection everything that is threatened today with extinction in the name of progress, efficiency, ideology, materialism, or even reason, for a certain abstract, inhuman use of reason and logic are becoming more and more allies of our murderous folly. It seems clear today that we have been merely doing to other species, and to yours in the first place, what we are on the verge of doing to ourselves."[9]

In contemporary art, the elephant has been selected as the herald of comprehensive global changes and imponderables in times of climate change, species extinction, and economic and political upheavals. A few selected examples serve to illustrate this phenomenon.

Robert Wilson's staging of Verdi's opera *Otello* in Baden-Baden in 2019 featured the corpse of a huge elephant lying on its side created by the sculptor Ralf Schira, and a blow-up of the fading eye of a dying elephant (Fig. 3). In Douglas Gordon's 2003 video installation *Play Dead; Real Time (this way, that way, the other way)*, the trained elephant cow Minnie is forced to lie on her side and stand up again while the camera almost voyeuristically circles her body and captures details of her body movements in close-up.[10]

In her sculptural work *The Skin Speaks a Language Not Its Own* (2006), the artist Bharti Kher, London-born but living in India since 1992, had a lifesize fiberglass elephant cow collapse enfeebled in the middle of an exhibition space designed as a white cube (Fig. 4). "Despite our familiarity with elephants, nothing prepares the viewer for the emotional experience of seeing Kher's elephant, huge and incongruous in the gallery space. With her head resting on the front foot, she is brought down to our level and her glassy black eye entreats a communion and proximity rarely encountered in the wild."[11]

The body of the elephant cow is painted with countless white *bindis*, the little dots the Hindu faithful wear in the center of their forehead. A *bindi* marks the energetic third eye, the sixth chakra and seat of esoteric wisdom. In Bharti Kher's work they are seen in an altered form with a sperm-shaped tail (Fig. 5). On the elephant's skin they form an overall pattern, one that electrifies the surface and sets it into a vortex of motion. The formation of these *bindi* lends the deflated body of the elephant cow an expression of indecisiveness, of transformation. It is surrounded by a palpable reserve of energy that augurs continuation and could be a promise of hope.

Whereas the renderings of a collapsed elephant by Bharti Kher and Ralf Schira dispense with iconic tusks, in the work of the Algerian artist Adel Abdessemed ivory takes the form of a mute cry—one could imagine it to be a last one.[12] Under the title *Cri* (2012), the terror behind a white, gleaming, seemingly innocent façade increases the horror of the picture motif. That motif was derived from the world-famous newspaper photograph by the 21-year-old Huỳnh Công Út, called Nick Uts, dated June 8, 1972, here rendered in three dimensions. The picture of the Vietnamese girl Kim Phúc has burned itself into the visual memory of "all who have seen it".[13] It became a collective visual experience. Her burning clothes already torn from her body and her mouth open in a desperate scream, she runs toward the photographer, stark naked, in the center of the picture, fleeing the napalm bombs reducing the village behind her to rubble and ashes. There is no going back.

Faithfully translated into three dimensions, *Cri* becomes the embodiment of a scream, the nine-year-old's body a cruel spasm. Her fragile arms are bent at her sides in a magical pose, as if she were trying to escape from her burning skin. This image of horror is further convulsed by the unreal elegance and gracefulness of her gestures: she resembles a dancer in her trancelike state of uncertainty. Expanded into three dimensions, she appears to want to shake off the very material she is made of—she does not want to touch herself. Here the alabaster quality of ivory seems as vulnerable as the girl's shimmering skin in the photograph. The figure is now actually running toward the viewers, their bodies are sharing the same space, so that viewers of the ivory sculpture become shocked participants—finally.

1 Kunst- und Antiquitätenbörse, www.kunst-antikboerse.de/angebot.php?detail=Hochwertige+Elfenbeinschnitzerei&id=1068 (accessed January 31, 2021).
2 Ibid.
3 Bertolt Brecht, *Stories of Mr. Keuner*, tr. Martin Chalmers, San Francisco: City Lights Books, 2001, p. 31.
4 See https://photos.willbl.com/big-tusker/ (accessed January 21, 2021).
5 This is described in the "human-elephant-conflict" (HEC) statistic. See: B.M.A. Oswin Perera, "The Human-Elephant-Conflict: A Review of Current Status and Mitigation Methods", *Gajah* 30 (2009), pp. 41–52.
6 Convention on International Trade in Endangered Species (CITES). See https://cites.org/eng (accessed March 18, 2021).
7 Caroline Good, Peter Tyrrell, Zhaomin Zhou, and David W. Macdonald, "Elephants never forget, should art museums remember too? Historic ivory collections as ambassadors for conservation education", *Biodiversity and Conservation* 28 (2019), pp. 1331–1342; online at: https://doi.org/10.1007/s10531-019-01735-6 (accessed February 3, 2021).
8 It presumably goes back to Ivan Andreyevich Krylov's fable "The Inquisitive Man", from 1814, the story of a man who during his visit to a natural history museum pores over the displays of the tiniest insects but fails to notice the exhibited elephant. See Jessica Ullrich, "Der Elefant im Raum", in: Sabine Schulze and Dennis Conrad, (eds), *Tiere. Respekt, Harmonie, Unterwerfung*, exh. cat. Museum für Kunst und Gewerbe Hamburg, Munich 2017, p. 252, note 1.
9 Romain Gary, "Letter to an African Elephant", *Life Magazine*, December 22, 1967; later published as "Monsieur et cher éléphant", *Le Figaro Littéraire*, March 1968. English text is available online at: https://www.les-racines-du-ciel.com/en/journal-mode-ethique-femme/romain-garys-letter-to-an-elephant/ (accessed March 17, 2021).
10 Douglas Gordon, video installation *Play Dead; Real Time (this way, that way, the other way)*, 2003, 2 projections, 1 video screen, 19:16 minutes, 14:44 minutes, 23:44 minutes, MMK Museum für moderne Kunst, Frankfurt am Main. See https://www.tate.org.uk/art/artworks/gordon-play-dead-real-time-this-way-that-way-the-other-way-al00339 (accessed January 31, 2021).
11 Zara Porter-Hill, Director of the Indian Department of Sotheby's auction house, quoted in Mark Brown, "Sotheby's to auction Bharti Kher's Indian elephant", *The Guardian*, May 24, 2010: online at: http://www.theguardian.com/artanddesign/2010/may/24/sothebys-auction-bharti-kher-indian-elephant (accessed January 31, 2021).
12 Sadly, it was not possible to obtain permission to reprint this work before going to press. It can be seen at: https://www.adelabdessemed.com/oeuvres/cri/ (accessed March 23, 2021).
13 Gisèle Freund, *Photography & Society*, tr. David R. Godine, Boston: David R. Godine, 1980, p. 216.

AN IVORY ABC

Are human fingernails made of ivory? What does an elephant tusk feel like? These and many other questions were asked by pupils of the City Elementary School, in the heart of Berlin near the Humboldt Forum. Their curiosity, ideas, and questions brought the ten-year-olds into preparations for the exhibition.

The following partially illustrated glossary of terms relating to elephants and ivory was compiled with them. Their contribution to this book, developed as part of an Outreach Project, exemplifies the Humboldt Forum's insistence that its exhibitions and programs be educational.

Asian Elephant
The Asian elephant doesn't look like an African elephant. For example, only the male elephants have visible tusks. And Asian elephants have smaller ears. Sadly, they too are killed for their ivory tusks.

Bull Elephants
The male Asian elephant can stand more than 3 meters (10 feet) tall and weigh more than 4,500 kilos (5 tons).

CITES Treaty
This international treaty protects endangered species all over the world. It regulates or bans international trade in the animals themselves and anything made from them. Today it protects 5,800 animal and 30,000 plant species. In many countries very wonderful animals have become either extinct or greatly endangered owing to illegal hunting.

Dumbo
There once was a little circus elephant who could fly and was very helpful. One day the locomotive pulling the circus train failed to start, so Dumbo flew to a ship and asked the captain whether he would take the animals to their next destination. The captain agreed. When Harry, the hippopotamus, tried to board, the gangway proved too small, but his friends got behind him and pushed him up onto the deck. Lots of other things happened on the ship, but if you want to know what came next you'll have to read the book yourself!

Ears
Elephants use their ears to cool themselves. They pump warm blood into their ears, where it is cooled as they wave their ears like fans. Asian elephants have big ears, but not as big as those of African elephants.

Food

Elephants eat grass, roots, bark, leaves, fruit, twigs, and tubers. They are strictly vegetarian. They require some 200 kilos (440 pounds) of food a day, and at least 70-150 liters (15-30 gallons) of water. To eat they use the end of their trunk to pick up bunches of grass or stalks. They can spend as much as 18 hours a day grazing for food.

Ganesh

Ganesh is an elephant-headed Hindu god, the son of Parvati and Shiva. He is known for overcoming obstacles, and stands for good beginnings. He is especially fond of sweets, so worshippers present them to him as offerings.

Holi Festival

In India's "Festival of Colors" people throw colored powders or dyed water at each other, and for once caste distinctions are disregarded. Elephants are painted in bright colors.

Ivory

Elephant tusks are made of ivory, which is very valuable, and that is why elephants are killed for their tusks. Other sources of ivory are narwhale and walrus tusks and hippopotamus teeth.

Jeopardized

Elephants are greatly in jeopardy because illegal hunters, called poachers, kill them for their tusks, which they then sell for a lot of money.

Kin

Asian and African elephants are related to manatees, or sea cows. And manatees, in turn, are related to hyraxes, which look nothing like them. These are the elephant's only relatives, since its closest one, the mammoth, became extinct some 4,000 years ago.

Lead Cow

In a herd of female elephants the oldest one serves as a lead cow, telling the others when to attack and when to run away. She also helps them find food and water and raise their calves.

Mammoth

In prehistoric times there were several kinds of mammoths, which were early relatives of elephants. Among them were the woolly mammoth and the steppe mammoth. The steppe mammoth could stand 4.7 meters (15.5 feet) tall, but the woolly mammoth was roughly the size of to-day's elephants. They roamed on cold savannahs in the far north and in Western Europe and other warmer regions.

M
Mammut

Es gibt zwei Elefanten der Vorzeit: das Wollhaar-mammut und das Steppenmammut. Das Steppen-mammut wird 4,7 m hoch. Das Wollhaar-mammut ist ungefär so groß wie ein heutiger Elefant und damit kleiner als das Steppenmammut. Mammuts leben in den Kältesavannen aber auch im Westeuropa und anderen wärmeren Gebieten.

Es gibt auch andere Mammutarten

Nose

The elephant's nose takes the form of a long, versatile trunk. With it the elephant not only breathes and drinks, but also places food in its mouth, scratches itself, greets friends, and fends off enemies.

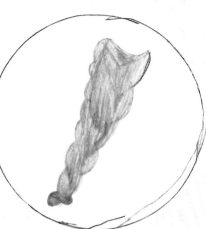

Other facts

Indian elephants were already being used as working animals two thousand years ago. Even in large herds they all know each other. They differ from African elephants in that their backs are rounded or "humped". Once the elephant's molars have worn down for the sixth time, they no longer grow back. And Tusks can never grow back.

Poaching

Because people like ivory jewelry and ornaments, elephants have always been hunted, or poached. In some countries it is still legal.

Question

Does the ban on trade in ivory mean that elephant populations are recovering? Or still in decline?

Rainforest

There are tropical rainforests in Central and South America, Africa, South Asia, and Australia. Forest elephants in Asia and Africa live in such habitats. But most African elephants live on grasslands, or savannahs.

Seeds

Forest elephants can be destructive, eating leaves and fruits and trampling on smaller plants. But the seeds they leave behind in their poop ensure that new plants grow to replace them.

Tusks

Tusks are enlarged, extra long teeth. Elephants use them in many ways: to peel bark from trees, to clear trails, to dig for roots and water, and to brandish as weapons.

Uses for Ivory

Ivory is used in many different ways: carved into figurines, plaques, and all kinds of other decorative objects; turned on lathes to make beads, handles, and knobs; and sawed into thin sheets applied to boxes, furniture, and musical and scientific instruments.

Vishnu

Vishnu, like Ganesh, is a Hindu god. He is held to be responsible for the world's upkeep, assuring a balance between good and evil.

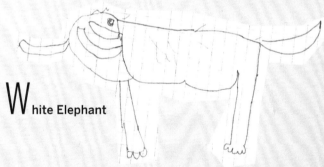

White Elephant

We can't think of anything beginning with *X*

Young

Newborn elephants are called calves. They weigh as much as 120 kilos (265 pounds). Calves suck on their trunks the way little children suck their thumbs.

Zaire

Zaire is home to more African Forest Elephants than any other country. Though they are hunted there as well, some are protected in a number of well-guarded national parks.

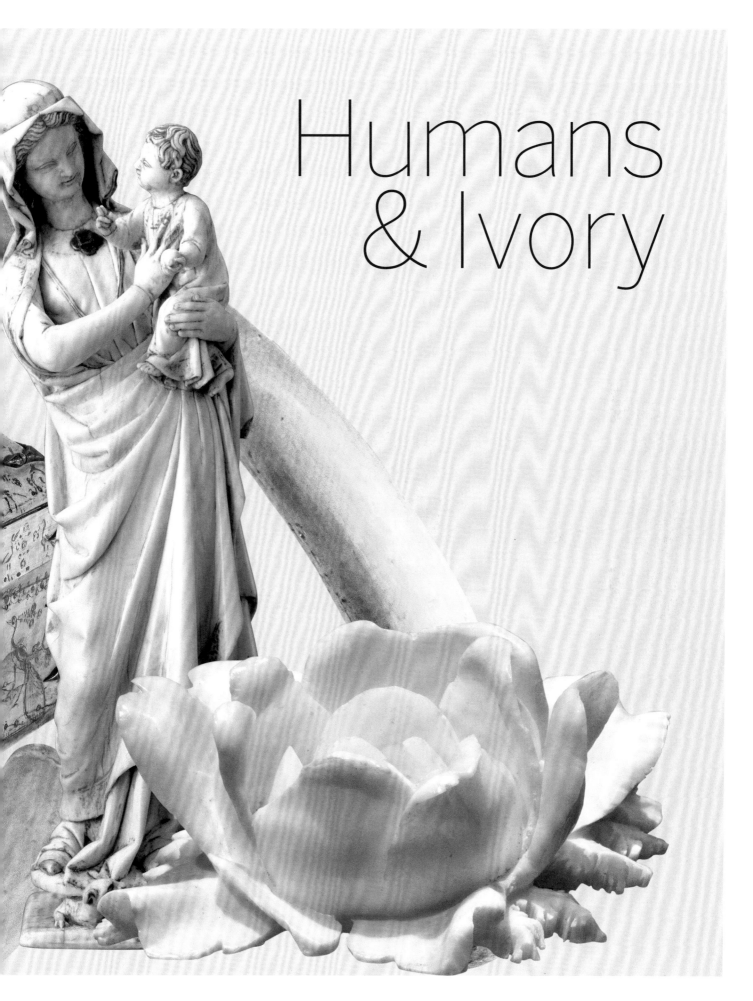

Humans
& Ivory

The Ivory Age

Mammoth Ivory Artifacts from the Swabian Aurignacian Period 40,000 Years Ago, and the Beginnings of Art, Music, and Religion

NICHOLAS J. CONARD

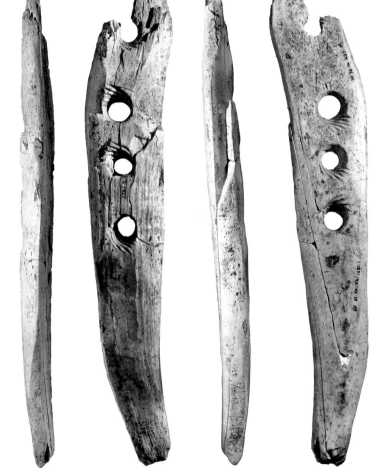

1 Aurignacian rope-making tool, Hohle Fels, mammoth ivory, 20.4 cm. Urgeschichtliches Museum, Blaubeuren.

2 Vogelherd Cave near Niederstotzingen in the Swabian Jura.

One often reads about the Stone Age, the Bronze Age, and even the Chalcolithic or Copper Age, but in the case of the Swabian Aurignacian it would not be out of place to speak of the Ivory Age. When we consider what makes the Aurignacian of the Swabian Jura of southwestern Germany unique and important, most of the key artifacts are made from mammoth ivory. Importantly, many of these finds are of great significance in the context of the evolution of both Paleolithic technology and symbolic behavior. This short essay examines why the concept of an Ivory Age is relevant in this context and presents some of the most remarkable finds of mammoth ivory from this period between roughly 42,000 and 35,000 years ago.

The Swabian ivories

The Swabian Aurignacian dates back 42,000 years, to when anatomically modern humans arrived in the upper reaches of the Danube Valley. The valleys of two tributaries of the Danube not far from the city of Ulm, the Ach and the Lone,[1] are the home to the UNESCO World Cultural Heritage sites of Geißenklösterle, Hohle Fels, Vogelherd (Fig. 2), and Hohlenstein-Stadel.

These sites have produced the earliest and richest assemblages of figurative art, personal ornaments with a culturally dictated form, musical instruments, and depictions of mythical or religious imagery in the form of lionmen. The makers of the Swabian Aurignacian carved all of these classes of finds, as well as numerous tools, from mammoth ivory. Since these artifacts are completely unknown among the many sites of Middle Stone Age modern humans in Africa, one can hypothesize that it was during the course of the spread of modern *Homo sapiens* out of Africa and into Eurasia that these cultural innovations occurred.[2] Whether or not the Upper Danube has a privileged place in human evolution as a key center of innovations is a matter of considerable debate among the proponents of monocentric and polycentric models for cultural evolution.

What is also remarkable about the Paleolithic record of the Swabian Jura is the radical contrast between the material culture of the Neanderthals of the Middle Paleolithic and the artifacts found in the Aurignacian deposits of the region. Neanderthals rarely used mammoth ivory for tools and never carved ivory into figurative art or musical instruments. In fact, there is very limited evidence that Neanderthals produced figurative representations in any medium or possessed a music tradition. This lack of symbolic artifacts could not contrast more sharply with the record from the Swabian Aurignacian, the first period associated with early modern humans in southwestern Germany, in which mammoth ivory formed the preferred material for an enormous range of tools and symbolic artifacts.

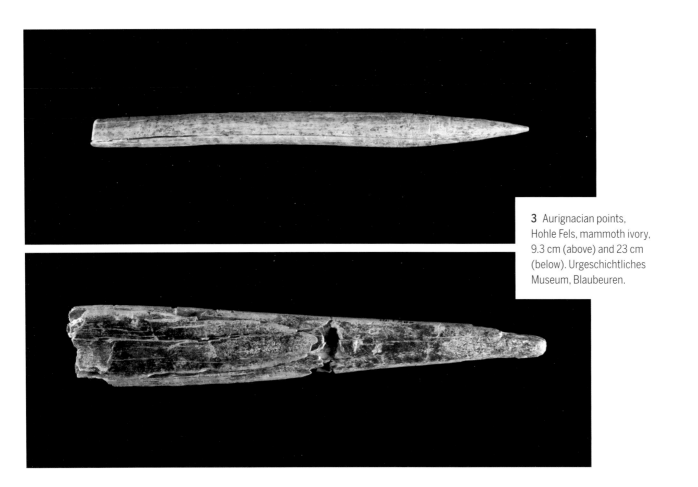

3 Aurignacian points, Hohle Fels, mammoth ivory, 9.3 cm (above) and 23 cm (below). Urgeschichtliches Museum, Blaubeuren.

The Ivory Age was made possible by several key environmental features, together with a wide range of new human adaptations. First, vast areas of the northern hemisphere during the last glacial period of the Ice Age provided the ideal environment for herds of mammoths and a wide array of other Ice Age animals. The paleontologist Dale Guthrie from the University of Alaska coined the term "mammoth steppe" to refer to this rich grassland that was the home of the woolly mammoth and many other Ice Age fauna.[3] Although cold during the winters, the mammoth steppe was also highly productive. Mammoths thrived in the open steppe and represented what is today often called a "keystone species" that played a critical role in creating and maintaining this now extinct ecosystem.

The mammoth steppe represented a challenging environment for archaic and modern humans, but with the right technology and a profound knowledge of the landscape and its rich plant and animal resources, human populations survived and at times thrived during the last glaciation. Perhaps in this setting it is not entirely surprising that mammoths provided key raw materials for early modern humans in Europe. Additionally, mammoths, which were the largest, strongest and most imposing terrestrial animals known to Ice Age peoples, count among the most frequently depicted motifs in the Aurignacian art of the Swabian Jura. Of the 33 carved ivory artworks that are complete enough to allow the subject matter to be identified, depictions of mammoths are the most numerous (9), followed closely by carvings of lions (8). The physical characteristics of ivory, with its beautiful, often homogeneous, color, great strength, robustness, and suitability for carving, made it the material of choice for artifacts, including hunting weapons, rope-making tools, figurines, and musical instruments. Each of these classes of artifacts reflects a high level of engineering skill, as is easily seen with the precisely carved spiral rifling that was used to twist and stabilize the plant fibers during rope-making (Fig. 1). This remarkable find from Hohle Fels and a similar tool from Geißenklösterle provide new insight into how rope was made 40,000 years ago. Although preserved rope and twine from the Aurignacian has never been recovered, these tools that were carefully carved from mammoth ivory help to explain how early modern humans in Europe made rope, a critical material with all sorts of practical applications. Similarly, whether of large or smaller size, ivory also provided a desired material for artifacts that likely served as hunting equipment, as can be seen among the finds recovered from the Aurignacian find horizons at Hohle Fels (Fig. 3).

Ornaments and figurative art

Another class of artifact, personal ornaments, has been part of the material culture of Middle Stone Age and Middle Paleolithic societies starting roughly 100,000 years ago, as is demonstrated by finds from southern Africa, north Africa, and the Levant. Interestingly, these earliest examples of personal ornaments are made by perforating marine shells to make jewelry, in other words modified natural forms. And in east Africa, starting around 50,000 years ago, people began making beads from ostrich eggshells. So the mammoth-ivory beads of the Swabian Jura are not the oldest examples of personal ornaments. They are, however, the earliest examples of personal ornaments with an arbitrarily defined three-dimensional form, and their many variants can be used to address issues of social identity and ethnicity at the onset of the Upper Paleolithic. Excavations at Vogelherd in particular have yielded roughly 600 examples, in all stages of manufacture, use, and disposal, of beads carefully carved from mammoth ivory with one or more perforations (Fig. 4). The other key Aurignacian sites of the region have similar but smaller assemblages of personal ornaments carved from mammoth ivory. Many of these finds, such as the numerous examples of double-perforated oval beads from the Ach and Lone valleys, are known only from the caves of the Swabian Jura, and form one key element of the unique social identity of the Aurignacian inhabitants of the region.

The Aurignacian era of the Swabian Jura is probably best known for the figurative art from Vogelherd, Hohlenstein-Stadel, Hohle Fels, and Geißenklösterle. The region has produced several dozen examples of figurines, a specific motif being identifiable in 33 cases. Most of these finds are small enough to hold in the palm of one's hand, and they likely served as artifacts among the personal possessions of these mobile hunter-gatherers. Many of the figurines have aesthetically attractive forms and textures that seem perfect. This is all the more remarkable since they stand at the beginning of global figurative art. The deepest Aurignacian layers, for example at Hohle Fels, have produced examples of female figurines, and other slightly younger layers have produced examples of a water bird, a horse, and a lionman. Vogelherd alone has produced

scores of fragmentary pieces of ivory figurines, most of which depict mammoths and lions. The artworks from the caves of the Swabian Jura are nearly all carved from mammoth ivory, and, with their dates ranging from about 42,000 and 35,000 years ago, they form the best record of the evolution of early figurative art identified thus far in the archaeological record. The perfection of many of these depictions suggests that figurative art evolved very quickly and immediately achieved an exceptionally high quality, rather than developing slowly, as many scholars have argued. This view is underlined by other examples of Aurignacian art, most notably the fabulous paintings of Grotte Chauvet, which also achieved something close to perfection near the beginnings of the known record of figurative representations.

4 Aurignacian ornaments, Hohle Fels and Vogelherd, mammoth ivory. Museum Alte Kulturen, Schloss Hohentübingen.

The figurines from the Swabian caves, which have been discovered over generations of excavation, include depictions of mammoths, lions, humans, bison, bears, fish, water birds, musk ox, and hare, and often show complex markings that conveyed information to the makers of the Aurignacian. Nearly all of the figurines were carved from mammoth ivory with great care and skill, underlining the importance of this material to the region's Aurignacian inhabitants. Today these finds are difficult to interpret with certainty, and dozens of potential explanations have been suggested over the decades. Some of the ideas include the following elements: shamanism, animistic representations, clan affiliation, fertility, gender identity, hunting magic, *l'art pour l'art*, etc. Clearly no single interpretation can explain the great variety of images. What is not disputed, however, is the beauty and exceptional quality of these artworks. This is demonstrated, for example, by the complete carving of a mammoth excavated at Vogelherd in 2006 (Fig. 5). The mammoth demonstrates another feature of the figurines, a successful mixture of a static depiction that yet conveys movement and a sense that something is about to happen. These characteristics are perhaps best illustrated in some of the depictions of lions low to the ground, as if stalking prey or about to pounce. In the case of the mammoth, many of the features, such as the small tail, the pronounced profile of the head and shoulder, substantial legs and curved trunk, successfully convey the main characteristics of a mammoth and are as readily recognizable to the viewer today as they would have been to the Aurignacian peoples of the mammoth steppe 40,000 years ago.

Lionmen

A particularly important class of depictions are the three lionmen from Hohlenstein-Stadel, Hohle Fels, and Geißenklösterle (Fig. 6). The famous lionman from Stadel is 31.1 cm high and originally weighs about 750 grams (Fig. 6, right). This find was deposited in the rear of the cave in what was likely part of a cache of symbolic artifacts. All of the other examples of carved mammoth ivory figurines are only a few centimeters in size and could easily be carried by their owners or caretakers. The lionman from Hohlenstein-Stadel seems to have been left at the back of the cave for later use, and the find seems to be specifically associated with this cave. Unlike all the other examples of carved ivory figurines found with many kinds of discarded material and refuse

from daily life, there was little evidence of mundane finds—such as debris from stone knapping or the preparing and consuming of food, or burnt material and hearths—found in the vicinity of this famous therianthropic depiction (combining human and animal features).

The much smaller relief of a lionman from Geißenklösterle and the figurine of a lionman from Hohle Fels were found among the refuse of daily life. Like the great majority of the other figurines, these finds likely belonged to a class of personal possessions that people carried with them as they moved across the Ice Age landscape. It is not by chance that, among the Aurignacian artworks from the Swabian caves, multiple therianthropic figurines have been recovered. Given the great difficulty of finding any examples of figurative art and the unlikelihood of such finds being preserved at all over tens of thousands of years, it is remarkable that three different caves in the Ach and Lone valleys have preserved depictions of lionmen. Since archaeologists have thus far excavated only an extremely small portion of the potential range of Aurignacian sites, finding three lionmen allows us safely to assume that such symbolic finds were much more common at the time and that the ideas and beliefs associated with them must have been familiar to the Aurignacian peoples of the region. The three lionmen document a system of beliefs in which humans and lions formed a fluid unity and in which people could transform into lions. These finds have often been interpreted as evidence for shamanism, and they provide insight into the earliest system of beliefs that has been documented archaeologically. That said, there is little reason to assume that all of the diverse ivory figurines from the Swabian caves can be seen to support a single interpretive framework. The two female figurines from Hohle Fels, for example, may reflect Aurignacian views of reproduction, fertility in the human context as well as in the broader world as a whole. Additionally, the many depictions of Ice Age animals have inspired numerous models to explain the meaning of Paleolithic art.

Music and theater?

Finally, the Swabian caves have produced about a dozen examples of flutes, most of which are made from bones of swans, vultures, and other birds. It is, however, the well-known flutes made from mammoth ivory that are in some respects the most impressive. The best example of such a musical instrument is the ivory flute from Geißenklösterle

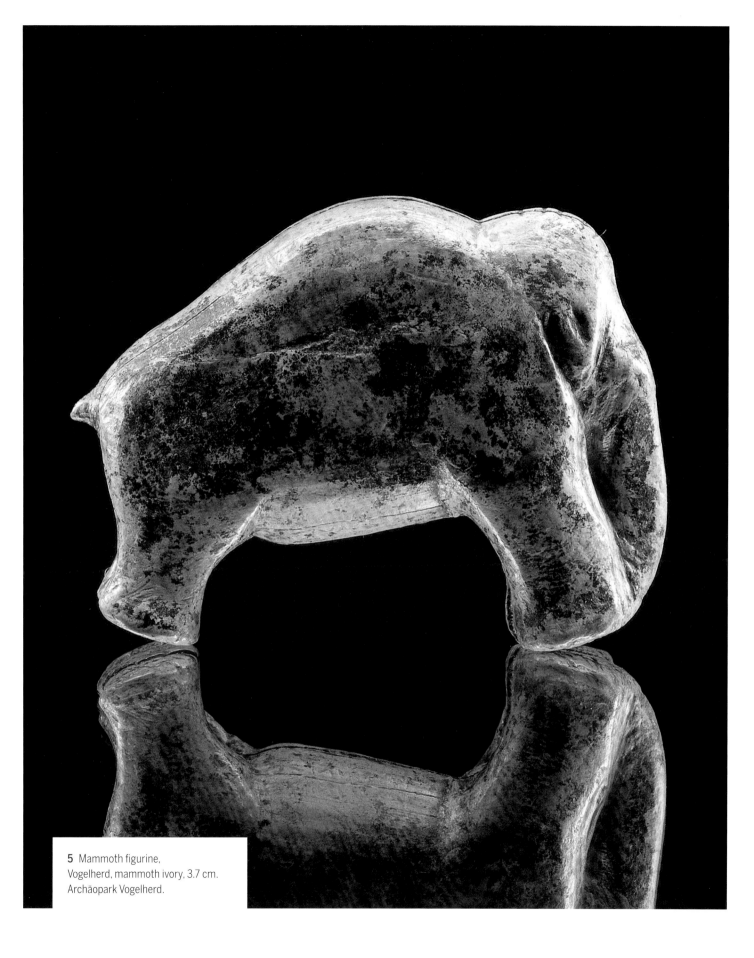

5 Mammoth figurine,
Vogelherd, mammoth ivory, 3.7 cm.
Archäopark Vogelherd.

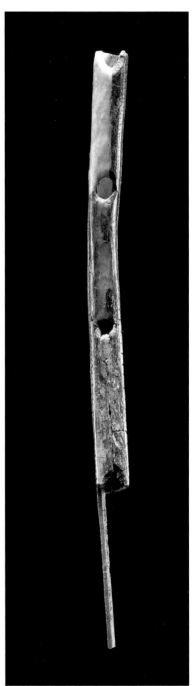

7 Flute, Geißenklösterle, ca. 38,000 BCE, mammoth ivory, 18.7 cm. Urgeschichtliches Museum, Blaubeuren.

6 Therianthropic figurines, so called Lion Men from Geißen-klösterle, 3.8 cm (top left); Hohle Fels, 2.6 cm (bottom left); and Hohlenstein-Stadel, 31.1 cm (right). All mammoth ivory.

(Fig. 7). When we identified this class of artifact in 2004, the proof that mammoth ivory was used to make flutes came as a great surprise to everyone familiar with the record of Paleolithic musical instruments. While a bird-bone flute can be made in about an hour by an expert craftsperson, a flute made from massive mammoth ivory requires roughly 100 hours to make when using chipped stone tools and technology available during the Ice Age. The main advantage of an ivory flute is the fact that it can be made to almost any desired size, while the size of a bird-bone flute was always determined by the size of the bones themselves. This means that the nature of the tones played on an ivory flute is defined by its maker. So far, fragments of ivory flutes have been found at Vogelherd, Hohle Fels, and Geißenklösterle. Together, the ivory and bird-bone flutes represent the earliest examples of musical instruments known. As is the case with the diverse and remarkable ivory depictions, the musical instruments are of exceptional quality, and by no means reflect rudimentary attempts to create sound. Indeed, these sophisticated musical instruments can be played using multiple techniques to produce a vast array of sounds and music.[4] The fact that the finds have all been recovered from cave deposits accords with the outstanding acoustical features of caves, making them ideal places for playing and listening to music. It is easy to imagine the combination of music, narratives, song, dance and perhaps moving shadows producing a kind of *Gesamtkunstwerk* inside the caves.[5]

Ivory and human creativity

Since Aurignacian peoples had all of our intellectual potential and creativity, we would be unwise to underestimate the range of cultural, artistic, and religious expression that accompanied the spread of modern humans across Eurasia. In areas such as the Swabian Jura, the ivory available on the mammoth steppe provided the main raw material for the expression of this creativity. Given that every society known to ethnography has created some form of abstract and figurative images, has maintained musical traditions, and has followed systems of religious beliefs to help make sense of the world around them and to answer the many practical and metaphysical questions that accompany human life and consciousness, the origins of art, music, and systems of beliefs help researchers to trace the development of symbolic life as we know it among all societies today. This makes the early mammoth-ivory figurines and musical instruments of outstanding universal value for all people, which explains why the caves of the Swabian Jura have been named UNESCO World Cultural Heritage sites.[6]

Finally, the figurative artworks, personal ornaments, ivory flutes, and diverse tools made from mammoth ivory demonstrate the virtuosity of the ivory carvers and justify the validity of the term Ivory Age to characterize the Swabian Aurignacian.

1   Nicholas J. Conard, Michael Bolus, Ewa Dutkiewicz, and Sibylle Wolf, *Eiszeitarchäologie auf der Schwäbischer Alb: Die Fundstellen im Ach- und Lonetal und ihrer Umgebung*, Tübingen: Kerns Verlag, 2015.
2   Nicholas J. Conard, "Cultural Evolution during the Middle and Late Pleistocene in Africa and Eurasia", in: W. Henke and I. Tattersall (eds), *Handbook of Paleoanthropology*, 2nd. ed., Berlin: Springer, 2015, pp. 2465–2508.
3   R. Dale Guthrie, *Frozen Fauna of the Mammoth Steppe*, Chicago: University of Chicago Press, 1990.
4   Anna Friederike Potengowski and S.C. Münzel, "Die musikalische 'Vermessung' paläolithischer Blasinstrumente der Schwäbischen Alb anhand von Rekonstruktionen, Anblastechniken, Tonmaterial und Klangwelt", *Mitteilungen der Gesellschaft für Urgeschichte* 24 (2015), pp. 173–191.
5   Nicholas J. Conard, "Paleolithic art and design", in: B. Franzen (ed.), *40,000 – A Museum of Curiosity*, 14th Fellbach Triennial, London: Koenig Books, 2019, pp. 395–437. English and German.
6   Nicholas J. Conard and Claus-Joachim Kind, *Als der Mensch die Kunst erfand: Eiszeithöhlen der Schwäbischen Alb*, 2nd ed., Darmstadt: Wissenschaftliche Buchgesellschaft, 2019.

Ivory

The Material that Makes Humans Human

HARALD FLOSS AND SIBYLLE WOLF

1 Female figurine (so-called Venus of Lespugue) from the Gravettian, Lespugue, mammoth ivory, 14.7 cm.

Various sciences contest the definition of the *conditio humana*. What is it that distinguishes us as humans? Is it our use of tools, our upright posture, or even that we create art? In this investigation, we have identified an interesting criterion that helps to define early humankind: the use of ivory.

The exploitation of elephants during the Pleistocene

Modern humans evolved during the Ice Age, at the same time as the elephant. The best-known example of Pleistocene elephants is unquestionably the mammoth, which was widespread in Eurasia between 110,000 and 14,000 years ago.[1] Humans used the tusks of the mammoth (Fig. 2) as raw material for numerous tools, ornaments, and artworks. In central and eastern Europe, tusks and other mammoth body parts were even used in the construction of dwellings, as in Gönnersdorf and Mezirici.[2] Our ancestors could use the tusks of hunted animals or collect them from fossil or dead animals in the permafrost of the vast Ice Age steppe landscape. Elephants provided humans with various raw materials, so in view of contemporary discussions it is important to point out that it was mainly the consumption of meat and fat that supported our ancestors in their development up into the present time. In addition, they also used the skins, sinews, and bones, in short, all the animal parts that hunter-gatherers might put to good use.

Tools made from elephant bones are known from Tanzania, for example, since the early Ice Age, more than a million years ago. During the Middle Paleolithic (roughly 300,000 to 40,000 years ago), most closely associated with the Neandertals, the creation of tools from elephant bones was common. In Salzgitter-Lebenstedt, more than 20 tools made from mammoth ribs or fibulae have been identified. From the late Middle Paleolithic and the so-called Châtelperonnian, we know of tools made from the shafts of long bones. The Châtelperonnian, named from the cave find site at Châtelperron in the Département Allier (France), designates a cultural complex dated from the Middle to Upper Paleolithic transition, and is presumably associated with the last of the Neandertals. Neandertals fed on mammoth meat and made tools from bones, but only rarely used ivory.

Early artworks, personal ornaments, and everyday objects

Mammoth ivory came to be universally used only with the beginning of the Upper Paleolithic (roughly 40,000 to 10,000 years ago). And with this we come back to our opening remark: this is also the time that anthropologists associate with the appearance of modern humans (*Homo sapiens*) in Europe.[3] These humans exploited the woolly mammoth extensively: they not only lived with the Ice Age animals, but also employed all available raw materials derived from them.[4] For example, the first roughly 40,000-year-old tools made from tusks come from the Aurignacian hunter-gatherers of the Swabian Jura.[5] The Aurignacian, named after a cave in the French foothills of the Pyrenees, was the first trans-regional cultural complex in Eurasia that can be linked with *Homo sapiens* in Europe. Best known are the famous Aurignacian ivory figurines of the Swabian Jura representing animals, humans, and hybrid creatures (see the essay by Conard in this volume, and Fig. 3).[6] These carvings came mainly from the Vogelherd Cave, with one prominent example, the lionman, from the Stadel Cave in the Lone Valley. Figurative artworks made from ivory are also known from the Geißenklösterle Cave and Hohle Fels Cave in the Ach Valley. Flutes, often made from bird bones, were also made from mammoth ivory. The use of

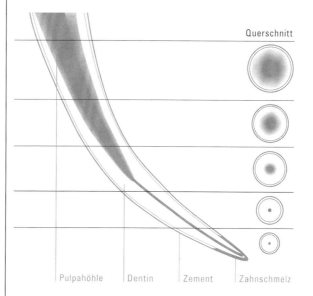

Querschnitt

Pulpahöhle   Dentin   Zement   Zahnschmelz

2 Structure of a mammoth tusk, schematic drawing, 2013. Museum Ulm.

3 Mammoth figurine, Aurignacian, Vogelherd, mammoth ivory, 5 cm. Museum Alte Kulturen, Schloss Hohentübingen.

ivory for artworks and musical instruments was a distinct technological innovation credited to *Homo sapiens*. At that time and in the subsequent Gravettian, mammoth bones were occasionally used in south-west Germany: the mammoth was accordingly not only a source of subsistence but also an important source of raw material.[7] The Gravettian culture that succeeded the Aurignacian was named after a site in western France, La Gravette. It followed the Aurignacian chronologically and is marked by a series of innovations in its utensils and its art.

Ivory was a perfect material for figurative carving, for tusks have great mass, and thus made it possible to fashion objects of an enormous range of sizes. This was a factor in the construction of flutes, for example, for with a bigger diameter lower tones could be produced than with bird bones (see the contribution by Lars-Christian Koch). Also, unlike antler and bone, of which only the compact outer layer can be worked, ivory is extremely homogeneous, simultaneously hard and elastic. Its durability also surely played a major role, not to mention its aesthetic and tactile charm; its soft, smooth surface after polishing clearly appealed to the humans of the early Upper Paleolithic.[8] Across Europe, Ice Age hunter-gatherers worked ivory using specific methods for more than 30,000 years.

4 Various bead types, Swabian Jura, Aurignacian, carved mammoth ivory, Museum Alte Kulturen, Schloss Hohentübingen: 1. double perforated bead, 2. double perforated bead with wedge-shaped appendix, 3. single perforated bead, 4. disk-shaped bead, 5. ring-shaped bead, 6. basket-shaped bead, 7. figure-eight-shaped bead, 8. Non perforated, constricted bead, 9. cone-shaped bead, 10. bulgy bead, 11. bead with single perforation and extension, 12. triple perforated bead, 13. blank for a bead, 14. bandeau.

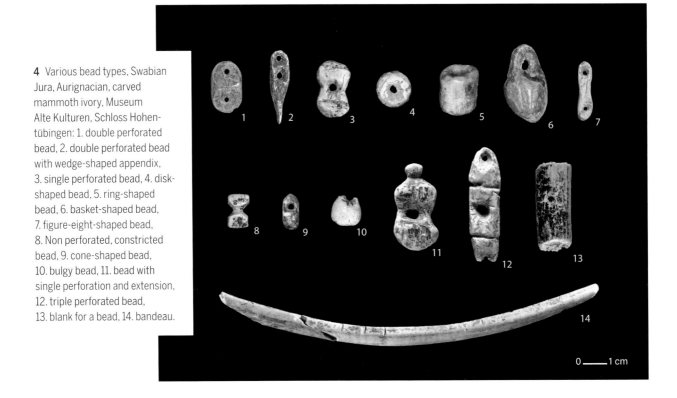

5 Mammoth figure from the Gravettian, Předmostí, mammoth ivory, 11.6 cm. Moravian Museum Brno.

During the Aurignacian, mammoth ivory was of great importance, particularly for the production of personal ornaments. Characteristic of the Swabian Jura was the serial production of very small, doubly perforated beads (Fig. 4).[9] To make them, a rod was carved from a mammoth tusk and rounded and smoothed. Blanks of the desired length were then sawed or broken off and the finished ornament made from them. The diameters of their perforations are generally less than a millimeter, a further indication of the craft skills of these hunter-gatherers. As with the previously mentioned finds, the production of items of personal ornaments from ivory is first documented in the Swabian Aurignacian. Along with serially produced beads, there are numerous individually worked pieces (Fig. 4). Finally, the use of personal ornaments is attested by small artifacts in ivory like the mammoth discovered in the Vogelherd Cave in 1931;[10] perforations between the legs indicate that the piece functioned as a pendant or amulet (Fig. 3). These were portable objects in mobile hunter-gatherer societies.[11]

Humans of the Early Paleolithic needed ivory not only to survive; they also used it for creative purposes and needs. This is true of all regions in the European Upper Paleolithic, more so of northern areas than Mediterranean regions. Ivory was also used in the making of everyday tools. Wedges, chisels, and multipurpose tools could be made from it, as exemplified by cylindrical utensils from find sites in Ukraine. Lance points and even entire lances of ivory are known. The strong yet elastic material was superbly suited for the manufacture of weapons of all kinds. Outstanding lances from straightened tusks have been excavated in Sungir (Russia), and an ivory boomerang was found in the Oblazova Cave (Nowa Biala, Poland).

For 30,000 years:
Female and animal figurines in ivory

Depictions of females play a special role in Paleolithic art. The oldest known female figure, created about 40,000 years ago, is from the Hohle Fels in Schelklingen; made from ivory like the animal figurines from the Swabian Jura and the lionman from Hohlenstein-Stadel, it dates to the Aurignacian. In the following Gravettian (roughly 30,000 to 20,000 years ago), depictions of corpulent females are very numerous in the Eurasian region, from the Atlantic to Siberia. The most famous of these is the so-called Venus of Willendorf (Lower Austria), discovered in the early 20th century. A large number of them were made of ivory, like the so-called Venus of Lespugue (Fig. 1). These are generally highly voluptuous in form, and only rarely pictured with elements of adornment like personal ornaments and rarely with individualized facial features.[12] There are several famous open-air sites in the present-day Czech Republic in which in addition to female figurines numerous animal figurines have been found that also date to the Gravettian. Noteworthy is an ivory mammoth figure excavated at Předmostí in 1895 (Fig. 5). A further example is the highly detailed female bison from Zaraysk (Russia), found in 2001. Attesting to the great virtuosity of the humans of the time, it shows that our ancestors could precisely judge the volume and structure of a tusk and that they knew how to make the best use of the material in their carving.

Ivory continued to be an important raw material for personal ornaments in the periods following the Aurignacian, and striking similarities in production methods can be seen across the entire continent. One peculiarity is the use of ivory to imitate other materials. For example, there is the Aurignacian ivory "shell" from La Souquette in the Castel-Merle Valley (southwest France), and a Gravettian ivory imitation of a deer's canine tooth from the Hohle Fels.[13] These finds highlight the enormous appreciation for the material and how with its help imitations of nature could be brought to perfection. In the Magdalenian (roughly 18,000 to 12,000 years ago), which followed the Gravettian and the Solutrean, the use of ivory waned, presumably because it became less available at the end of the last Ice Age. Named after the site of Solutré (Burgundy, France), the Solutrean is a cultural complex which dates from the last glacial maximum and is distinguished by an extraordinary production of flint tools in the form of bifacial leaf points, while the Magdalenian is named after the site La Madeleine in the Dordogne (France)—the last major culture at the end of the last Ice Age. Nonetheless, pieces like the swimming reindeer from Montastruc (Haute-Garonne) (Fig. 6) and the barbed end of a spear thrower from Abri de la Madeleine (Tursac, Dordogne), which pictures a young bison, highlight not only the considerable manual skill of these hunter-gatherers, but also the use of this outstanding material up to the end of the last Ice Age.

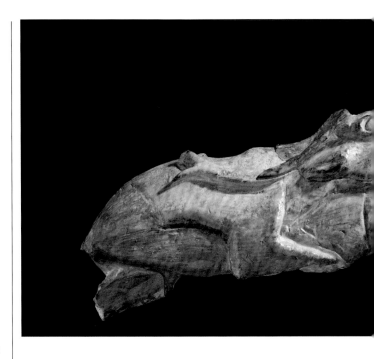

Importance of mammoth ivory to Ice Age humans

This brief overview has indicated the central role of ivory in the early history of humankind: the great value of the mammoth to hunter-gatherer societies of the Ice Age is underscored by the numerous archaeological finds and also by the many depictions of the animal in cave paintings and as small sculpture.[14] For millennia mammoth ivory was the favored material for personal ornaments and small carvings, attesting to our ancestors' fascination with it. No major development in the techniques of ivory working can be seen in the more than 30,000 years of humankind's early history. Strategies for its handling and uses that still applied in the advanced Upper Paleolithic were already fixed in the Aurignacian. Despite the availability of many other materials, ivory was used for the production of pieces of personal adornment and small figurines in nearly every Ice Age culture. From this it can be concluded that it was the favored raw material with which to convey symbolic content. This surely also points out the outstanding importance of ivory and the mammoth in the collective imagination of hunter-gatherers and in their particular social activities. It thus makes sense that the use of ivory can be considered an essential criterion in the definition of modern humans.

6 Swimming reindeer from the Magdalenian, Montastruc, mammoth ivory, 21 cm. The British Museum, London.

Conclusion

After the Paleolithic, the ivory-working tradition gradually disappeared from Europe, a clear consequence of the shrinking of mammoth populations some 11,000 years ago; the last died on the Wrangel Island (Russia) some 4,000 years ago.[15] Ivory has lost none of its appeal to this day, as is shown by the massive decimation of walrus and elephant populations in various parts of the world. The virtually industrial-scale recovery of mammoth ivory from Siberia's permafrost is surely one solution, but one that is not unproblematic ecologically. Currently there are also various attempts to bring the mammoth back to life, by way of extracting the DNA of the animals frozen in Siberia—an approach we cannot support.

1   See Ralf-Dietrich Kahlke, "The maximum geographic extension of Late Pleistocene *Mammuthus primignius* (Proboscidea, Mammalia) and its limiting factors", *Quaternary International* 379 (2015), pp. 147–154.
2   See Gerhard Bosinski (ed.), *Gönnerdorf, Eiszeitjäger am Mittelrhein. Eine Ausstellung des Landesmuseums Koblenz*, exh. cat. Landesmuseum Koblenz (Veröffentlichungen des Landesmuseums Koblenz 7), Koblenz 1981.
3   See Sibylle Wolf and Carole Vercoutère, "L'exploitation de l'ivoire de Mammouth au Paléolithique", *L'Anthropologie* 122, no. 3 (2018), pp. 579–587.
4   See Chantal Conneller, *An Archaeology of Materials: Substantial Transformations in Early Prehistoric Europe*, London and New York: Routledge, 2011; Shumon Hussain and Harald Floss, "Sharing the world with mammoths, cave lions and other beings: linking animal-human interactions and the Aurignacian 'belief world'", *Quartär* 65 (2015), pp. 85–120.
5   See Sibylle Wolf, *Schmuckstücke. Die Elfenbeinbearbeitung im Schwäbischen Aurignacien*, Tübingen: Kerns Verlag, 2015.
6   See Gustav Riek, *Die Eiszeitjägerstation am Vogelherd im Lonetal*, Tübingen: Die Kulturen, 1934; Harald Floss, "L'Art mobilier aurignacien du Jura souabe et sa place dans l'art paléolithique – Die Kleinkunst des Aurignacien auf der Schwäbischen Alb und ihre Stellung in der paläolithischen Kunst", in: Harald Floss and Natalie Rouquerol (eds), *Les Chemins de l'Art aurignacien en Europe – Das Aurignacien und die Anfänge der Kunst in Europa. Colloque international, Aurignac 2005*, Aurignac: Éditions Musée-forum Aurignac 4, 2007, pp. 295–316.
7   See Laura Niven, *The Palaeolithic Occupation of Vogelherd Cave. Implications for the subsistence behavior of late Neanderthals and Early Modern Humans*, Tübingen: Kerns Verlag, 2006.
8   See Riek 1934 (as note 6); also Conneller 2011 (as note 4).
9   Wolf 2015 (as note 5).
10   Riek 1934 (as note 8).
11   See Floss 2007 (as note 6).
12   See Sibylle Wolf, "Eine neue Venusstatuette vom jungpaläolithischen Fundplatz Dolni Vestonice (Mähren)", *Jahrbuch des Römisch-Germanischen Zentralmuseums Mainz* 55 (2008), pp. 1–42.
13   See Stefanie Kölbl and Nicholas John Conard (eds), *Eiszeitschmuck. Status und Schönheit*, (Museumsheft 6), Blaubeuren: Urgeschichtliches Museum, 2003.
14   See Hussain and Floss 2015 (as note 4), Wolf 2015 (as note 5).
15   See Adrian Lister and Paul Bahn, *Mammoths: Giants of the Ice Age*, Berkeley: University of California Press, 2007.

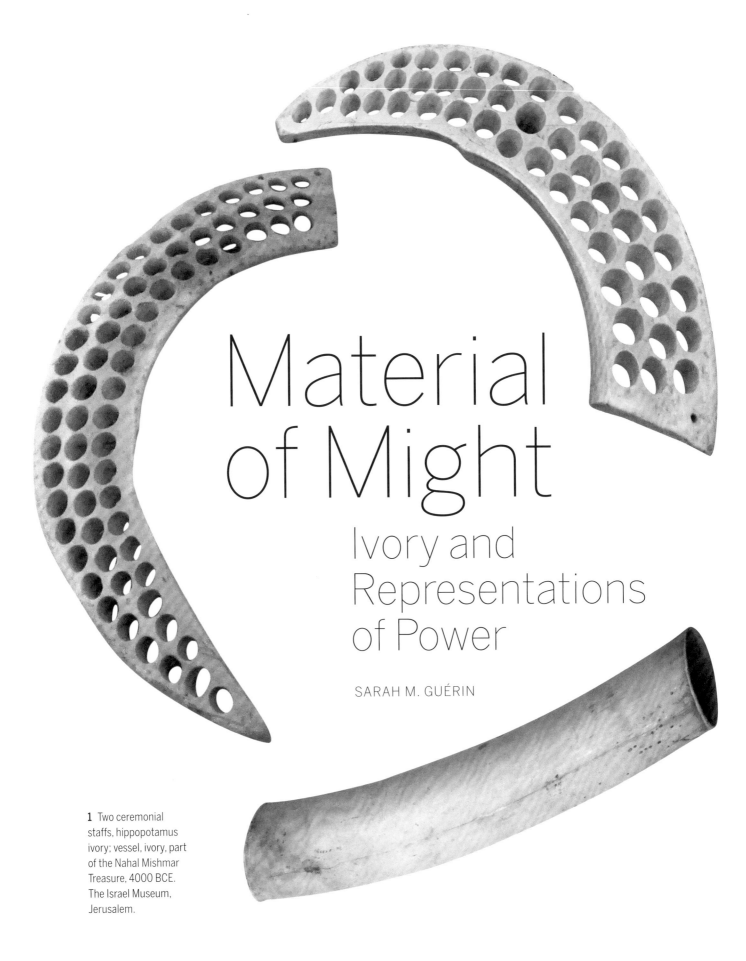

Material
of Might
Ivory and
Representations
of Power

SARAH M. GUÉRIN

1 Two ceremonial
staffs, hippopotamus
ivory; vessel, ivory, part
of the Nahal Mishmar
Treasure, 4000 BCE.
The Israel Museum,
Jerusalem.

Prehistoric

Human beings have always appreciated elephantine ivory's silky texture, fine grain, and unique ability to be carved with extreme delicacy and virtuosity. The earliest known artifact carved by modern humans, *Homo sapiens*, is the Hohle Fels Venus that dates to approximately 38,000-33,000 BCE, that is, 10,000 years before the Venus of Willendorf and 20,000 years before the Lascaux cave paintings.[1]

This miniature woman with exaggerated breasts and swollen pudenda forces us to consider the deep history of humans using ivory to fashion social order and represent power relations. The Hohle Fels Venus was carved from the ivory of a mammoth, a relative of the modern Asian elephant on the *Elephantidae* family tree, which became extinct in western Europe with the last Ice Age, around 11,000 BCE. though in Siberia some may have survived until as recently as 3,700 years ago. The enormous tusks of this impressive beast figure strongly in the arts of our distant ancestors, not only among the first symbolic objects, but also among the representations on the walls of caves. The Rouffignac cave in the Périgord, France, for example, pictures the impressive animals with their extensive tusks in the very centuries when they were disappearing from western Europe[1] (Fig. 2). As the mammoth is an animal generally less frequently represented in cave arts, the 158 mammoths inscribed and outlined on its walls make this an unusual site. As with all Paleolithic cave paintings, the meaning, function, and significance of the Grotte de Rouffignac mammoths remain mysterious, though we might note that the mammoths' tusks are prominent. Even more indicative of the value ascribed to mammoth ivory, and its

role in nascent social structures, is its use in personal ornamentation.

A ca. 28,000-year-old Paleolithic site at Sungir, about 200 kilometers east of Moscow, revealed elite members of a community draped in ornamentation made of mammoth ivory.[2] In the three burials, of an elderly man and two children, there were over 13,000 beads—the man wore 25 arm bands (Fig. 3)— and a sculpture of a mammoth itself. Archaeologists have estimated that each bead took about an hour to make, thus the burials evidence a community where the labor of many benefits (that is contributes to the ornamentation of) the few who wield power. That two children have been thus adorned suggests, already at this early date, a system of birthright rather than power adhering around a strongman based on merit. Ivory, worked with both patient labor and technological ingenuity—for example, the invention

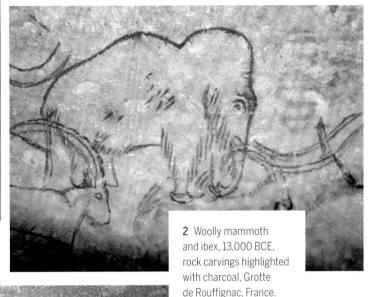

2 Woolly mammoth and ibex, 13,000 BCE, rock carvings highlighted with charcoal, Grotte de Rouffignac, France.

3 Burial place of an adult male from the Early Paleolithic, Sungir, Russia, replica, Parque de la prehistoria, Teverga, Spain.

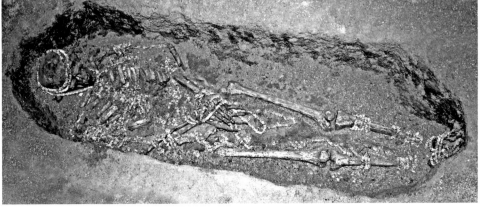

4 The Woman at the Window (furniture fitting), Nimrud, 900–700 BCE, ivory, 11 x 9 x 1 cm. The British Museum, London.

of hematite polishing dust to finish the beads—was the choice material to mark social distinction in the Paleolithic Siberian Steppe.

As the mammoth gradually exited the world stage, the trade in the elephant tusks filled the void, transporting the material—in either raw or worked form—from regions in Asia and Africa where modern species thrived. Of these, there are three: the African savannah elephant (*Loxodonta africana*), prized for its large tusks with diameters of solid ivory well above 11 cm (a rule-of-thumb measurement that has provided historians with a useful threshold for distinguishing savannah tusks from others); the more diminutive elephant of the African forest zones (*Loxodonta cyclotis*); and the Asian elephant (*Elephas maximus*). Only the males of the latter species grow tusks, which are smaller than those of their African "cousins". In the ancient world, the elephant thrived in many more regions than it does today, covering much of Asia and Africa, including parts of the Middle East, North Africa, and the

Sahara. And elephant ivory was a frequent trade good. The Nahal Mishmar treasure, for example, found in 1961 in a cave in the Judaean desert, can be dated to at least ca. 4000 BCE, if not earlier. It contains not only remarkable finds of copper-alloy ritual objects and weapons (including 240 mace heads), but also five "wands" of hippopotamus ivory and a carefully rendered vessel fashioned from a large elephant tusk (Fig. 1).[3] With time, trade intensified. The Uluburun shipwreck (ca. 1400 BCE) carried not only at least ten tons of copper ingots—standardized and manageable forms appropriate for trade—and other goods in commercial-sized quantities, but also small amounts of a wide variety of luxury goods including 14 hippopotamus teeth, and one large section of elephant tusk.[4] Ivory tusks, from the elephant as well as from other megafauna such as the hippopotamus, were thus one of the luxury commodities traded in the Bronze Age. The circulation of ivory over long distances to satisfy a persistent desire for the material should be considered the rule rather than the exception.

Ancient Near East

The cosmopolitan court cultures of the Ancient Near East in the first millennium BCE readily employed elephant ivory in the formation of symbols of power. The raw material was obtained both locally, from the herds of Asian elephants that still roamed the region, and from trade, notably with Egypt and the Indus Valley.[5] Inscriptions on the pavement stones of the temple of Urta at Calah (Nimrod) record that Ashurnasirpal II, king of Assyria from 883 to 859 BCE, received impressive tribute from Sangara, king of the Hittites, including elephant tusks and furniture inlaid with ivory.[6] Such models of kingship and modes of exchange were cemented in the Western imagination via the Hebrew Scriptures, where King Solomon of Israel (ca. 10th century BCE), among the lavish accoutrements for his palace and the temple, had made "a great throne of ivory: and overlaid it with the finest gold. It had six steps: and the top of the throne was round behind: and there were two hands on either side holding the seat: and two lions stood, one at each hand" (1 Kings 10: 18–20).

The shared appeal of luxury elephant ivories across the ancient world is best illustrated by the cache of figural appliqué plaques found in Nimrod, the capital city of Ashurnasirpal II. The ivories had been discarded by conquering invaders in 612 BCE, at the fall of the Assyrian Empire. After having been stripped of their gold, the dentine, which could not be melted down, was instead thrown down a well, the victors jettisoning a medium particularly associated with the conquered ruling elites. The stylistic plurality of the objects excavated at Nimrud seems to support the emphasis on ivory tribute documented by the textual tradition. Generations of art historians have argued about which plaques were carved where. It is clear some were made more locally, though inspired by foreign models, like the probably Phoenician plaque shown here drawing on an Egyptian style (Fig. 4), while others were brought from much further afield. Marian Feldman has written eloquently about the works that testify to a shared "stylistic community", in a visual mode appropriate for elites across the ancient world. [7]

Rome

The ancient Mesopotamian and Egyptian empires served as models for the nascent self-fashioning of Rome, first Republican then Imperial, which looked to models farther east as prototypes of power. The earliest reference to elephants in Latin texts is to *Lucas bovis*, Lucanian bulls, after the Romans' first encounter with the animals during the Pyrrhic War (280–275 BCE) in the territory of Lucania, modern southern Italy.[8] *Elephas*, borrowed from the Greek for both ivory and the animal, was initially reserved for describing luxury products associated with the Hellenistic world. Only later was the term used primarily for the animal, and *ebur* adopted for the material from their tusks, itself derived from the Egyptian Demotic *yb*.[9]

As the Roman Empire expanded, so did its infrastructure, stretching from the Atlantic Ocean to the Caspian Sea, and from Hadrian's Wall to Aswan on the First Cataract of the Nile, facilitating interregional trade. The Roman elites enjoyed ready access to African elephants in Egypt, Nubia, and the North African provinces of Mauritania (Morocco and Algeria) and Africa Proconsularis (Algeria, Tunisia, and Libya), as well as undoubtedly Asian elephants from various Eastern parts of the Empire. In his eleventh *Satire*, Juvenal (fl. ca. 100), in mocking the luxuries of Roman banqueting, names the places of origin for elephant ivory—at least those possible in the poet's imagination. He notes that the snobby dinner guest loses his appetite:

"Unless the great round tabletop is held up by a massive ivory pillar, a rampant snarling leopard made of tusks imported from the Gate of Syene

[Aswan], by the swift North Africans (*Mauri celeres*) or even [the people] of 'India'; Tusks that the elephants drop in the glades of Nabatea (Sinai Peninsula), when they prove too large to carry."[10]

North Africa, "India"—a geographic designation to which we shall return—Aswan on the Nile, or the Sinai Peninsula: undoubtedly Juvenal's passage is an eclectic and supercilious mix of far-flung locales from where a Roman sophisticate might imagine ivory to have come. All are in fact possibilities. Scholars have generally dismissed the *Mauri celeres* as a purely poetic invention. But recent scholarship has shown not only that elephants might still have roamed north of the Sahara and Atlas mountains in the 1st century, but also that the Garamantes, the ancient civilization of Libya, an indigenous Amazigh culture later called by the derogatory terms "Moors" or "Berbers", actively participated in interregional, namely trans-Saharan, trade.[11] Excavations demonstrate that trade across the more verdant Sahara of the Roman period was frequent, and likely provided Carthage with gold bullion, and perhaps Rome with some of its ivory.

Yet, by the Late Roman period, a combination of overhunting and climate change forced the extinction of the North African elephant population. In the 4th century, the rhetorician and Roman senator Themistius warned that the beast was about to disappear, or had. His text is chillingly familiar, juxtaposing the extinction of megafauna and racial cleansing after conquest:

"[We] feel pain when elephants are wiped out from Libya, lions from Thessaly and hippopotami from the Nile marshes; in the case of a race of men—even if one could by all means say barbarian, yet still men—impoverished, downtrodden and consenting to submit to our rule, shall we not admire him who does not wipe them out completely but cares for and spares them?"[12]

Emotions evoked by the extinction of charismatic beasts should also, Themistius warns, be stirred by the suffering of the conquered. The intertwining of extinction, environmental resource management, and post-conquest ethics are issues that still resonate deeply with us today.[13]

As the North African elephant was becoming extinct, trade relations were developing with the Horn of Africa, securing Roman access to elephants much farther afield and allowing the carving of ivory to in fact flourish throughout the Empire precisely as local resources were diminishing. The kingdom of Aksum, the main political power in the Horn of Africa, covered modern Eritrea and the highlands of northern Ethiopia.[14] As Aksum rose to importance in the Late Antique period, Romans began to produce some of their most lavish ivories, such as the consular diptychs (Fig. 5). These pairs of large-scale ivory panels very probably made from the remarkable tusks of savannah elephants (many panels being well over 11 cm wide) are first attested in 387 CE when the distribution of such ivory diptychs (*diptycha ex ebore*), together with gifts of gold, was limited to consuls alone.[15] Thus the first evidence of consular diptychs is a sumptuary law, already attempting to limit, perhaps, the overuse of the rare material, a symbol of power.

The enormous, five-part panel at the Louvre depicting a 6th-century Byzantine Emperor, likely Justinian (r. 527–565), sitting astride his rearing mount, has a central panel which measures 19 cm high, 12.5 cm wide, and 2.6 cm thick (see fig. page 82). The bottom plaque depicts in traditional Roman iconography four personifications of subject territories bearing tribute to the Emperor, flanking a central Victory. To the left are two individuals dressed as Persians or Scythians, with their loosely fitting pants, offering a crown and a container filled to the brim, probably with gold; to the right are two bare-chested men wearing sarongs, identified in the literature as "Indians".[16] The first, carrying a staff, walks comfortably in step with a tiger, an apex predator indigenous to Asia and the Indian subcontinent. His companion stands beside a small elephant and holds a tusk of moderate size—though he too might represent an Indian from the subcontinent, the geographical designation "India" in the Late Roman period confusingly also included Aksum: because "India", for Romans, comprised all southerly territories east of the Nile. The impressive relief thus strives to demonstrate the origins of the material from which it is made. Emphasis is placed on tribute and dominion, even if there was a relatively vague understanding of exactly which territories bore what tribute. Yet the enormous ivory panel itself suggests through its morphology, being 12.5 cm wide, that the material came from an African savannah elephant likely from Aksum.

Medieval to modern

Such imperial ivories and consular diptychs were among the many objects that passed into ecclesiastic collections with the decentralization of the Roman Empire in the Middle Ages, serving as aspirational objects for future leaders of Church and State who wished to promote their power. These antique

models fed the continued demand for elephant ivory, even after the North African elephant had become extinct and trade relations with Aksum were severed in the 7th century. Charlemagne and his court in the 8th and 9th centuries provide a compelling example of demand for ivory exceeding supply. The carvers of Carolingian ivories not only revived Roman formats, in a determinedly Roman style, but moreover reused Late Antique ivories: the reverse of many objects reveal planed-down carvings. The ivory is recycled.[17] Even if the early European Middle Ages did not enjoy the vast trading networks typical of the Roman world, models from the height of empire continued to inspire and ignite desire for elephant ivory.

This period of lack was followed by the so-called "ivory century" around the Mediterranean Basin, when the craft of ivory carving flourished in Al-Andalus, Byzantine Constantinople, Fatimid Egypt, and in the lands of the Germanic Ottonian Empire. Although some of the increase in elephant ivory in the Mediterranean is surely linked to growing trade relations between Muslim Swahili merchants and the Red Sea in the 10th century, and thus access to Egyptian markets,[18] it is also a period that coincides precisely with the growing involvement of Umayyad Iberia and Fatimid North Africa with caravan trade southwards across the Sahara.[19] Trans-Saharan trade provided these states with West African gold that funded their military campaigns and ornamented their courts.[20] Savannah elephant ivory too was borne across the Sahara by caravan. Indeed, it is Sicily and southern Italy's continued close relationship with North Africa (modern Tunisia) and trans-Saharan trade that explains their continued carving of elephant ivory in the 11th and 12th centuries, a time when northern Europe had to make do with more locally available replacements, such as walrus ivory.

The ivories of Ummayad Iberia, in particular, speak strongly of their connection to the members of the courts at Córdoba or Madinat al-Zahra by means of their lavish inscriptions. For example, the pyxis now at the Victoria & Albert Museum in London bears an Arabic inscription that states it was made in 969–970 for Ziyad ibn Aflah (Fig. 6), the year he was made prefect of police under the caliph al-Hakam II (r. 961–974). It pictures a man, presumably the prominent bureaucrat himself, in three settings appropriate to the highest orders of society: seated cross-legged administering justice, hawking, and traveling in state on a palanquin itself mounted upon an elephant.[21] Mariam Rosser-Owen has suggested that it was the powerful, ambitious and

5 Emperor Triumphant (Barberini Diptych),
ca. 500–550 CE, ivory with traces of inlay,

6 Pyxis made for Ziyad ibn Aflah, prefect of police in Córdoba, ca. 970, ivory, h. 19.4, dia. 12.2 cm. Victoria and Albert Museum, London.

conniving vizier al-Mansur (r. 978–1002) who was most active in the commissioning and gifting of ivory pyxes and boxes, reserving them as markers of favor. Indeed, Ziyad ibn Aflah had been a co-conspirator of al-Mansur's when the inscription and iconography were carved; with this ivorine gift,

Ziyad ibn Aflah seems to be promised continued status and power in return for his complicity.

The proto-industrial developments of the textile industry in northern Europe in the 13th century led to an increase in commercial activity in general, and an increased connectivity between the textile-producing regions of Picardy, Flanders, Hainaut, and Brabant (modern northern France and Belgium) with North Africa in particular.[22] This was facilitated by innovations in shipbuilding that allowed direct sea access to the Atlantic through the Straits of Gibraltar. Northern Europe enjoyed much stronger connection to the endpoints of the trans-Saharan routes, primarily for chemicals necessary to the textile industry—namely alum, an essential mineral fixative for the dying process—but the increased connection with trans-Saharan routes also brought a range of West African exports for sale to European merchants: exotic animal skins, leather, Grains of Paradise (a gingery spice), ebony, specialized shields made from oryx skins, ostrich eggs and feathers, parrots, indigo-dyed cotton—and savannah elephant ivory.

Such were the economic conditions that allowed the remarkable flourishing of ivory carving in Europe during the Gothic period. Thousands of extant works, ranging from large-scale religious statues to knife-handles and toiletry sets with charming courtly scenes were produced. One of the most impressive is a statuette of the Virgin and Child made for Sainte Chapelle (see fig. page 83), the palace chapel of the French monarchy founded by Louis IX in 1241. The statuette was mentioned in the first inventories of the royal foundation (drawn up between 1279 and 1285), and it was likely a commission instigated by or for the Capetian king—possibly in the last years of the reign of Louis IX himself (d. 1270). Carved from a single enormous African savannah elephant tusk, and standing 41 cm high and 12.4 cm wide at the integral base, the statuette, in its size and refinement, reflects the apogee of ivory carving in the Gothic period. It also reflects an ambition to publically demonstrate access to trans-Saharan trade, and a certain control of those resources; one might recall that the saintly king died while on his second crusade, not to the Holy Land, but to Tunisia, a key outlet of trans-Saharan commodities, including West African gold.[23]

Like the Romans before them, there is little evidence that northern Europeans understood the true origin of the material used for their sumptuous mirrors, devotional objects, writing tablets, or hair parters. The first evidence of European knowledge of the long-distance relay network linking northern Europe to West Africa comes in the form of the Catalan Atlas (Fig. 7) likely made by the Majorcan cartographer Abraham Cresques for the French king Charles V between 1375 and 1380.[24] This six-paneled object charts the state of Europe's geographic knowledge at the height of the Gothic period, incorporating evidence from Jewish and Italian portolan charts, such recent travel accounts as Marco Polo's (accurate or not), as well as information from more traditional Arabic and European sources. It not only tracks current geographical knowledge, but moreover foreshadows geopolitical developments of the next 100 hundred years—presaging the Age of Discovery.

A caption along the coast of West Africa on the first of two panels depicting this territory offers the first unequivocal evidence that Europeans, in the 14th century, might have understood that elephant ivory, the immensely popular and prestigious artistic material, came to Europe from sources in West Africa. The badly abraded caption reads:

"Cape Finisterre in West Africa. Here Africa begins, and it ends in Alexandria and Babylon [i.e. Fustat]. It begins here and comprises all the coast of Barbarie, towards Alexandria, and towards the south [towards] Ethiopia […]. On these beaches much ivory is found, for the [multitude] of elephants […]." (my translation)

Sub-Saharan West Africa is thus clearly identified as the source of elephant ivory circulating in the Gothic Mediterranean. If Charles V ever had the opportunity to examine this magnificent map, he would have understood the origins of his enormous collection of Gothic ivories. While Charles might have deduced that the means of transport for those ivory tusks was at the time still largely by Amazigh-led camel caravan, as per the depiction next to the inscription, a low-slung galley flying the flag of Majorca sailing along the edge of the coast of Mauritania points instead towards the dawning of the Early Modern world.

The inscription beside the ship reads: "Jaime Ferrer's ship departs for the River of gold on the feast of St. Laurent [Lawrence] which is the 10th of August, in the year 1346" (my translation). Although the mission of the Catalonian Jaime Ferrer was unsuccessful, and nothing else was heard from the adventuresome captain, European interest in direct connection to West Africa, not only for gold but increasingly for enslaved labor to man sugarcane plantations—first in the western Mediterranean, and then across the Atlantic in the New World—would forever shift the ethical balance of the ivory trade. With the so-called Age of Discovery, that is, emerging European colonialism, the overconsumption of elephant tusks figured among the exploitative practices typical of Europeans encountering the world—not just along the West African coast (Fig. 8), but along the Swahili coast, in India, and in Asia. Henceforth, ivory trade and objects carved from elephant tusks would be intrinsically and directly linked to the mechanisms of oppressive colonialism.

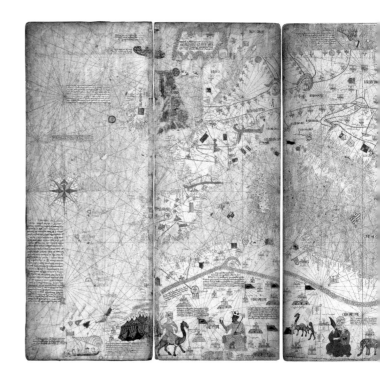

7 Abraham Cresques, Catalan Atlas, 1375–1380,
vellum on wood, 6 double leaves, each 64 x 50 cm.
Bibliothèque nationale de France, Paris.

8 Detail of Fig. 7: bottom recto and verso of double leaf II, showing West Africa.

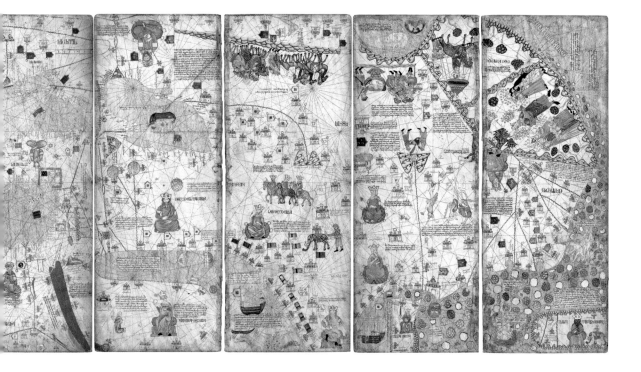

1 Claude Barrière, *L'Art pariétal de Rouffignac*, Paris : Picard, 1982.
2 Randall White, "The Dawn of Adornment", in: James M. Bayman and Miriam T. Stark (eds), *Exploring the Past: Readings in Archaeology*, Durham, NC: Carolina Academic Press, 2000, pp. 391–395.
3 Pessah Bar-Adon, *The Cave of the Treasure: The Finds from the Caves in Nahal Mishmar*, Jerusalem: Israel Exploration Society, 1980.
4 Joan Aruz, Kim Benzel and Jean M. Evans (eds), *Beyond Babylon: Art, Trade and Diplomacy in the Second Millennium B.C.*, New York: Yale University Press, 2008, pp. 289–310.
5 Thomas R. Trautmann, *Elephants and Kings: An Environmental History*, Chicago: University of Chicago Press, 2015.
6 Daniel Luckenbill, *Ancient Records of Assyria and Babylonia*, vol. 1: *Historical Records of Assyria from the Earliest Times to Sargon*, Chicago: University of Chicago Press, 1926, § 476.
7 Marian H. Feldman, *Communities of Style: Portable Luxury Arts, Identity, and Collective Memory in the Iron Age Levant*, Chicago: University of Chicago Press, 2014.
8 Pliny, *Natural History*, Vol. III, Books 8–11, trans. H. Rackham, Loeb Classical Library 353, Cambridge: Cambridge University Press, 1940, 8.6; and Jo-Ann Shelton, "Elephants as Enemies in Ancient Rome", *Concentric: Literary and Cultural Studies* 32.1 (January 2006), pp. 3–25.
9 Charlton T. Lewis and Charles Short, *A Latin Dictionary*, Oxford: Clarendon Press, 1879, under *ebur*.
10 "latos nisi sustinet orbis / grande ebur et magno sublimis pardus hiatus / dentibus ex illis quos mittit porta Syenes / et Mauri celeres et Mauro obscurior Indus, / et quos deposuit Nabataeo belua saltu / iam nimios capitique graues." Susanna Morton Braund, ed. and trans., *Juvenal and Persius*, Loeb Classical Library 191, Cambridge, MA: Harvard University Press, 2004, pp. 410–411 (XI. 122–127), my translation.
11 D.J. Mattingly (ed.), *The Archaeology of Fazzān*, 4 vols, London: Society for Libyan Studies, and Tripoli: Department of Antiquities, 2003–2013, vol. 1, pp. 346–362.
12 Themistius, *Orations X*, trans. in Peter Heather and John Matthews (eds), *The Goths in the Fourth Century*, Liverpool: Liverpool University Press, 1991, pp. 33–46, here 44.
13 Sarah M. Guérin, "Ivory and the Ties that Bind", in: Andrew Albin and other (eds), *Whose Middle Ages?: Teachable Moments for an Ill-used Past*, New York: Fordham University Press, 2019, pp. 140–153.
14 David W. Phillipson, "Aksum, the Entrepôt, and Highland Ethiopia, 3th–12th Centuries", in: Marlia Mundell Mango (ed.), *Byzantine Trade, 4th–12th Centuries: The Archaeology of Local, Regional and International Exchange*, Burlington, VT: Ashgate Press, 2009, pp. 353–368.
15 Clyde Pharr, ed. and trans., *The Theodosian Code and Novels and the Sirmondian Constitutions*, Princeton, NJ: Princeton University Press, 1952, p. 435 (Cod. Theod. 15.9.1).
16 Anthony Cutler, *The Hand of the Master: Craftsmanship, Ivory, and Society in Byzantium (9th–11th Centuries)*, Princeton, NJ: Princeton University Press, 1994, pp. 22–23.
17 Anthony Cutler, "Reuse or use? Theoretical and Practical Attitudes Towards Objects in the Early Middle Ages", *Settimane di Studi del Centro Italiano di Studi Sull'alto Medioevo* 46 (1999), pp. 1055–1079.
18 Mark Horton, "The Swahili Corridor", *Scientific American* 257, no. 3 (1987), pp. 86–93.
19 Avinoam Shalem, "Trade in and the Availability of Ivory: The Picture given by the Medieval Sources", *Journal of the David Collection*, 2.1 (2005), pp. 25–36; Sarah M. Guérin, "Forgotten Routes? Italy, Ifriqiya and the Trans-Saharan Ivory Trade", *Al-Masaq* 25 (2013), pp. 70–91.
20 Kathleen Bickford Berzock (ed.), *Caravans of Gold, Fragments in Time: Art, Culture, and Exchange across Medieval Saharan Africa*, Princeton, NJ: Princeton University Press, 2019.
21 Mariam Rosser-Owen, "A Córdoban Ivory Pyxis Lid in the Ashmolean Museum", *Muqarnas* 16 (1999), pp. 16–31, esp. 20–21.
22 Janet L. Abu-Lughod, *Before European Hegemony: The World System A.D. 1250–1350*, Oxford: Oxford University Press, 1991; more specifically, see Sarah M. Guérin, "'Avorio d'ogni Ragione': The Supply of Elephant Ivory to Northern Europe in the Gothic Era", *Journal of Medieval History* 36.2 (2010), pp. 156–174.
23 Cf. Ronald Messier, "The Christian Community of Tunis at the Time of St. Louis Crusade, AD 1270", in: Eleanor Cogdon (ed.), *Latin Expansion in the Medieval Western Mediterranean*, Farnham: Ashgate Variorum, 2013, pp. 295–310.
24 The atlas (BNF MS. Esp. 30) is now fully digitized with a detailed catalogue entry by the Bibliothèque nationale de France on Gallica, online at: http://gallica.bnf.fr/ark:/12148/btv1b55002481n.r=atlas%20catalan?rk=64378;0 (accessed August 2019).

Prestige, Power, Purity

Elephants and Ivory in the Benin Kingdom and Elsewhere in Africa

KATHY CURNOW

The supremacy and might of elephants have impressed African artists for tens of millennia. When the Sahara was still rich grasslands, a skilled hand used stone to engrave an image of the animal into a Libyan massif (Fig. 2). One of numerous ancient elephant representations across what is now desert, it includes no hunters and conveys a sense of freedom and movement. The grandeur and strength of this, the world's largest land animal, became synonymous with power across the continent, its ivory tusks evoking both the elephant's sovereignty and the prestige of this luxury material. Because of the continent's vastness and the long timespan of elephant representations and ivory objects, this essay can provide only a limited view of the topic. The objects discussed, however, are meant to hint at the subject's great scope, and its manifestations in both small-scale societies and major states during the past half-millennium. As such, the spotlight on the Benin Kingdom—the site of rich elephant associations as well as the greatest concentration of surviving African carved ivories—provides a sense of the abundant cultural associations elephants and their ivory have throughout the continent.

2 Elephant in movement,
ca. 10,000–7000 BCE, petroglyph,
Tadrart Acacus region, Libya.

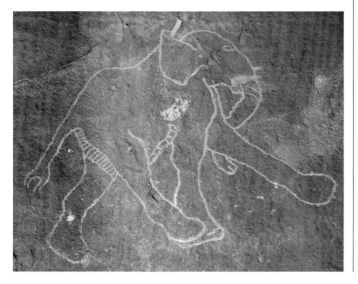

3 Bamileke male artist, before 1913 (late 19th or early 20th century), Bafoussam, Cameroon, wood, 100 x 41 x 26 cm. Ethnologisches Museum der Staatlichen Museen zu Berlin - Preußischer Kulturbesitz.

Elephants: Visual and verbal

The awe that elephants inspire has linked them to wisdom, superiority, and great accomplishments. Leaders coopt their size and power through hyperbole. Ghana's Akan peoples say "No one follows the elephant in the bush and gets wet from the morning dew", referring to the way "big men" protect their followers from consequences. Even the High God is praised through elephant comparisons. Nigeria's Igbo people devised the panegyric: "He who swallows what swallowed the elephant."[1]

Elephants are also represented visually throughout much of the continent. In West Africa, many masqueraders embody them through stylized masks, particularly among the Guro, Baule, and Yaure of the Côte d'Ivoire, the Igbo of southeastern Nigeria, and Cameroon's various Grassfields Kingdoms.[2] Their purposes vary. Baule examples (Fig. 1) are part of a dance ensemble that performs for entertainment, sometimes miming a hunt, while Guro elephant masks are part of a troupe of sacred animal and human masquerades that appear at funerals, as

do the performers of the horizontally worn elephant masks of the Cameroon Grassfields (Fig. 3). The animal's tusks, trunks, and ears wax or wane in scale, depending on the region, and may be geometricized. The characteristic massiveness of an elephant's head is usually eschewed in order to facilitate the dancers' performance. While costumes vary, they do not mimic the animal's skin.

Cameroon's Bamileke people create an aristocratic herd through performances by the select Kwosi society, composed of royals and influential chiefs. Its members' high status is reinforced at biannual celebrations and at members' funerals and commemorative festivals through the elephant masquerade (Fig. 4). The costumes' imported beads, expensive indigo-patterned cloth, and leopard pelt all suggest leadership and exclusivity, as do some dancers' headdresses, which may be topped by hundreds of red tail feathers from the African grey parrot or even some ostrich or peacock plumes. The elephant itself is abstracted to the point of unrecognizability (Fig. 5). Its ears are waggling disks, its trunk is flat and broadened into two long flaps of the hooded cloth mask,

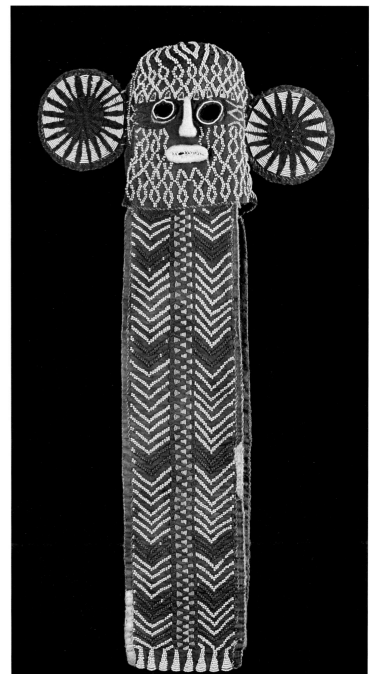

5 Bamileke male artist, elephant mask of the Kuosi society, Cameroon, 20th century, raffia, cotton, and glass beads, 100 x 55 x 5 cm. Staatliche Museen zu Berlin, Ethnologisches Museum.

6 Sultan Njimoluh Seidou (r. 1933–1992) of the Bamum capital of Foumban, Cameroon, seated in his office, two tusks flanking his desk, ca. 1950s–1960s. Staatliche Museen zu Berlin, Ethnologisches Museum.

7 Lega male artist, *Mumtu*, instructional object, Democratic Republic of Congo, probably first half 20th century, ivory, 14.9 cm. Afrika Museum, Berg en Dal.

8 Igbo male artist, *Ikenga*, Umuleri/Aguleri region, Nigeria, first half of the 20th century, wood, pigment, 61.0 cm. Sidney and Lois Eskenazi Museum of Art, Indiana University.

9 Igbo chiefs blowing *okike* ivory trumpets, Nigeria, 2018.

and a human nose and mouth anthropomorphize it. While its characteristic tusks are absent, many performers hold a beaded flywhisk whose forked handle forcefully recalls these two external teeth. The performers frequently wear ivory jewelry, reinforcing the animal association. The hood's patterned surface regularly incorporates triangular designs that allude to a leopard's markings. Both animals are royal symbols, and the ruler is believed to be able to transform into either.

Elephants appear as caryatids on many Cameroon monarchs' informal travel stools, and as motifs on other royal objects, such as brass pipe bowls. Ivory itself also has leadership connotations. Bamileke rulers are said to be buried with a tusk placed between their legs, and formal 20th-century photographic portraits of Grassfields monarchs frequently portray them resting their feet on tusks or sitting on thrones flanked by huge examples. The latter were apparently ubiquitous enough to be incorporated into informal palace settings as well (Fig. 6).

Ivory and its value

The date African artists created the first ivory objects is unknown, but by the 4th or 5th millennium BCE, pre-Dynastic Egyptian tombs included ivory figures and knives. The material's prestige associations continue to the present. Many communities throughout the continent have fashioned ivory hairpins, bracelets, labrets, combs, and other precious objects prized for their color, smoothness, and associations with a powerful animal not easily felled before the advent of guns.

Esteemed ivories were not limited to ornaments. For the Lega of the Democratic Republic of Congo, they served as an educational tool of the highest order (Fig. 7). The village-based Lega were self-regulated by a supervisory society called Bwami. Both men and women could be initiated into Bwami through initiation, to then progress through a series of grades and sub-levels as they mastered degrees of wisdom, perception, and morality. Bwami instruction often referenced the once-common elephant through proverbs, and elders adopted costume elements that used their bones, ears, tails, or skins, all metaphors of leadership. The animal's ivory also alluded to varied concepts of power in veiled ways. The maxim "mushrooms do not grow on ivory" underlines the material's invulnerability to time, speaking to Bwami's ethical continuity over generations.[3]

Kindi, the highest level of Bwami initiation, was distinguished by ownership of ivory figurative elements. Elders carried these objects in bags and used them instructionally, paired with esoteric proverbs, songs, and dances that conveyed societal values. When their owner died, these objects were temporarily placed on his grave and then kept in reserve until a worthy successor emerged, such as a newly initiated Kindi member who then received an ivory figure to validate his position as a senior Bwami professor.[4] Although a few of these ivories were stock types with common meanings, most were specific to the owner, their associated aphorisms shifting as students advanced within the society. The figures are typically abstract with concave, heart-shaped faces and coffee-bean eyes. Oil, pigment, and scent were added before each usage in a process that mimicked Bwami members' own cosmetic treatments, producing appealing patinas; sometimes kaolin and a specific charcoal were also applied. The power inherent in these ivories was also used for healing; fine dust or scrapings from the pieces were mixed with water and drunk.[5]

Ivory as an Igbo social marker

Igbo men from eastern Nigeria advance socially by assuming different levels of titles, each with attached fees and privileges. The supreme male title is that of *ozo*, which commands wide respect. It serves as a gateway to influence, political activities, and societal respect, but at its essence *ozo* is a kind of ancestral priesthood with personal purification as a requirement. As such, whiteness—of clothing and ivory—is a hallmark of participants.

Ivory was so critical to Igbo status that it was depicted in other mediums. Until recent decades, most ambitious men owned personal wooden altars to accomplishment called *ikenga*, the "power of the right arm". These were usually figurative, with considerable formal variety. Even abstract examples, however, included a stool and horns, respectively suggesting a titled man's stool or a ram's masculinity and aggression. Men sacrificed to their *ikenga* to maximize success through their personal efforts. Some larger and more complex examples indicate a male age-grade commissioned them for joint use, a proclamation of its members' solidarity and united drive for legendary success (Fig. 8). While many personal *ikenga* depict warriors holding both a weapon and an enemy head, some emphasize the aspirational status of a titled man. Markers here include a

10 Elephant tusk with carving from a royal memorial altar. Staatliche Museen zu Berlin, Ethnologisches Museum.

11 The late Oba Erediauwa, who died in 2016, playing an ivory gong while dancing in the 1994 Emobo ceremony, gong made by an Edo male artist, Benin City, Nigeria, second half of 20th century.

backed stool (a marker of rank, for the *ozo* man cannot sit on the ground), *ichi* forehead scarifications like those that had adorned the former titleholder, an iron staff used to serve the ancestors, and an ivory trumpet.

The trumpet was a key piece of *ozo* regalia, and some titleholders owned multiple examples. The material itself signals expense and respect, its whiteness underlining the concept of purity. The Igbo differentiate two ivory trumpets, both with undecorated surfaces. *Ozo* men carry the smaller of the two to festivals and daily occasions, and blow it in imitation of speech to salute fellow titleholders and neighbors. Its use today extends to those with high political posts and status, even without *ozo* membership. The *ikenga* shown here, however, displays the larger of the two trumpets, the *okike* (Fig. 9). As it is the ultimate status symbol, the titleholder plays it at festivals, funerals, installations of fellow *ozo* members, and on any occasion when his superior social rank calls for recognition. He does not deign to carry it himself, instead assigning that task to a junior male

relative. One of the Igbo High God's praise-names is Chukwu Okike, a reference to the elephant's power and magnitude, traits that are also accorded to the *okike*-owning titleholder. As Chris Ebighbo states, "The elephant, *enyi*, is not a common animal and should not be regarded as such. Acquisition of its tusk means an end to social achievement in Igbo, meaning metaphorically that God-*Chukwu*, as elephant, is behind my success."[6] For over 40 years, however, the unavailability of ivory has meant that most contemporary *ozo* men possess ivory trumpets only if they inherited them from fathers who were also titleholders.

Nigeria's Benin Kingdom: Site of Africa's most prolific ivory carving

Pre-colonial Igbo communities were egalitarian city-states, ivory being used to mark an individual's recognized achievements. Larger polities, however, had the wherewithal to both collect more tusks and develop specialized carvers. Nigeria's Benin Kingdom (11th century to present, now under Nigerian national jurisdiction) exemplifies the density of artistic representation through both elephant motifs and many varieties of ivory figures and other objects with relief ornamentation. Its monarch, the Oba of Benin, held rights to one tusk from a felled elephant, as well as the privilege to buy the second. A village of royal elephant hunters stood just outside the capital, for forest elephants were once numerous. The palace coffers were not limited to locally hunted elephants, however; tribute from subject states would have swollen their contents. Benin's extant carved royal ivories outnumber those of any other African culture, though most are now scattered in museums worldwide. The capital was never abandoned nor successfully invaded until the British forcibly attacked in 1897 in their efforts to subjugate what is now Nigeria. Their attack on Benin City stripped the palace and many chiefs' homes of thousands of treasures in brass, ivory, and wood[7]—see Figs. 10, 12, 13—colonial plunder that continues to prompt demands for restitution. The dispersed works permit a rare uninterrupted look at more than 500 years of royal African art from a single culture—a continental corpus unmatched outside ancient Egypt. Benin's ivories, like its other artworks, reveal a sophisticated encoding of historical events, personalities, and worldview.

Although the elephant is a Benin royal symbol, the leopard surpasses it. The latter is identified solely with the monarch, while an elephant can represent power in the abstract, the majesty of the Oba, or, particularly in 18th-century art, Chief Iyase, a rebellious war chief whose transformation into an elephant fomented destruction. Today, a naturalistic elephant joins the leopard as a flanking element on the Oba's coat-of-arms, but in the past depictions of a complete elephant were uncommon. They do show up as toppers on several brass and wooden *ukhurhe*, tall staves placed on all ancestral altars. Modeled after a bamboo-like stem that recalls a lineage's segments, their finial imagery is restricted by status. Some royal *ukhurhe* show an elephant, a privilege shared by carvers' guild members. Certain others depict the Oba standing on an elephant's back, a triumph over the oppositional chief.[8] The elephant's head by itself, however, is a widespread motif. They are portrayed with modest ears and tusks, often in extreme abstraction, emphasis being on the animal's trunk, which ends in a human hand to signify its prehensile abilities. This generally clutches leaves, indicating powerful supernatural

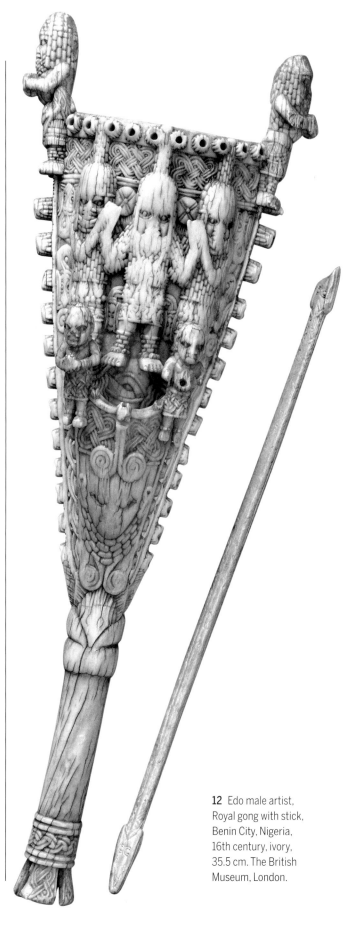

12 Edo male artist, Royal gong with stick, Benin City, Nigeria, 16th century, ivory, 35.5 cm. The British Museum, London.

53

13 Edo male artist, waist pendant representing Oba Esigie's mother, Idia, Benin City, Nigeria, 16th century, ivory, 24.5 cm. The British Museum, London.

bush medicines, dually alluding to esoteric knowledge and formidable abilities.

Sumptuary laws restricted ivory's use to the Oba and the select few to whom he granted favor. No one, however, could compete with his ownership of raw tusks and carved objects. The latter were numerous and varied, including decorative palace items (door latches, a rasp for the royal feet, combs, containers for beads and kola nuts, human and leopard sculptures), ceremonial objects (flywhisk handles, musical instruments, armlets, waist pendants), and sacred articles such as royal ancestral altar tusks (Fig. 10), and medicine containers. Only royal brasses—another elite material that the Oba controlled—surpassed the profusion of ivory objects. Royal demand for art was constant and considerable, warranting a hereditary royal guild of wood and ivory carvers with its own city ward.

Like other Benin artworks, ivories often extol the monarch. They do so by incorporating symbolism that summarizes history as well as relationships between this world and that of spirits. The inherent complexities of such visual expression are exemplified by a 16th-century work used for an annual ceremony (Fig. 12). This object, an ivory version of a double metal gong, includes now-worn imagery. At the upper front, the Oba is the central figure in a triad of nearly identically dressed men. He looks straight ahead, they turn slightly to support him with upraised hands. This triad, a standard Benin motif, dates to at least the 15th century, and indicates the interdependence of a ruler and his people. In this work it depicts Oba Esigie, together with Osa and Osuan, two priest-chiefs. They held key roles in Esigie's reign (ca. 1517–1580s): Osuan was his advisor before he took the throne, while Osa counselled his half-brother and rival Prince Arhuaran—yet still supported Esigie.

The vertical extension of their headgear (oro) still appears on both the crown, the hats of these chiefs, and as attachments for the Uzama (a select group of seven chiefs) and a few priests. Osa and Osuan no longer wear beaded attire; its use is apparently more restricted today than before. The Oba's attire is distinguished here by a large bead at mid-chest, as well as a belt with mud-fish-shaped extensions on each side. The bead was magically imbued with the power to make others tremble in the monarch's presence, while the belt held medicinal energy with a similar function. All mudfish are liminal creatures that can cross from water to land—and thus symbolize kings, priests, and witches who cross from human to spirit realms—but this 16th-century gong specifically portrays electric mudfish, whose paralyzing ability the Oba shares.

The instrument's upper edges and front feature two male pairs, each holding a globular object. The upper figures are chiefs; the lower ones lack their elaborate headgear and the high beaded collar worn by the Oba, upper-level chiefs, and some royal family members. All are playing the *ukuse*, a calabash gourd whose loose netted cover of beads or other objects supplies percussive rhythm. An attached secondary gong displays a worn face with the same aristocratic collar, and represents Esigie's mother, Idia. Her efforts, both martial and supernatural, put him on the throne, and he elevated her with a title equal to that of his generals. Below her chin is the abstract head of a sharp-beaked bird, an association the gong's reverse clarifies.

If the gong's front demonstrates the social roles of its key figures, its reverse shows them in their night guise as supernatural beings. The Oba here exchanges his political role from the triad to identify with Olokun, deity of the sea, rivers, and wealth. In each hand he masters a dangerous crocodile, gripping them by one foot. In their mouths, these reptiles each form a huge fist with upright thumb—a sign of good fortune. Electric mudfish replace Oba's legs, reinforcing his awe-inspiring abilities. Below, in a supportive position, a snake-winged bat supplants Idia's face. Night birds—like the one on the gong's front—and bats are liminal creatures linked to witchcraft, a skill Idia is said to have mastered and used to her son's advantage.

A handful of these ivory gongs, most with nearly identical imagery, survive (Fig. 12). The majority show wear and breakage, but the monarch never disposed of "retired" examples no longer in use. Additional gongs were used in 20th- and 21st-century annual Emobo ceremonies (Fig. 11) held just outside the palace walls where Esigie's quarters once stood. This festival's limited participants feature Ogbelaka guild drummers. The Oba and a few other courtiers dance decorously around the percussionists before returning to the palace. There a chief raises a royal *ukhurhe* and commands any lingering spirits to depart for Udo, about 30 kilometers to the north.

Through allusion, rather than reenactment, Emobo historically commemorates a supernatural problem that had a clever solution. It refers to events that occurred during and after Esigie's triumph in a war of succession with his half-brother, Arhuaran. Idia was involved, tipping its balance by feeding Arhuaran's soldiers enchanted soup, thus inducing them to switch allegiance. Cornered at a lake in Udo, Arhuaran planned suicide in the face of defeat. He first removed the large pendant bead of kingship his father had previously bestowed upon him, cursed

14 Temne or Bullom male artist, hunting horn for a Portuguese patron, Sierra Leone, late 15th or early 16th century, ivory, 48.2 cm. The British Museum, London.

it, and hung it on a bush. He then drowned himself as Esigie's men approached.

Placing the cursed necklace around his own neck, Esigie began to move erratically and speak gibberish. His mental condition—if observed by the populace in the capital—would have resulted in dethronement. In order to convey him safely to Benin City without arousing concern, the Ogbelaka members who had accompanied him to Udo imitated Esigie's movements and garbled "lyrics". As they passed the citizens, the latter assumed the palace had introduced a new dance and songs in a foreign tongue. Crisis averted, the Oba was cured, an iron gong being used in the restorative process. The final invocation for all stray spirits to "go to Udo" after sacrificial feeding is meant to appease Arhuaran, whose unrecovered body never had a funeral, thus causing his spirit to remain unsettled.[9]

The Emobo gong's portrayal of Esigie and his mother in both their supernatural and social guises comments on the dual power sources that enabled both victory and recovery. While the entourage and the elite material itself reinforce the status of the participants, the substitution of ivory for iron also asserts one of the material's critical functions. In Benin, ivory is a protective medicine. Like many African mystical ingredients, it is an animal part that is destructive or defensive. Ivory's abilities are so highly ranked that the carving guild saves even the "sawdust" from their work for medicines that provide strength, protection, and the ability to make any action more efficacious.[10]

A contemporaneous pendant of Idia (Fig. 13), identified by the late Oba Akenzua II,[11] constitutes another Emobo-related ivory. She again wears the aristocratic high collar generally owned by men, but has a female coiffure—tiny upstanding braids, each capped by a coral bead—behind a crest of bearded Portuguese faces. A handful of Portuguese fought for Esigie, but here they double as references to Olokun's world because of their sea travel and luxury trade goods. Iron once inlaid her stylized frown[12] and pupils, and also outlined her eyes, but is now mostly missing. It indicated her determination and power, creating a resolute, indomitable gaze. Idia's reputation as a formidable witch stretches to the present, with songs that extol her "chalk-white belly" (pure heart). This reference is a euphemistic inversion, since insulting a witch is foolhardy.

15 Edo male artist, export spoon, Benin City, Nigeria, late 15th or early 16th century, ivory, 26 cm. Weltmuseum, Vienna.

16 Kongo-Vili male artist, decorative export tusk, purchased in Chinchoxo, Cabinda region, Angola, 19th century (before 1876), ivory, length (entire tusk) 63 cm. Staatliche Museen zu Berlin, Ethnologisches Museum.

A near-identical example in the Metropolitan Museum, made by the same artist from the same tusk, served as a pendant. Along with other pendant pairs—leopard heads, the triad—these were strung around the royal waist, serving as apotropaic devices that kept the monarch invulnerable to Arhuaran's spirit. All suffered wear-and-tear and were periodically replaced, but, once again, damaged examples were not discarded for they had medicinal power. In 1897 the British invaders, in sacking the palace, discovered them in a box in the Oba's bedroom. Their superior quality was instantly recognized, and these stolen goods were divided among some of Britain's most important colonial and military figures in the region. Ralph Moor, Commissioner and Consul-General of the Niger Coast Protectorate, took the two twin examples, while others went to Henry Gallwey, who had served as Deputy Commissioner and Vice-Consul of the Oil Rivers Protectorate, and to Robert Allman, the invasion force's Principal Medical Officer. Only one early example passed immediately into a dealer's hands; two dating from a much later period are now in museums in Berlin and Lagos. More recent versions are still sometimes worn but are not inevitably part of royal Emobo dress.

Carved ivory for export: From the 15th–20th century

Although known exports of raw tusk date to Nubia's commerce with ancient Egypt, we cannot be sure when traffic in worked African ivories commenced or how widespread its destinations were. Bracelets made from cross-sliced tusks are likely to have been the first such works and are still distributed overseas. In the Early Modern period, exported carved ivories were traded to Europe via the Portuguese from the early 15th century onwards, but remained limited. Made in already established carving centers such as coastal Sierra Leone, the Benin Kingdom, and the coastal Kongo region, these so-called Luso-Portuguese ivories were both commissioned works and royal gifts whose recipients considered them exotic curiosities. Albrecht Dürer wrote that he had bought "two ivory salt-cellars from Calicut" (India, today Kozhikode) in Antwerp in 1520, contributing to a confusion regarding the ivories' origins that persisted for centuries.

European forms influenced most of these Luso-African works:[13] spoons, saltcellars, horns, and the occasional knife hilt or ecclesiastical vessel. In some cases, European tastes dominated both shape and iconography. Hunting horns from coastal Sierra Leone (Fig. 14) were end-blown, lacking the African transverse mouthpiece. They usually included imagery drawn from printed sources, suggesting a direct commission—here the armillary sphere, the cross of the Military Order of Christ, and the angel-supported coat-of-arms all relate to King Manuel, while a centaur, harpy, crowned lion, and various stag-hunting scenes are also foreign in inspiration. Nonetheless, the artist included two crocodiles and a coiled snake, nods to more familiar local denizens.

Export ivories from the Benin Kingdom were fewer in number than those of Sierra Leone. Dominated by delicate spoons whose bowls followed a Portuguese pattern, nearly all their handles bore imagery wholly African in inspiration. The spoon illustrated here (Fig. 15) depicts a bird with a fish in its mouth, a Benin reference to the natural order of hierarchy; a virtuoso open-worked element follows, but the finial—a hand gesturing in Catholic blessing—is a rare European insertion.

An even smaller group of Kongo ivories had reached Europe by the 17th century, but these showed little adaptation to foreign tastes. The trade in carved exotica for external consumption dwindled, bursting forth anew in the mid 19th century. Kongo-Vili artists then began producing large numbers of non-functional tusks, small figures, and related works. This trade was centered at Loango but extended to nearby coastal ports (Fig. 16), continuing until World War One. The tusks number about 600, featuring similar compositions of Europeans and Africans marching along a spiral groundline. This example's scenes include a climbing palm-wine tapper, one African threatening another with decapitation, a drummer, a human-headed bird, and an amorous couple, as well as many figures toting rifles.[14]

While this last group could depict a war party, it likely represents elephant hunters. The international ivory trade proliferated in the 19th century with an influx of guns, a major upsurge in foreign traders, and an escalation of demands for Indian brides' bangles and industrially produced European pianos, billiard balls, and trinkets. This precipitated the wholesale destruction of herds throughout the continent and indirectly led to the current elephant crisis. Even though plastic has replaced ivory and the protective laws have been enacted, decreased elephant numbers have in fact raised ivory's commodity value. Poachers, warlords, and smugglers—particularly to China and other Asian countries—continue to undercut the millennia of respect and esteem Africans held for the elephant and its ivory, once expressed through the latter's restricted use.

* Artists not known by name are referred to as male because the activity of ivory carving in the cultures discussed here was reserved exclusively for men.

1 Edwin Anaegboka Udoye, *Resolving the Prevailing Conflicts between Christianity and African (Igbo) Traditional Religion through Inculturation*, Münster: LIT Verlag, 2011, p. 39.

2 Doran Ross (ed.), *Elephant: The Animal and its Ivory in African Culture*, Los Angeles: UCLA Fowler Museum of Cultural History, 1992.

3 Daniel Biebuyck, *Lega Culture: Art, Initiation and Moral Philosophy among a Central African People*, Berkeley: University of California Press, 1973, p. 174.

4 Daniel Biebuyck, "The Kindi Aristocrats and their Art among the Lega", in: Douglas Fraser and Herbert M. Cole (eds), *African Arts and Leadership*, Madison: University of Wisconsin Press, 1972, pp. 7–20; Elisabeth Lynn Cameron, "The Stampeding of Elephants: Elephant Imprints on Lega Thought", in: Doran H. Ross (ed.), *Elephant: The Animal and its Ivory in African Culture*, Los Angeles: UCLA Fowler Museum of Cultural History, 1992, pp. 295–305; Elisabeth Lynn Cameron, *Art of the Lega*, Los Angeles: UCLA Fowler Museum of Cultural History, 2001.

5 Cameron 2001 (as note 4), p. 94; Daniel Biebuyck, *The Arts of Zaire*, vol. 2: *Eastern Zaire*, Berkeley: University of California Press, 1986, pp. 53, 191. Biebuyck 1972 (as note 4), p. 19; Biebuyck 1973 (as note 3), pp. 144, 167, 173–175, 179; H. Kellim Brown, "Crossing the Lega Ivory Spectrum: A Contemporary Ride Through 'Heavy' Things in Maniema, Part One", in: Marc Leo Felix (ed.), *White Gold, Black Hands: Ivory Sculpture in Congo*, vol. 5, Qiquher Heilungkiang, China: Gemini Sun, 2013, p. 258; and H. Kellim Brown, "Crossing the Lega Ivory Spectrum: A Contemporary Ride Through 'Heavy' Things in Maniema, Part Two", in: *White Gold, Black Hands* (as this note), vol. 6 (2013), p. 38.

6 Chris Ebighgbo, "The Trumpets: Okike, Odu-mkpalo, and Enenke as Ethnography in Igbo Social Commitments", *Gefame Journal of African Studies* 6, no. 1 (2009), n.p.; Herbert M. Cole and Chike C. Aniakor, *Igbo Arts: Community and Cosmos*, Los Angeles: Museum of Cultural History, 1984.

7 A.F.C. Ryder, *Benin and the Europeans, 1486–1897*, New York: Humanities Press, 1969; Barbara Plankensteiner, "The Benin treasures: difficult legacy and contested heritage", in: Brigitta Hauser-Schäublin (ed.), *Cultural Property and Contested Ownership*, London: Routledge/Taylor & Francis, 2016, pp. 133–155.

8 Paula Girshick Ben-Amos, *Art, Innovation, and Politics in Eighteenth-century Benin*, Bloomington, IN, Indiana University Press, 1999.

9 Kathy Curnow, *Iyare! Splendor & Tension in Benin's Palace Theatre*, Cleveland, OH, 2016, pp. 136–137, 144–145; Barbara Blackmun, "Double Gong and Striker", in: Barbara Plankensteiner (ed.), *Benin: Kings and Rituals*, Ghent: Snoeck, 2007, p. 315.

10 Kathy Curnow, "Ivory as Cultural Document", *Curator* 61, no. 1 (2018), pp. 61–94.

11 Paula Ben-Amos, *The Art of Benin*, London: Thames and Hudson, 1980, p. 81.

12 Joseph Nevadomsky and Joseph Aisien, "The Clothing of Political Identity", *African Arts* 28, no. 1 (1995), p. 65.

13 Kathy Curnow, "The Afro-Portuguese Ivories", PhD diss., Bloomington: Indiana University 1983; Ezio Bassani and William Fagg, *Africa and the Renaissance*, New York: Center for African Art, 1988.

14 Z.S. Strother, *Humor and Violence: Seeing Europeans in Central African Art*, Bloomington: Indiana University Press, 2016, pp. 82–152, 295–300, 319–332; Nichole N. Bridges, "Novel Souvenirs: Loango Coast Ivories", in: *White Gold, Black Hands* (as note 5), vol. 1 (2010), pp. 254–269; Della Jenkins, "Nineteenth Century Loango Coast Ivories", PhD diss., University of California, Santa Barbara, 2003.

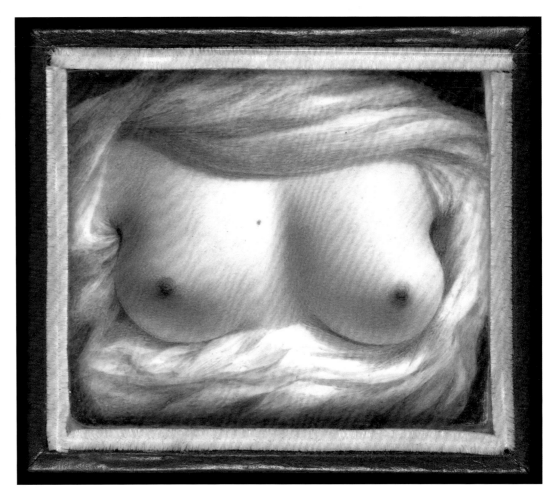

1 Sarah Goodridge, *Beauty Revealed*, 1828, watercolor on ivory, 6.7 x 8 cm. The Metropolitan Museum of Art, New York.

Encounters with Ivory

Body Image, Body Contact, Body Replacement

ALBERTO SAVIELLO

In addition to its preciousness, there is another central reason why ivory has been treasured across cultures and through millennia: it is closely associated with the human body. The tusks of the elephant (and the mammoth), called ivory, are made of dentin, an organic material from which—in a compound that is chemically very similar—human teeth are formed as well. Our relationship with ivory, even though we are not always aware of it, is influenced by this fundamental association, and is reflected in various ways in myth and in art. The Olympian gods, for example, had the missing shoulder of the dismembered prince Pelops replaced with a piece of ivory, so as subsequently to be able to revive him in all his former beauty. In the Spanish Baroque, sculptors used the dentin of elephants to depict the teeth in the martyred body of Christ, thereby creating an image of his suffering as realistic as possible (Fig. 2).

The physical affinity between humans and ivory is clearest in touch. Ivory is a sensuous material. It is heavy and dense, generally with an appealing smoothness and, since it is a poor conductor, a relatively warm surface. It seems pliable to the touch, almost like a living body. Direct contact with it has always been considered pleasing, as seen by the fact that craftsmen have frequently used ivory for handles and mouthpieces (e.g. of wind instruments, pipes, etc.) . A look back at history reveals the manifold relationships between ivory and ourselves, at times literally getting under our skin, and shows the many different values and qualities that have been ascribed to the material.

The beauty of ivory

From a psychological perspective, teeth stand for strength, health, beauty, and sexuality.[1] These same attributes have also been associated with ivory and with objects made of it. This is apparent from love poetry. Poets of various epochs have compared the body of the beloved or specific parts of it to ivory. Already in a Sumerian love song from the Old Babylonian period (ca. 1800 BCE) the body of the goddess Ishtar is described as a lustrous pillar of ivory.[2] Better known are the erotic verses of the Old Testament Song of Songs, in which lovers praise each other's beauty. Whereas the woman praises "his belly as of ivory, set with sapphires", the woman's neck is likened to a "tower of ivory" (Song of Songs 5: 14, 7:5). In Arabic and Persian poetry, in followers of Petrarch, and in European Baroque poetry, the skin and specific parts of the body like the cheeks, the neck, the forehead, the fingers, and the breasts are likened to ivory in their smoothness and flawlessness. This may have been what inspired the artist Sarah Goodridge to create in 1828 the first known "breast selfie" (Fig. 1). The painter apparently pictured her own breasts in this 7 x 8 cm miniature and sent the image to her beloved.[3] Set off by a beauty spot and small, delicate pink nipples, her breasts have a snow-white pallor. In addition, the picture, like many love tokens and personal mementos of the time, was painted on ivory. Thus the notion of ivory breasts is here doubly realized.

2 Gregorio Fernandez, *Dead Christ*, 1627, wood, ivory, polychromy (detail with the head of Christ). Museo Nacional de Escultura, Valladolid.

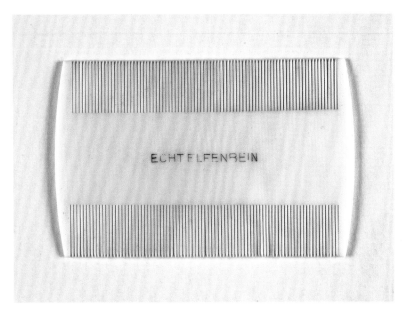

3 Nit or dust comb with the inscription "ECHT ELFENBEIN" ("genuine ivory"), Germany, early 20th century, ivory, ca. 8 x 10 cm. Stiftung Stadtmuseum Berlin.

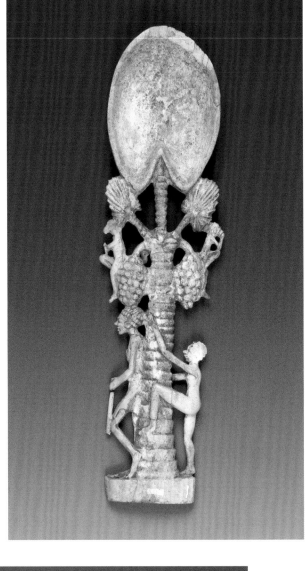

4 Cosmetic spoon, Egypt, 18th Dynasty (1550–1292 BCE), elephant or hippopotamus ivory, h. 20 cm. Museu Calouste Gulbenkian, Lisbon.

5 Double-sided comb with depictions of the Annunciation and the Nativity, Italy (?), mid-15th century, ivory, 11 x 14.4 cm. Staatliche Museen zu Berlin, Kunstgewerbemuseum.

Ivory has not only been a common motif in the description of human beauty, it has also served to preserve it. The material has been employed in personal hygiene in various ways. Ivory has been popular in the manufacture of utensils that come in direct contact with the skin. The most widespread example is the comb. It is thought to be the oldest grooming implement. The ancient Greek word for comb was κτείς, which can be translated in a secondary meaning as "hand with splayed fingers" and describes the implement's basic form. Interestingly, not only the form of the comb remained constant in all regions of the world since its 'invention', the use of ivory in its manufacture can also be traced back to at least to the 4th millennium BCE. Modern examples, like a machine-made comb from the early 20th century, were purposefully advertised as having been made of "genuine ivory" (Fig. 3).

Other grooming implements have also frequently been made of ivory. From pharaonic Egypt, where cosmetics had cult significance, countless cosmetic objects have been preserved as grave goods: small vials for oils, salves, and pigments, as well as cosmetic spoons (Fig. 4), in which pigments were mixed with binding agents. These were made from both elephant and hippopotamus teeth. Styluses (Arabic *mīl*) used to apply makeup to the skin were also often made of dentin.

Though real ivory is rarely used in personal grooming today, the myth of ivory-like beauty and above all the association of ivory with flawless light skin has survived to this day. This is apparent from the number of modern beauty products like skin cremes and skin lighteners branded with names incorporating the word "ivory".

6 Robert Testard, *Pygmalion Taking his Figure to Bed*, late 15th century, book illumination, from *Roman de la Rose*. The Bodleian Library, Oxford.

Not only clean, but also pure

Ivory toilet utensils became more widespread in Europe during the Middle Ages. Early examples are the princely caskets and boxes produced in the 10th and 11th centuries in Córdoba, the capital of the Umayyad caliphate. These often served as containers for scent, and in their decoration and poetic inscriptions illustrated courtly ideals.[4] In the late 13th and 14th centuries, Paris was a production center for luxury articles in ivory. Combs, hairpins, mirror cases, and caskets from this time frequently present figural scenes from the sphere of courtly love, the era's highly regulated knightly lovemaking. Among these depictions were conventional courtly love gestures like a gentle stroking of the chin, men and

women playing chess, or allegorical themes like the "Attack on the Castle of Love". With such gifts from the realm of personal grooming, lovers could not only express their affection, but also hope to come closer, at least indirectly, to the body of the beloved.

Even though images on toiletry items often have to do with love, the depictions are rarely blatantly physical. There was also an ethical, moral aspect to such objects as instruments of hygiene. Instead of promoting lust, most ivory implements convey a restrictive sexual morality and physical restraint. For example, a depiction of the Annunciation on the back of a comb (Fig. 5) does not necessarily point to its use in a clerical environment—though bishops and priests were ritually combed before the Mass:[5] as an ideal image of female virtue, the depiction of Mary was also appropriate for the comb of a secular owner.

Particular importance was accorded to the material in this regard. Thanks to its homogeneous structure, light coloring, and firm surface, ivory was considered a symbol of purity and innocence in Christianity. Descriptions of elephants by ancient writers contributed greatly to this interpretation in Europe. In his *Natural History* (ca. 77 CE), Pliny the Elder describes the elephant as the animal that most resembles man thanks to its mental and social characteristics. Since it venerated the stars, the elephant even had a form of religion. It was a bashful creature that coupled only every two years and did not know "adultery" (Book VIII, Chapter 12). Pliny's report on the elephant's virtue was given a Christian interpretation in the nature textbook *Physiologus* (2nd–4th century CE). There the elephant bull and cow are perceived to "represent the persons of Adam and Eve".[6] Since the elephant was essentially free of sexual desire, propagation occurred only after seduction by the elephant cow, following the pattern of the Fall. As a purported archenemy of the serpent, the elephant moreover took on Christological associations. The animal's virtue was transferred to its tusks as well. Augustine of Hippo and Hrabanus Maurus understood ivory to be a symbol of the subjection of the flesh and of purity.[7] The Church teacher Saint Peter Damian went so far as to draw a parallel between the ivory body (*venter eburneus*) of the Song of Songs and the belly of Mary, which bore the Son of God in chastity and without sin.[8] In the 12th century, "ivory tower" (*turris eburnea*) came to be used as a reverent epithet for the Virgin Mary.

Corresponding to its ethical value, pharmaceutical powers were also ascribed to ivory, and it was employed as a medicine. In his *Puch der Natur* (Book of Nature) from the mid-14th century, Konrad von Megenberg, for example, maintained that burnt ivory could repel snakes and neutralize poisons.

Ivory appetites and procreative powers

Thanks to its being equated with the body of the beloved, ivory could also become an object of human desire. A literary highlight of sexuality involving ivory is the story of King Pygmalion as told in Book 10 of Ovid's *Metamorphoses*. Having been scared by real women, the king of Cyprus, a trained sculptor, carved his ideal woman in ivory, only to fall in love with the figure. He treated the statue as a lover, and even shared his bed with it (Fig. 6). On the feast day of Venus, Pygmalion made sacrifice to the goddess of love and begged for a wife resembling his sculpture. Returned home, the king began to caress the ivory woman as usual, only this time the figure became soft and alive under his kisses.

In almost all epochs and regions of the world, beginning with one of the earliest known figural depictions, the Old Stone Age Hohle Fels Venus, ivory has been a favored material in which to create figures with a distinctly erotic or sexual expressiveness. One virtuosic and voyeuristically titillating carving shows Adam and Eve lying in, or more correctly standing in front of, a bed. The bit of cloth covering their lower bodies can be removed, so that the depiction of the couple gazing at each other in ecstasy takes on an explicitly sexual, almost pornographic, quality (Fig. 7). Ivory depictions of naked or largely unclothed couples are also found in other cultures with different meanings and functions: for example, as depictions of heavenly lovers (Maithuna) in India, whose sexual union has ethical and religious meanings (Fig. 8).[9]

The tusks of the bull elephant are considered signs of its strength and are important in the sexual selection of elephants. This, as well as their curved shape and hardness may explain the association of tusks and the material ivory with the male penis. Countless carvings of phalluses in ivory from various regions and epochs document the association of the substance with male sexuality and procreation. The roughly 30,000-year-old Venus XIV from Dolní Věstonice in present-day Czech Republic was probably employed in cult practice (Fig. 9). Depending on how it is placed, the roughly 8.5-cm-tall figure can be interpreted as an abstracted female with breasts or as a phallus with testicles. The use of phallus figurines as amulets, as the drill holes suggest, is already documented in prehistoric times, and was widespread in antiquity in Europe, Asia, and Africa. These phallus pendants were made either of ivory or less precious materials, and had a mostly apotropaic function, that is to say they served to ward off the "evil eye". In a ritual among the Swazi, described by Zimbabwean anthropologist Hilda Kuper in 1944, the material's association with the male member is explicit. On the fourth day of the annual Incwala festival, celebrating the bond between royalty and nature, as well as the social hierarchy, the king walked past his people clad only with a cap of ivory covering his penis. At the end of the ceremony, he retired to his hut to have sex with his wife.[10]

In Europe, ivory dildos, which have mostly survived from the 18th and 19th centuries, were used as sex aids. An especially sophisticated example, with a built-in pump to simulate ejaculation, was

7 Zacharias Hegewald,
Adam and Eve as Lovers,
ca. 1630, ivory, h. ca. 20 cm.
Schwäbisch Hall,
Kunstkammer Würth,
Sammlung Würth.

8 Mithuna Image (Heavenly Pairing), Srirangam, end of 17th century, ivory with inlaid rubies, h. 20.2 cm. Staatliche Museen zu Berlin, Museum für Asiatische Kunst.

9 Venus XIV, stylized figure, Dolní Věstonice, 29,300–25,570 BCE, mammoth ivory, h. 8.5 cm. Moravian Museum, Brno.

10 Dildo with ejaculation simulator, France (?), 18th century, ivory and wood, h. ca. 17 cm. Science Museum, London.

found hidden in an armchair in a former convent in Paris (Fig. 10).

Just as ivory, as a "pure" substance, was considered to be an antitoxin, various scholars have assumed a medicinal effect in the realm of sexuality as well. In doctor Michael Herr's *Neues Tier- und Arznei Buch* (New Animal and Medicinal Book) from 1546, we read: "Such fresh ivory, which is beautifully white, and especially that derived from the teeth, when shaved and subsequently pounded into a fine powder, is said to be a very effective and proven medicine for strengthening the heart and the spirit. Apothecaries call it *ebur,* and it is always used in a number of precious concentrated juices and sweets, but above all in certain special practices or standard procedures for making infertile women fertile, for which it is said to have a specific inherent natural property, as the most excellent ancient doctors amply attest."[11] Similar comments are found in other physicians of early modern times, for example in Conrad Gessner's *Thier-Buch* (Book of Animals) of 1551–1558, which was still being reprinted in the mid-17th century.

Religious devotion

People have sought contact with ivory not only in the hope of greater beauty, offspring, or the satisfaction of sexual desires. Religious devotions have involved physical practices in which ivory objects were employed. Examples of this are the pax- or kissing-plaques passed around during the Christian Mass on special occasions and kissed by the faithful. On the front of these plaques made of ivory (but also of wood or metal) are depictions from the story of Salvation—very often Christ's crucifixion.

Because of the purity ascribed to it and its association with the chastity of Mary, ivory was especially well suited for depictions of the Corpus Christi untainted by original sin.[12] The use of ivory emphasized the theologically important corporeality of the Son of God, and, given the material's pleasant feel and durability, it offered at the same time a surface that could attract physical devotion and suggest to the faithful an intimacy of experience and direct participation. Many an ivory sacred figure reveals obvious wear on the extremities, indicating that the carving was very often grasped or kissed. One touching example is a roughly 8-cm-tall crucifix from 17th- or 18th-century Japan (Fig. 11). The ivory's smooth surfaces suggest that the figure was carried and touched again and again over many years, probably decades, by a Japanese Christian. This close physi-

cal bond seems all the more moving when one considers that at this time Catholicism was forbidden in Japan, and could be exercised only in secret.

In general, religiosity in the Christian Middle Ages and early modern times was strongly experienced and practiced by way of the body. This naturally included handling images of saints, which were washed, dressed, and caressed by the faithful, treated almost like living beings. The practice has been continued in various congregations to this day. Along with depictions of the sufferings of Christ, small figures of the Christ Child were especially popular. We know that in nunneries such sculptures were cared for like real children and formed a part of physical devotions. Though the figures were generally smaller than real infants or toddlers, it can be assumed that such ivory children were also objects of physical affection. A sleeping Christ Child, very probably fashioned in the context of the Indian Catholic mission (Fig. 13), was at least at a later point not only furnished with a crown, shirt, and gold shoes, but also provided with a full canopy bed with bed-linens of French lace and numerous votive gifts.

There are also comparable practices that include physical interactions with images in other religions and denominations. For example, the sculptures of the Bwami society of the Lega people (Democratic Republic of the Congo) featured in social initiation rites (Fig. 12) undergo intensive preparation. The human- or animal-like figures represent positive or negative role models, but also have quite personal meanings. Before each rite, they are cleansed like the initiates themselves and rubbed with colored palm oil. This treatment creates a link between the figures and the bodies of the ritual's participants,[13] both prepared for a higher status through initiation. Cared for and used for generations, the figures take on an increasingly dark, shiny patina expressive of their age and significance.

Medical ivory

Along with the pharmaceutical uses already described—in the 19th century, as a result of the industrial processing of elephant-tusk ivory, increasingly available ivory dust was cooked into a supposedly especially nutritious jelly—ivory fulfilled other medicinal functions. As in the fine arts, it was a favored material for depictions of the human body. Scantily clad "doctor's ladies" from China, for example, are said to have allowed genteel ladies to indicate the location of their complaints without having to undress in front of the doctor. Ivory anatomical figures and models of body parts such as eyes, ears, and noses were probably employed as visual aids in teaching. Because of its material qualities and stability, ivory was also used in the manufacture of medical instruments, handles especially. Here ivory again came into direct contact with the human body. At times it was literally "ingested with mother's milk": before plastics came on the market, ivory was a favorite material for nursing caps. These were placed over the nipples of mothers who found nursing painful so that babies could suck mother's milk through the holes in the ivory (Fig. 14).

Ivory was already used to make artificial teeth in antiquity. These were probably mainly employed post mortem, so as to restore the deceased's full rows of teeth at least in the afterlife. The first full dentures were created in the 17th century. The main material used for them were the teeth of the hippopotamus, as they proved to be stronger and retained their color better than elephant ivory. But even this practice could not prevail, for ivory in the mouth soon took on an unpleasant odor. Doctors also experimented with human and animal teeth inserted into an ivory matrix. The American president George Washington wore such dentures. Such ivory denture matrices are known primarily owing to the "Waterloo teeth" set into them—teeth of the fallen on the battlefields of the Napoleonic Wars were extracted and sold as replacement teeth (Fig. 15).

Finally, ivory penetrated even deeper into the human body as a bone replacement. In the mid-19th century, Berlin clinics especially experimented with ivory implants. In 1890, the surgeon Themistocles Gluck could already boast of a number of implanted prostheses (knee, hand, and elbow joints) made of ivory. If the implant was inserted in sterile conditions, such interventions were altogether successful. In 1913, the surgeon Fritz König even reported that ivory pegs inserted to help fuse bone were fully resorbed by the human body.[14] In the 1960s, the technique was adopted by the surgeon San Baw in Myanmar, who over the course of more than two decades replaced 300 hip joints with ivory prostheses. One of his patients is said to have lived without restriction for 20 years after the implant, as the physician and researcher Bartek Szostakowski determined.[15]

"Bloody" and "living" ivory

The use of animal remains and body parts has been a substantial, irreplaceable element of human cul-

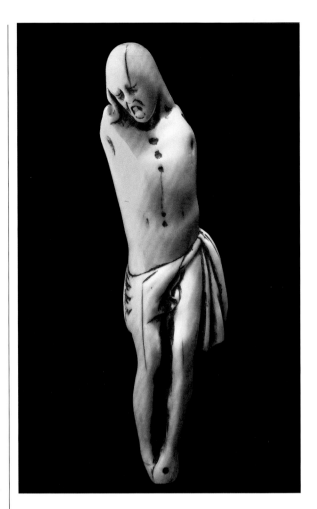

11 Netsuke in the form of a crucifix, Japan, 17th–18th century, ivory, h. 8.5 cm. Musée Guimet, Paris.

ture since the earliest times. And the use of animal materials occasionally took on heightened significance in that certain qualities were ascribed to them beyond their actual characteristics. This was the case with ivory, especially, since such attributes ascribed to the elephant as power, strength, dignity, virtue, and purity were also transferred to its tusks. Paradoxically, it was this special respect for the animal that made the possession and use of its tusks so attractive.

Anyhow, the pleasant feel and appearance of ivory have been difficult to reconcile with the animal's possibly violent killing. Various mediums needed to suppress ivory's largely bloody extraction in favor of an unsullied delight in the material. In his *Natural History* (Book VIII, Chapter 4), Pliny tells

12 Animal figurine, Lega (Democratic Republic of Congo), dyed ivory, 14 cm. Nationaal Museum van Wereldculturen, Amsterdam.

13 *Sleeping Christ Child in a Canopy Bed*, India and Myanmar, figure (ivory), probably 17th century; bed and amulets 18th–19th century, h. 39 cm. Victoria and Albert Museum, London.

14 Nipple caps, Great Britain, 1790–1850, silver, glass, and ivory. Private collection.

the misleading story that the elephant breaks off his tusks in order to avoid being killed by human hunters. Modern advertising for ivory products has also attempted to divert consumers attention away from the real and cruel fate of elephants—and that of the native bearers who were required to transport the tusks to coast ports and who were frequently sold as slaves at the end of their journey. In a 19th-century advertising illustration, the elephant appears not only to survive the removal of its tusk by a proud African unharmed, but even to voluntarily permit it (Fig. 16).

Around the middle of the 19th century, Western markets developed an increased awareness of the violence involved in the retrieval of ivory and the danger of the complete extermination of African elephants. Even ivory dealers occasionally pointed this out.[16] As a reaction, the tagua nut was rediscovered for the production of smaller objects, and the first synthetic resins came on the market, promoted as a substitute material in the manufacture of figures and billiard balls. The makers of these products not only advertised their economic, ecological, and ethical advantages, they also attempted to approximate the look and feel of ivory as closely as possible. Despite the tremendous advantages these new materials offered, some customers complained that plastic was a dead substance. Holding or cleaning an ivory billiard ball felt like caressing a young girl's shoulder, while those made of synthetics felt as lifeless as stones.[17] This judgment, suggestive of an old man's fantasy, plays on ancient myths about the ivory shoulder of Pelops and the transformation of King Pygmalion's ivory sculpture, but such a display of

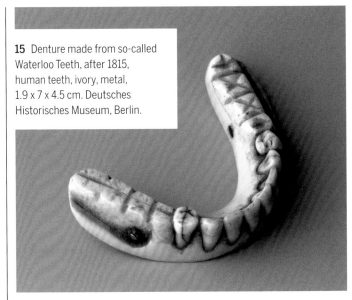

15 Denture made from so-called Waterloo Teeth, after 1815, human teeth, ivory, metal, 1.9 x 7 x 4.5 cm. Deutsches Historisches Museum, Berlin.

humanistic learning can hardly mask the fetishizing of ivory balls.[18] Perhaps the delusion of "living" ivory reflects an increased yearning for direct contact with nature felt as a result of the increasing urbanization and industrialization of the 19th century. Unlike the anonymous materials of industry, ivory was considered a living substance precisely because of its biological origin, its irregularities, and the frequently visible growth lines on its surface. In analogy with the idea of religious sacrifice, even the elephant blood shed for it may have contributed to the evocation of a hidden vitality or power in such

16 Advertisement from Harvey & Ford, Philadelphia, for billiard and pool balls, fittings for umbrellas, whips, sticks, wooden pipes and ivory jewelry, ca. 1867. Smithsonian Institution, National Museum of American History.

"tooth relics". Although the romanticization of ivory as a powerful, pure and living substance may strike us as outdated and unenlightened, its contemporary antithesis, the rejection of plastic as a dead and supposedly unnatural material, is today perhaps more prevalent than ever.

1 Sigmund Freud had already identified a connection between human sexual drives and dreams involving teeth, see Sigmund Freud, *Die Traumdeutungen* (1900; *The Interpretation of Dreams*), Hamburg: Severus Verlag, 2016, pp. 365–367.
   The psychosomatic importance of teeth is also reflected in modern dentistry. See also Marco Fisch, "Psychologische und psychosomatische Aspekte in der Zahnmedizin", in: Boris Luban-Plozza, Walter Pöldinger, and Friedebert Kröger (eds), *Der psychosomatisch Kranke in der Praxis*, Berlin and elsewhere: Springer, 2013, p. 135. I am grateful to Simone Lämmersdorf from the library of the Universität Frankfurt's Zentrum der Zahn-, Mund- und Kieferheilkunde for her assistance in sourcing literature.
2 See "Botschaft des Lu-dingirra", in: Volkert Haas, *Die hethitische Literatur: Texte, Stilistik, Motive*, Berlin and Boston: De Gruyter, 2008, pp. 282–283.

3 Sarah Goodridge, *Beauty Revealed,* 1828, watercolor on ivory, The Metropolitan Museum of Art, New York; see https://www.metmuseum.org/art/collection/search/14521?&searchField=All&sortBy=Relevance&ft=Sarah+Goodridge&offset=0&rpp=20&pos=3 (accessed August 26, 2019).
4 Francisco Prado-Vilar, "Circular Visions of Fertility and Punishment: Caliphal Ivory Caskets from al-Andalus", *Muqarnas* 14 (1997), pp. 19–41.
5 For the use and ornamentation of combs, see Julia Saviello, "'Purgat et ornat' – die zwei Seiten des Kamms", in: *Dinge im Kontext. Artefakt, Handhabung und Handlungsästhetik zwischen Mittelalter und Gegenwart*, ed. Thomas Pöpper, Berlin and Boston: De Gruyter, 2015, pp. 133–144.
6 See *Physiologus: A Medieval Book of Nature Lore*, trans. Michael J. Curley, Chicago and London: Chicago University Press, 1979, p. 31.
7 Sancti Aurelii Augustini Hipponensis Episcopi Enarrationes in Psalmos, in: Patrologia Latina Database, vol. 36, Ps. XLIV, 23, col. 508; Beati Rabani Mauri Fuldensis Abbatis et Moguntini Archiepiscopi De Universo Libri Viginti Duo, in: Patrologia Latina Database, vol. 111, Liber 17, chap. VI, col. 0464B.
8 B. Petri Damiani Sanctae Romanae Ecclesiae Cardinalis, Episcopi Ostiensis Ordinis S. Benedicti, Sermones ordine mensium servato, in: Patrologia Latina Database, vol. 144, Sermo LXIII, col. 0860B. See also Avinoam Shalem, *The Oliphant: Islamic Objects in Historical Context*, Leiden and elsewhere: Brill, 2004, pp. 82–88.
9 See Prithvi Kumar Agrawala, *Mithuna. The Male-Female Symbol in Indian Art and Thought*, New Delhi: Munshiram Manoharlal Publisher, 1983, p. 8.
10 Hilda Kuper, "A Ritual of Kingship among the Swazi", *Africa: Journal of the International African Institute* 14/5 (1944), pp. 230–257, here p. 247.
11 Michael Herr, *Das neue Tier- und Arzneibuch des Doktor Michael Herr A.D. 1546*, ed. Gerhard E. Sollbach, Würzburg: Königshausen und Neumann, 1994, pp. 41–42.
12 See Stefan Trinks, "Eingehüllt in Gold und Bein – Die techné des Chryselephantin als 'Mitstreit' im Mittelalter", *Zeitschrift für Kunstgeschichte* 79, no. 4 (2016), p. 486.
13 Elisabeth L. Cameron, *Art of the Lega*, Los Angeles: UCLA Fowler Museum of Cultural History, 2001, p. 120
14 Fritz König, "Ueber die Implantation von Elfenbein zum Ersatz von Knochen- und Gelenkenden", *Beiträge zur Klinischen Chirurgie* 85 (1913), p. 93.
15 Bartek Szostakowski, Jakub Jagiello, and John A. Skinner, "ArtiFacts: Ivory Hemiarthroplasty: The Forgotten Concept Lives On", *Clinical Orthopaedics and Related Research* 475, no. 12 (2017), pp. 2850–2854. I thank Mr. Szostakowski for a most informative telephone conversation regarding hip implants.
16 See Heinrich Ad. Meyer, *Elfenbein. Gewerbe- und Industrieausstellung*, Hamburg 1889, p. 7. The Hamburg firm Heinr. Ad. Meyer produced ivory articles and even organized its own caravans in East Africa for the importation of tusks. To counter the threat of extermination, the taming and breeding of African elephants is here proposed as a remedy.
17 See John Frederick Walker, *Ivory's Ghosts: The White Gold of History and the Fate of Elephants*, New York: Atlantic Monthly Press, 2009, pp. 102, 105.
18 For fetishism in modern societies, see Hartmut Böhme, *Fetischismus und Kultur. Eine andere Theorie der Moderne*, Reinbek: Rowohlt, 2006.

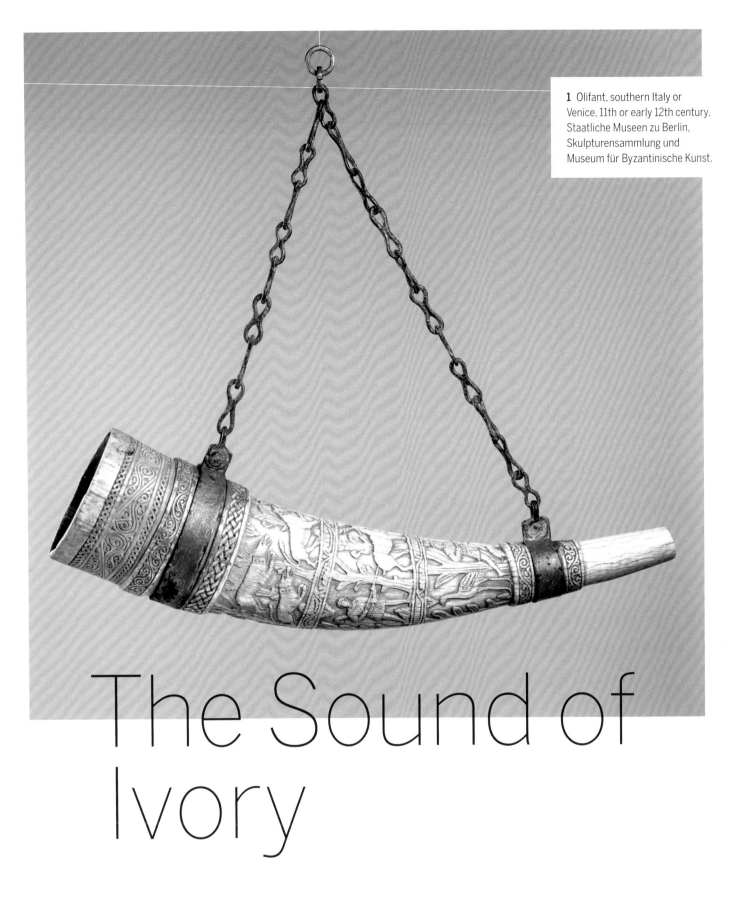

The Sound of Ivory

LARS-CHRISTIAN KOCH

In its various biological and material forms (mammoth ivory, walrus ivory, elephant ivory, etc.), ivory has been a favorite material for technological and artistic uses in numerous cultures for millennia. Harvested from animals killed in hunting, it was readily available, and because of its unique composition (though hard, it could be intricately carved with various tools) it was used at a very early date in what we now interpret as artistic contexts. It is important to understand that many of the ivory pieces from the Paleolithic, though not all, were ritual objects, or at least employed in ritual contexts. This was certainly the case with the many instruments for the production of sound in early cultures.

The first known musical instruments date from the Aurignacian, the Upper Paleolithic, during which anatomically modern humans (*Homo sapiens*) spread across large areas of western, central, and eastern Europe some 40,000 years ago.

Flutes from Geißenklösterle

In 1990, a flute 12.6 cm long was found in Geißenklösterle in the Swabian Jura. Fashioned from the radius bone of a whooper swan, it has clearly worked notches and finger holes that have been carved flat, clearly identifying it as a handmade flute. The finger holes on this flute-like instrument were obviously carefully placed, probably calculated to produce the desired pitches. As yet, to be sure, it is not altogether clear whether it is a flute in the narrower sense, since the mouthpiece has not survived: it could have been a wedged flute, a type in which the upper opening is fitted with a V-shaped wedge to serve as a mouthpiece, or even a reed instrument like the oboe or clarinet. Acoustic experi-

ments with exact copies have shown that both are possible. Another badly fragmented flute of the same type was found at the same spot, and in a third find at Geißenklösterle separate fragments came to light that could suggest a flute formed of two concave lengths of mammoth ivory cemented together after carving. The first pieces had already been discovered in the late 1980s, but it would take several more years before this find could be identified as a flute. It is estimated to be around 40,000 years old, which means that it is among the oldest musical instruments known (Fig. 2).

3 Young man playing the *siwa*, a side-blown horn of ivory.

2 Flute, Geißenklösterle, ca. 38,000 BCE, mammoth ivory, 18.7 cm.Urgeschichtliches Museum, Blaubeuren.

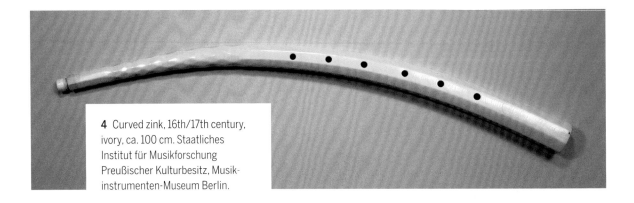

4 Curved zink, 16th/17th century, ivory, ca. 100 cm. Staatliches Institut für Musikforschung Preußischer Kulturbesitz, Musik-instrumenten-Museum Berlin.

5 François Balthazar Solvyns, *Sarinda Player*, colored drawing.

This third instrument is remarkable for the great amount of labor involved in its manufacture, for the other finds show that simpler ways of making a flute were known. Its precise ornamentation is striking, also its larger size, for both of which ivory was particularly well suited. It is highly probable that this was an instrument for use on special occasions, for flute-like instruments made of birds' bones require far less labor, though this does not exclude the possibility that they were also used in religious rites.

Ivory horns and other wind instruments

In Europe, the use of ivory in the making of musical instruments has continued through antiquity, the Middle Ages and the Renaissance right up to the present day. Acoustically, ivory does not appear to be particularly outstanding, though this might be disputed in certain cultures. For example, the *rabab* (a bowed lute) in the Indonesian gamelan orchestra was made of ivory up to the second half of the 20th century, as a special acoustic quality was attributed to it. Compared to wood, ivory has a higher density and is not as elastic, and it does not transmit sound as well as certain tonewoods (woods with tonal qualities), spruce for example. Because of this, and because it is easily polished, it was still best suited for wind instruments, though even here no significant difference from special hardwoods is apparent.

Whereas in the Paleolithic ivory was available in great quantity thanks to mammoth hunting, and was mainly used for certain objects because of its outstanding structure, in antiquity and the Middle Ages, owing to the greatly reduced availability of the material, ivory artifacts became prestige objects. One example was the medieval instrument called the olifant (or oliphant; from Old French *olifant* [elephant], properly *cor d'olifant*), an ivory horn; the name alone indicates the material from which it was made (Fig. 1). Beginning in the 10th century, such instruments made their way to central Europe, frequently by way of Byzantium, and came to signify power and dignity. Olifants became meaningful attributes in the realm of knighthood: a king might, for example, bestow an important office by presenting the candidate with an olifant instead of a document.

In the *Song of Roland*, written in France around 1100, the olifant plays a major role. Roland, one of the Emperor Charlemagne's paladins, formed with his retinue the rear guard of the main army at an important battle in the Pyrenees. Encircled by the enemy, he called help from Charlemagne's main army with his horn. According to the legend, Roland blew so hard that the veins in his temples burst, and the excessive pressure even cracked the horn. Nonetheless, Charlemagne heard the signal, but the battle had been lost by the time the imperial army arrived. To this day several surviving olifants are claimed to be Roland's actual horn, but without definitive proof.

The tonal range of an olifant is limited to two or three notes of the harmonic series—usually the tonic, fifth, and octave—and is therefore hardly suited for the production of melodic phrases. Its sound can be highly penetrating, like that of many horns made of other materials. Olifants were made into the 17th century, bovine horn taking the place of ivory. Horn is softer, however, and more susceptible to moisture, and of only limited value for extended use. Because of their great importance in the Middle Ages, a considerable number of them were made, so it is not surprising that more examples of olifants survive than of any other musical instruments of that time; it is estimated that from 60 to 80 are preserved. The majority were made by Arab craftsmen in southern Italy in around the 11th century.

Directly related to the olifant in type and function, though from a different period, is the most important ceremonial horn in the music of the Swahili, the ivory *siwa*, for a long time part of a ruler's insignia (Fig. 3). It was sounded on important occasions, for example at weddings. Today other instruments are used for such special events, probably owing primarily to the numerous influences from cultures with which the Swahili maintained trading contacts. Swahili wind instruments can be divided into cross-blown natural horns of African origin, Arabic-Persian flutes, and European trumpets. The latter are played in processional music. Also belonging to the group of African wind instruments is the cross-blown antelope-horn *baragumu*, used by the Swahili in the 19th century as a battle horn, and still commonly used ceremoniously to convene assemblies.

The zink, or cornetto, is a wind instrument that at first glance might be taken for a flute because of its finger holes. On closer inspection, however, one notes the mouthpiece, which resembles that of a trumpet, a type common to brass instruments in general. Zinks combine the sound-production technique of brass instruments (cup mouthpiece) with the fingering technique of woodwinds. Between the

6 *Sarinda*, a bowed instrument decorated with carved angels, flowers, and imaginary creatures, ca. 1700, ivory, 59.7 x 16.1 x 13 cm. The British Museum, London.

7 The bridge of a *rudra vina*, originally ivory, here staghorn. Staatliche Museen zu Berlin, Ethnologisches Museum.

8 Bechstein piano, 1862, rosewood, ivory, 119.5 x 133.5 x 62 cm. Staatliches Institut für Musikforschung Preußischer Kulturbesitz, Musikinstrumenten-Museum, Berlin.

15th and 17th centuries, the zink was one of the most important musical instruments, and in large part defined the music of the European Renaissance, especially in its role as a solo instrument. As a rule, it was made of wood or ivory. Because of the way its sound is made, it is now numbered among the brass instruments. There are various types: the curved zink, the straight zink, and the still zink; in the latter, the mouthpiece is carved into the instrument itself as a fixed component. All three types were made in different sizes (as a rule between 50 and 70 cm), depending on their musical roles. They also differ in form: the curved zink (Fig. 4), as the name suggests, is slightly bent, and is frequently covered with leather or parchment, while the still zink is either straight or only slightly curved and has a mellower sound, often softer as well. In Renaissance music, it was felt that the zink best imitated the human voice. Once the violin became increasingly featured for this same quality, the zink gradually lost importance. In many Renaissance pieces, it played a solo role as a soprano instrument—a few zink players were great virtuosi, comparable to violinists of the time still famous to this day—a role steadily taken over by the violin. By the beginning of the 19th century, zinks had essentially disappeared from musical life in Europe, and it was only in the 1920s, with the return to historical performance practice, that it was revived.

Ivory in string and keyed instruments

The *sarinda* is a bowed, short-necked lute with a bowl-shaped body with two prominent swellings. The instrument is made from a single block of wood into which two chambers are carved, one above the other, the one below covered with animal skin. Stretched across the bridge, which sits on the membrane over the lower chamber, are three to four melody strings (*tar*), a main string, and two or three bourdon strings. The fingerboard is without frets, so is ideally suited for producing glissandi, an important feature of Indian music. Among the *sarinda's* more outstanding features are the striking indentations in its body, which are meant to facilitate bowing. The body is generally formed of wood, but in exceptional cases of ivory. As a rule, performers play seated on the ground (Figs. 5, 6). It varies in length between 60 and 70 cm.

The *sarinda* was produced in many different styles, depending on the owner's social standing and native region, some already in its present form in the 18th and 19th centuries.

The Santal in northeastern India (Odisha/Bengal) used a type of *sarinda* called a *dhodro banam* ("hollow instrument"). When played, the usually single string is shortened with the upper surface of the fingernails of the left hand. These instruments are adorned with human figures, for according to Santal mythology the wood used came from a human being. Human body parts are associated with parts of the instrument, the closed sound chamber at the bottom with the stomach, the open part with the breast, the peg box atop the neck with the head.

In 19th-century Bengal, the *sarinda* was already played by sadhus or "holy" men, many of them homeless vagrants. The instrument is generally strung with two gut strings, and like the *sarinda* of the Santal can be decorated with carved animal or human figures on the peg box. It is used to accompany religious songs or in a kind of singing competition on religious themes.

In India, ivory was used mainly on stringed instruments such as the *sarinda* and the *rudra vina*, a large plucked instrument, but because of its limited hardness and susceptibility to moisture it was employed only as ornamentation or for smaller accessories like fine tuners and bridges (Fig. 7). It did not play a prominent role in an instrument's construction, and today is no longer used.

Still today a number of concert pianists prefer keyboards to be faced with thin slices of ivory. The practice became especially popular in the 19th century (Fig. 8), and demand steadily increased up to the end of the 20th century. To many musicians, the material combines an optimal feel when playing, it warms quickly, is smooth but not slippery, and is thus considered superior to synthetic materials especially for long and challenging performances such as concertos.

In the first half of the last century, ivory was considered the standard material for piano keys, and was only gradually replaced by synthetic materials. In the early 1990s, ivory from stored inventories was briefly used on a few concert grand pianos and on other instruments when it was specifically requested by the customer. Today, some kind of synthetic material is standard, in most cases Ivoplast, an acrylic-glass bond. But there are also substitute materials that have all the positive qualities of ivory, such as Ivorite, developed by Yamaha, a plastic based on acrylonitrile butadiene styrene (ABS) in combination with inorganic hardening agents. The names of both substitutes allude to the word "ivory", underscoring the importance of the original material. All these synthetic materials have one advantage over ivory: they are more durable. Real ivory has microscopically small holes in the surface, and in time can become discolored and cracked.

No grand or upright pianos have been produced with ivory keys since 1992; piano manufacturers were quick to change over to synthetics. When the

European Union's ban on the importation of ivory went into effect in June 1989, more than 200 African elephants were dying every day, most of them slaughtered solely for the ivory in their tusks. By that time, their numbers had been reduced from 2.3 million in 1970 to fewer than 700,000. Starting in January 1990, trading in ivory products was also banned.

Prices provide an especially clear indication of how shadowy trading in ivory already was at that time. Since the 1960s, the price of ivory has risen nearly twentyfold, even though at the beginning of the 1990s there was an estimated inventory of nearly 50 tons in the German Federal Republic. With it, firms using ivory could have continued production for years if not decades without new imports. Nevertheless, the decision by the European Union commission was understandable. To prevent global trade from growing out of hand, it established a universal import ban. With it, the use of ivory in the manufacture of musical instruments has disappeared.

Literature
Anthony C. Baines, "Oliphant," in: Stanley Sadie (ed.), *The New Grove Dictionary of Musical Instruments*, London and New York 1985, 3 vols, vol. 2, p. 815.
Joep Bor, "The Voice of the Sarangi: An illustrated history of bowing in India", *National Centre for the Performing Arts, Quarterly Journal*, vol. 15, nos. 3, 4 (September–December 1986), and vol. 16, no. 1 (March 1987).
Nicholas J. Conard, Maria Malina, Susanne C. Münzel, and Friedrich Seeberger, "Eine Mammutelfenbeinflöte aus dem Arignacien des Geißenklösterle", *Archäologisches Korrespondenzblatt* 34 (2004), pp. 447ff.
— , Maria Malina and Susanne C. Münzel, "New flutes document the earliest musical tradition in southwestern German", *Nature* (June 24, 2009).
Karl Greininger, *Instrumente in der Musik des Abendlandes*, Munich: Beck, 1982.
Lars-Cristian Koch, "Immer noch entscheidend für das Spielgefühl? – Elfenbeinbelag bei Klaviertastaturen", *musikhandel* 6 (1989), pp. 265–266.
— , "rudra vina – Die Herstellung eines indischen Saiteninstruments in der Tradition Kanailal & Bros", Museum Collection Berlin Audiovisuell / DVD-Reihe der Abteilung Musikethnologie, Medientechnik und Berliner Phonogramm-Archiv, 2007.
R.R. Marett, "The Siwa in East Africa", *Folklore* 25, no. 4 (December 31, 1914), pp. 499–500.
Hermann Moeck and Helmut Mönkemeyer, *Zur Geschichte des Zinken*, Celle: Moeck Verlag, 1973.
Curt Sachs, *Reallexikon der Musikinstrumente*, Berlin 1913.
— , *Die Musikinstrumente Indiens und Indonesiens. Zugleich eine Einführung in die Instrumentenkunde*, Berlin 1915.
— , *Der Musikinstrumentenkunde*, Berlin 1919, 2nd ed. Leipzig 1930.
Avinoam Shalem, *The Oliphant: Islamic Objects in Historical Context*, Leiden: Brill, 2004.

Ivory Objects

Between Masterpiece and Mass Production

The tusks of mammoths and later elephants have probably always been considered to be of great value. Already in prehistoric times ivory was used not only for single, virtuosic carvings, but also for the serial production of valuable objects. This has continued up to our own day. The following pages picture objects from various epochs. Masterpiece or mass production? It is not always easy to determine.

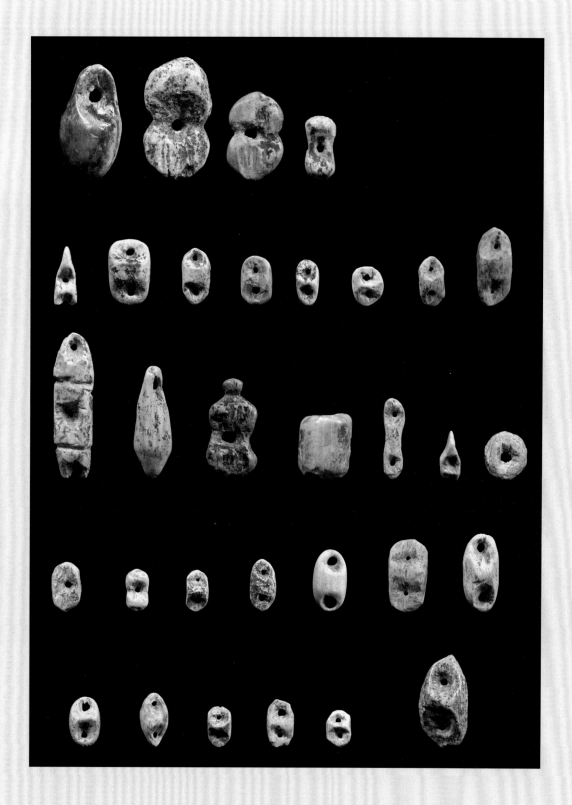

Miscellaneous beads from the Aurignacian, ca. 33,000–26,000 BCE, found in the Vogelherd Cave (Swabian Jura), mammoth ivory. Museum Alte Kulturen, Schloss Hohentübingen

Fragments of decorative netting comprised of several hundred such ivory beads have been found among Stone Age grave goods. Division of labor was the practice even then.

**Aurignaciain figure of a horse, ca. 30,000 BCE, found in the Vogelherd Cave (Swabian Jura),
mammoth ivory, 4.7 x 2.5 x 0.8 cm. Museum Alte Kulturen, Schloss Höhentübingen**
This small wild horse, one of the earliest known figural depictions in the history of humankind is striking for its pronounced realism.
It has taken experimental archaeologists a full 30 hours to reproduce it using Stone Age tools.

Relief with figure of a seated lioness, Phoenician, 8th century BCE, found in Nimrud (Iraq), ivory, 14 x 11.4 cm. The British Museum, London

This open-work relief probably served as a furniture mounting. It was found during excavations in the ruins of the Assyrian capital Nimrud, along with several thousand other ivory fragments. These were probably either booty or tribute from the Phoenician city states along the Mediterranean coast.

Consular diptych of Justinus, Rome, ca. 540, ivory, each panel 33.5 x 13 cm.
Skulpturensammlung und Museum für Byzantinische Kunst, Staatliche Museen zu Berlin
So-called consular diptychs, which were coated with wax on the undecorated inner sides and so could be used as writing tablets,
were made by the hundreds and given out to supporters by Roman consuls on their assumption of office.

Virgin and Child from Sainte-Chapelle, Paris, before 1279, ivory, 41 x 12.4 cm. Musée du Louvre, Paris
This carving of the Virgin is one of the finest pieces of medieval sculpture in France.
The curve of the tusk was expertly exploited for the Gothic figure's elegant S-shape.

Casket with ivory veneer, Sicily (?), 12th century, wood, ivory, gilt brass, polychrome, 16.5 x 35.7 x 19.8 cm.
Museum für Islamische Kunst, Staatliche Museen zu Berlin
Thin ivory facings applied to a wooden body give the casket a sumptuous appearance yet required only a small amount of material.
The joins in the ivory veneer were masked with decorative painting.

Ivory casket, Kōṭṭe (Sri Lanka), ca. 1541–1543, ivory, gold filigree edging, rubies and sapphires, 18 x 30 x 16 cm. Schatzkammer der Residenz, Munich
This casket, made of solid slabs of ivory and decorated with exquisite pictorial scenes, was a diplomatic gift
from the king of Kōṭṭe (in present-day Sri Lanka) to the royal Portuguese House of Avis.

Markus Heiden, Centerpiece, Coburg/Weimar, 1639, ivory, silk, 115.3 x 31 cm. Kunsthistorisches Museum, Vienna
The Baroque sculptor Markus Heiden indicated in his description of this table centerpiece made for Duke Wilhelm of Saxe-Weimar
that the tusk he created it from weighed 140 pounds and was selected from a stock of 300,000 tusks.

Good Shepherd, Diu (?), India, 17th century, ivory, height 20.5 cm. Kunsthistorisches Museum, Kunstkammer, Vienna
Figures like this "Good Shepherd" testify to the global trade in ivory in early modern times. Tusks were transported to India from East Africa and there worked in series by native craftsman after European patterns. The figures were then sold in Asia, Europe, and South America.

Joseph Gabler, organ with stop knobs of solid ivory, 1737–1750, Basilica of St. Martin, Weingarten
Ivory was also frequently used in the building of musical instruments, its sound and material qualities generally of less importance
than its costliness, which was meant to emphasize an instrument's high quality.

**René Lalique, binding for the score of Richard Wagner's opera *Die Walküre*, ca. 1893/1894,
Morocco leather, ivory, silver, 50 x 40 cm. Calouste Gulbenkian Museum, Lisbon**

René Lalique, one of the leading artists of Art Nouveau, presented this binding with motifs from the Nibelungen saga at the salon of
the Société des Artistes Français in 1894. It was his first work in ivory, one in which he revived the tradition of medieval book bindings.

Josef Karl Klinkosch, tea service, ca. 1910, silver, ivory, height 12.7 cm. Bröhan Museum, Berlin
The pleasant feel of ivory made it a favored material for handles. Precious tableware and cups for hot beverages were therefore enriched in this way. Also a factor was the fact that ivory is a poor conductor, and therefore serves as insulation.

Set of six champagne whisks, Mr Doderay, 1938, ivory, 13 x 6 cm. Musée du quai Branly, Paris
If the champagne was too bubbly, one might make use of a champagne whisk. The *haut monde* used whisks of ivory.

Billiard balls, Mr Doderay, 1938, ivory, dia. 6.1 cm each. Musée du quai Branly, Paris
Billiards became a popular sport in Europe and America in the 19th century. This led to an enormous increase in the demand for ivory, the favored material for balls owing to its elasticity and hardness. But elephant populations were endangered by the massive slaughters, and the "raw material" became scarce, so soon the search was on for alternative substances.

Seated Buddha figure confiscated by Berlin customs, before 1997, 16.5 x 9 x 4 cm. Deutsches Historisches Museum, Berlin
Although the international community banned trade in ivory with the CITES Treaty in 1989,
many thousands of pounds of illegally traded ivory are impounded by customs officials each year.

HUMANS
& ELEPHANTS

1 *Hatari!*
"The Baby Elephant Walk":
The bathing scene is one of
the most popular elephant
appearances in film history.
USA 1962, film still.

2 *Hatari!*
Paradise on earth.
Howard Hawks, *Hatari!*,
USA 1962, film still.

THE **ELEPHANT** AS
FILM STAR

A LOOK BACK
AT A CAREER IN
CINEMA

DOROTHEE WENNER

Elephants can hardly compete with the popularity of cats in videos on YouTube. This is mainly owing to their size; they are by no means house pets, after all, so animal lovers rarely have a chance to post personal encounters with them or their amusing antics on the Internet. But this does not detract from their special role as actors in the history of film. There is probably no other species that has played such varied roles—tragic, comic, dramatic, mythological. In contrast to meerkats, Dalmatians, dolphins, and sheep, elephants are no temporary fad; they have been a presence through all of film history, from children's films to adventure stories, love stories, and documentaries.

In the following I present a few important examples of the range of depictions of elephants—based on a subjective selection from an inexhaustible fund and with no claim to completeness. I also indicate the special importance of elephants in our perception of Africa, for the continent as the setting of any number of European and American films has served as a gigantic projection screen.

3 *Bal Ganesh*
Bal Ganesh shortly after his rebirth as a hybrid: a little boy with an elephant's head. Pankaj Sharma, *Bal Ganesh*, India 2007, film still.

TEMBO, THE JACK-OF-ALL-TRADES

The special role of the elephant in the Western cinematic animal kingdom can be introduced especially well by the example of *Hatari!*, the Hollywood classic from 1962 directed by Howard Hawks. The film takes place in a station dedicated to trapping wild animal in contemporaneous Tanzania. The boss of the small operation, far from the nearest city, is the grumpy Sean Mercer (John Wayne). Under his command is a group of hard-boiled types who track down animals for zoos all over the world, capture them, place them in crates or cages, and ship them off. In spectacular tracking scenes, for which the film became famous, rhinoceroses are depicted as especially dangerous. Enraged, they ram the hunters' vehicles, badly wound one of them, and are clearly the most menacing of game animals—zebras, gazelles, buffalo, crocodiles. Elephants are not hunted in this film. Instead, the big-game hunters come upon a dead mother elephant in the bush, and in search of help her orphaned calf runs through the tall grass toward the men. They bring the baby elephant back to the station. Sean wants to shoot the adorable creature because it is not yet viable on its own, but Dallas (Elsa Martinelli), an animal photographer from the Basel zoo who happens to be visiting the station and turning the men's heads, promises to raise the

baby with goat's milk and gives him the name Tembo. Sean only reluctantly accepts this adoption in his bailiwick, suspecting that the little elephant has the power to call into question the hard-won authority of man over the animal kingdom. And in fact there follows a chain of comical events caused either directly or indirectly by the awkward little beast. The new member of the family changes the group dynamic and brings about a gradual change in the somewhat puzzled men, who find their tender feelings breaking through their emotional insensitivity. Dallas, who has initiated their transformation by assuming the role of Tembo's adoptive mother, is honored by the station's African neighbors in a bizarre fantasy rite and elected "Mother of Elephants". In a questionable directorial shift, there is at this point a reference to a colonially determined, unquestioned intimacy between Africans and the animals in their surroundings. In the logic of the film, this is presumed to be "only natural" and serves to explain why the event is "talked about" in the district and why two more small elephants are sneaked into the station. The newly found bliss is expressed in a bathing scene in the river, when Dallas splashes with her three elephants to joyous music. It is a brief, utopian moment of utter harmony between man and beast, of paradise regained, to which the elephant has helped the people in the film as well as in the cinema audience. But Hollywood filmmaking requires a different ending. Without betraying the joyous mood of the bathing scene, the film finds two ways to sweeten the expulsion from paradise. First, there is a jealousy scene: Joke, a rambunctious mother elephant, contests the position of her human competitor and thereby sees to it that man and beast find their way back into their own worlds. But Tembo is too small, too fixed on Dallas, to let go of her as his substitute mother when her love relationship goes bad. But in the meantime, the men have learned something, after all, and with the young elephant form a strategic alliance so as to bring about a "happy ending". In a wild gallop, the men and elephant race through a hotel lobby and a supermarket, with no thought of damages, finally ending at the marriage bed. In this film, Tembo is a creature who brings men luck, and combines everything positive that men ascribe to the species. The film is a landmark in any consideration of elephants in film history.

ANIMATED BABY ELEPHANTS AND THEIR FAMILY HISTORIES

The Indian animated film *Bal Ganesh* (Pankaj Sharma, 2007) deals with a very different elephant childhood, one that could hardly be more closely intertwined with humankind. The four-armed god with the head of an elephant, a human torso with a protruding belly, and a rat as avatar, is one of the most popular figures in the gigantic Hindu pantheon. The faithful turn to him as a god of wisdom, when there are difficulties to be surmounted or new endeavors to be undertaken. In *Bal Ganesh* one can experience—as though in a crash course—what makes Hindu beliefs so suitable for cinema compared to those of other religions. Each of the Hindu deities embodies a different aspect of the supreme god Brahma, and is moreover endowed with very human qualities, positive and negative. Their relationships with each other are marked by characteristic strengths but also weaknesses: they are motivated by anger, rage, vanity, imperiousness, and envy. The sacred writings of Hinduism, above all the epic *Mahabharata*, are a virtually inexhaustible fund of tragedies and love stories. Traditionally, these tended to be narrated on Indian stages rather than performed, especially if miracles are involved or deities are transformed into other beings. With the arrival of cinema, with its ability to depict the supernatural, India exploited that ability by first filming so-called "mythologicals". These enjoyed enormous popularity from the start, which explains, at least in part, why the Indian film industry managed to become the largest in the world. As the story of a god, *Bal Ganesh* stands in this tra-

4 and 5 *The African Queen*
When the elephants appear on the riverbank, the two on board the *African Queen* find love.
John Huston, *The African Queen*, UK 1951, film stills.

dition. Ganesh's greatest weakness is his craving for sweets, which is why children can readily identify with him—also why he enlists the sympathies of grown-ups. It was obvious that a film about Ganesh might use his excessive consumption of sweets as a leitmotif. Surprising, however, is the explicit depiction of the beheading of the infant Ganesh by his own father with a sword: it happens in the heat of the moment, when Ganesh angers him and provokes his rage. The body of the child now lies before the grown-up gods, his head rolled to the side. Because his mother threatens suicide if her son is not immediately brought back to life, it is necessary to find a substitute head quickly. In the version of the myth presented in *Bal Ganesh*, the helpers dispatched by the gods find a young elephant, which also has to be beheaded for the purpose—but viewers are spared these details. All the more impressive is the creation of a new being worthy of veneration out of a child and an elephant, accompanied by such visual effects as sprays of golden sparks. Awakened to life, Ganesh immediately delights all the grown-ups with his charm, and is considered a perfect synthesis of man and elephant. The animation gives this film Ganesh giant saucer eyes with incessantly fluttering long lashes, the complete opposite of the often remarkably small eyes of real elephants. Ganesh not only combines the human and animal in his outward form, he also combines an adorable childlike nature with

the elephant's social sense, and constantly fights for greater justice.

The narration of the animated Canadian-French film *Babar: The Movie* (Alan Bunce, 1989) functions in a similar way. The film is set in an elephant world where in a long flashback Babar, the kind-hearted elephant papa, tells of his childhood to his little sons and daughters, who are dressed in light blue and pink pajamas. In this story, too, the young elephant is a model social creature; even as a child, he is highly cultured and courageously champions the weak and despairing. The adversaries in the film are rough-and-ready hippopotamuses, characterized as evil uncles and drunkards. By contrast, the elephants in *Babar: The Movie* occasionally take their children in their arms, pull handkerchiefs from their purses with their trunks when tears flow, and are not only loving parents, but also, like Bal Ganesh, "superior people".

THE INFLUENCE OF ELEPHANTS ON HUMAN MORALITY

The positive influence that elephants can have on human character development is also related in the British feature films *The African Queen* (John Huston, 1951) and *White Hunter, Black Heart* (Clint Eastwood,

1990). The latter can be described as a fictional version, after an interval of nearly 40 years, of the making of *The African Queen*, and in both films elephants have highly important, though very different, roles.

In *The African Queen* there is only one brief but crucial scene in which, thanks to an elephant sighting, the love story between the prim lady missionary Rose (Katherine Hepburn) and the rakish boat captain Charlie (Humphrey Bogart) reaches a turning point. On their river journey in the eponymous *African Queen*, the pair, fleeing from the Germans—the film takes place during World War One in what was then German East Africa—are again and again required to negotiate huge rapids and waterfalls. Animals on the banks of the river accompany and reflect the development of the love story with a precise crescendo of symbolism: for example, it is when in the afternoon light Charlie begins an imaginary conversation with some apes that Rose erupts in a liberating fit of laughter, finally breaking the ice between the two so very different people. Later, during a romantic sunset, a small herd of elephants appears on the riverbank, and at precisely this moment—and by no means coincidentally—Charlie declares his love: "Pinch me, Rosie! Here we are going down the river like Anthony and Cleopatra."

The editing of the film makes it clear that the exaltation the pair experiences in this crucial scene

6 *The Elephant Man*
John Merrick (John Hurt) as the Elephant Man
at high tea in elegant London society.
David Lynch, *The Elephant Man*, USA/UK 1980, film still.

when they become lovers is owing to the appearance
of the elephants. Enraptured by the sight of them,
they are able to put aside their very different natures,
which seemed so incompatible at the beginning of
the film, and Charlie can finally tell Rose: "I lost my
heart, too!"

When Clint Eastwood made *White Hunter, Black
Heart*, serving as the film's director and lead actor,
he assigned an entirely different role to the elephants. Eastwood plays a Hollywood director by the
name of John Wilson, who is in Africa shooting an
adventure film titled *The African Queen*. But he is really only obsessed with the idea of shooting an elephant himself. Everything has to be subordinated
to his ultimate male fantasy; his fixation defines the
entire course of the film's narrative. Even as he is
arriving in Africa, a virtually emblematic aerial
shot just before Wilson lands at the Entebbe airport
along with his screenwriter Pete (Jeff Fahey) estab-
lishes a magnificent elephant as a main actor in the
film. A short time later, over a first beer next to the
hotel pool—the film people wearing safari gear, of
course—there is shop talk with a seasoned big-game
hunter. Wilson tells the expert that while in Africa
he wants to hunt elephants, but it is clear that he
knows little about what that entails. He doesn't even
know that to kill an elephant it is best to aim at a
spot 12 centimeters below the eyes. Spurred by this
new information, Wilson soon heads for the Congo
and penetrates deeper and deeper inland. His desire
to kill an elephant seems to be greater than his

desire to make a good film—the dialogue thoroughly
exploits the double meaning of "to shoot". In an
interesting subplot, the hunt-obsessed Wilson is,
however, revealed to be a morally more complex
character: he defends his Jewish screenwriter when
the woman at his table makes anti-Semitic comments, and a little later he fearlessly fights a white
racist who has insulted a Black waiter. Despite these
nobler reactions, he initially retains his elephant
obsession. On his first encounter with a bull elephant—a huge beast that Wilson wants to kill at
all costs—his companions urgently dissuade him,
warning that it is too dangerous, for there are
elephant cows in the immediate vicinity that could
become enraged. One of the people warning him
is Kivu (Boy Mathias Chuma), an African with
whom Wilson has felt a special bond ever since
their first meeting. He lets himself be talked out
of his intention and doesn't shoot. Pete, Wilson's
screenwriter friend, observes the scene from a safe
distance through binoculars, and exclaims to himself, the driver, and to us, the audience: "I've never
seen an elephant outside a zoo. They're so majestic.
So indestructible, part of the earth. They make us
feel like lesser creatures from some other planet.
Without any dignity. You believe in God again,
the miracle of the Creation. Fantastic. They're
part of a world that no longer exists. A feeling of
an invincible time."

After the encounter with the huge bull elephant—
the hunter and game seen together in a single shot
to prove the authenticity of film—Wilson still fails
to abandon his plan: on the contrary. He belittles
the screenwriter, who now considers shooting elephants a crime, and disregards his warnings. During a filming pause, Wilson finally makes another

attempt to shoot the bull. This time he takes only Kivu along. Soon Wilson and the elephant stand eye to eye as two alpha males. Kivu again warns that it is too dangerous, and suddenly the bull charges Wilson. In the following dramatic sequence, Kivu saves Wilson's life but becomes a victim himself. The elephant gores Kivu, tosses him into the air, then tramples him. After the fatal accident Wilson returns to the village a broken man. Drums announce the death of the villager with the news: "White hunter, black heart." In his obstinacy, Wilson has been responsible for a man's death and committed a crime. Eastwood's film shows the elephant to be a more moral being than man; the bull is the only thing that can finally bring the irrational and narcissistic Wilson to his senses. The elephant's superior strength is brutally and punitively displayed, but ultimately with justification, for in this story it is the Hollywood director who is solely to blame for Kivu's death.

AN ELEPHANT TRAUMA IN REAL-LIFE LONDON

The true story of the life and suffering of the Englishman Joseph Merrick, who lived at the end of the 19th century, was filmed by David Lynch in 1980 in *The Elephant Man*. Merrick, called John in the film, suffered from the disorder neurofibromatosis. His head was greatly enlarged, his body badly contorted, and he could barely walk. As a historical drama, the film shows the causes of the ailment as explained to Merrick by his mother: according to her account, an accident had occurred at a parade of elephants during her pregnancy and she had fallen. So in the prologue to the film, the mother's pained face appears in a double exposure in which a number of elephants nightmarishly and aggressively trample on people lying on the ground. Merrick apparently believed this story up to the time of his death in 1900 at only 27.

Lynch's film relates how Merrick was mistreated by Victorian society, exhibited as a monster in freak shows, and exploited for medical research, but also loved by a few people for his gentleness and sensitivity. In addition to recognizing the artistic achievements of its actors, director, and designer, response to this very successful black-and-white drama revolved around the issue of what feelings the Elephant Man, played by John Hurt, evoked in viewers. As it happens, Lynch opens up a range of possible interpretations in that on various levels and with visual subtlety he plays on people's fear of elephants. Yet as a film

figure, Merrick reflects the unfathomable nature of that fear and illustrates something puzzling that remains hidden to the direct gaze.

TOPSY AND PROFESSOR GRZIMEK: ON ELEPHANTS AND THE ROLES ASSIGNED TO THEM IN WESTERN DOCUMENTARIES

On January 4, 1903, the female elephant Topsy, which had killed her keeper and two other men on Coney Island, was electrocuted. The 97-second film *Electrocuting an Elephant* (Jacob Blair Smith or Edwin S. Porter, 1903) documents the killing, staged as a spectacle, in the style of the early "cinema of attractions". Around 1,500 people were in attendance as Topsy collapsed from the electric shocks in a cloud of dust. To this day the film is the subject of Internet discussions about animal welfare, for Topsy, named after the slave girl in the novel *Uncle Tom's Cabin*, had probably been tortured by her keeper. Since then,

7 *Kein Platz für wilde Tiere (No Room for Wild Animals)*
He shaped the image of Africa in post-war Germany: Professor Bernhard Grzimek, filmmaker, author, TV presenter, behavioral researcher, zoo director. Bernhard and Michael Grzimek, *Kein Platz für wilde Tiere (No Room for Wild Animals)*, Germany 1956, film still.

the majestic animals have been pictured as victims of human activity in countless documentaries and television films.

In Germany, for example, it is worth recalling the period when television was still national, when there were popular serials and TV personalities that everybody knew. Professor Bernhard Grzimek, with his extensive film and TV appearances, was one of them. Along with Albert Schweitzer, he was one of the figures who helped to form the public perception of Africa in the German-speaking world, with ramifications to this day. Like Schweitzer, Grzimek created in his work a superficially benevolent Africa narrative, but one that on closer inspection was able to be so successful only because it was based on a foundation of colonial thinking and specifically German sensitivities. Whereas Schweitzer, as a doctor, made the charitable turn to Africa the leitmotif of his work and its treatment in the media, the zoologist Grzimek focused on ecology and conservation. Grzimek "discovered" or "conquered" Africa for the German film and television public as a paradise of natural wonders.

In 1956, the still young Federal Republic was busy rebuilding the country and its own reputation when the film *Kein Platz für wilde Tiere* (*No Room for Wild Animals*; Bernhard and Michael Grzimek, 1956),

the winner two Golden Bears at the Berlinale, or Berlin International Film Festival, arrived in cinemas. Berhard Grzimek directed the film, initially with his son, but Michael Grzimek died in a plane crash while it was being shot. The film is a fervent plea for the creation of nature reserves; one hears Bernhard Grzimek's distinctive voice as commentator almost constantly warning, explaining, and alerting: "Nature is being encroached upon more and more. Even where the last nature reserves have been set aside, in Africa, more and more cities, roads, railways are being constructed. The last paradises are being encircled. The heavy machinery of technology is even rolling over the Dark Continent." In the film, Grzimek and his son travel from Nairobi into the Congo, where with the help of two locals, Cassimo and Eoini, they find the rare forest elephants. In somewhat jagged film logic, in this sequence the camera assumes their perspective, gazes in an unusual close-up into the eyes and hearts of the elephants. The paternalistic commentary completes the visual assault of the white film team, which here becomes the mouthpiece for the acting locals: "Never does a white man get to see them, even if he marches through the jungle for weeks or months. Cassimo and Eoini are familiar with all the creatures of their forest, and either love or fear them."

At the end of the film, another elephant on a riverbank dies from a hunting wound in extended, heart-wrenching agony. The political subtext of the film, which can be seen as a media precursor of the German ecology movement, promoted a view of Africa in which the continent's peoples, frequently reduced to secondary roles, disturb or threaten nature. Grzimek's films, and not only this one, establish the elephants as symbols of a proxy war in which such complex political, social, and ecological power relationships between Africa and the rest of the world are faced with to this day.

A CHANGE OF PERSPECTIVE: ELEPHANTS IN TWO DOCUMENTARY FILMS FROM ZIMBABWE AND SOUTH AFRICA

In 2002, Tsitsi Dangarembga, a filmmaker from Zimbabwe, opposed this view with an African perspective in her film *Elephant People*. She lets Zimbabwe village people who live at the edges of the large nature reserves, and are at the mercy of elephants, speak. The animals regularly destroy their fields and occasionally attack people, trampling grown men and goring little children with their tusks. Yet the

8 *Elephant People*
A family mourns after a teenager was killed by an elephant while tending the cattle.
Tsitsi Dangarembga, *Elephant People*, Zimbabwe 2002, film still.

9 *Sisters of the Wilderness*
A young South African woman sees an elephant in the wild for the first time. Karin Slater, *Sisters of the Wilderness*, South Africa 2018, film still.

people have no choice but to submit to coexisting with the animals. Tourism in this part of Africa thrives only when *white* tourists get to see elephants, and tourism offers them a better chance for income than agriculture. At the end of the film, the sole *white* person in it is interviewed, an older woman who runs an "elephant orphanage" and receives so many donations for the little ones' upbringing from all over the world that they are better cared for than many of the human babies in the vicinity.

Finally, a recent South African documentary focuses on the perspective from which we view wild elephants and other animals. For *Sisters of the Wilderness* (2018), Karin Slater, one of the few successful camerawomen in the field of wildlife film making, accompanies five teenage Zulu girls on a several-day hike through the Hluhluwe iMfolozi Game Reserve. Like the director, the young women grew up near the park but had never been on a safari.

The majority of South Africa's blacks know the "big five"—to big-game hunters and safari experts the five most sought-after animals, whether for killing or photographing: the elephant, black rhinoceros, Cape buffalo, lion, leopard—only from television. The young women are hoping that the hike will have a therapeutic effect. They have been traumatized by the murder of a parent, by teenage pregnancies, and similar misfortunes. And in fact, during the course of the film you can see the effect, especially on the women's faces, that many feature films ascribe to elephants when they are presented as friends to humankind and bringers of good luck. The women are profoundly moved by their encounter with the animals in their native habitat. At the end of the hike, they begin to talk about themselves and their problems much more openly than at the beginning. Mixed in with their individual stories are reflections on their perceptions of nature and how they are influenced by social privileges and limitations, by traditions and education. In South Africa, where the apartheid system continues to have its effect to this day, many of these mechanisms are more apparent than elsewhere. The young women become aware of this on their hike: of the neglect and injuries they have experienced as non-privileged citizens, but also of their feelings when from a high cliff they see elephants striding through a spectacularly beautiful river valley or watch them feeding up close. *Sisters of the Wilderness* is thus a promising attempt to find answers to the question of why there are countless films of Western provenance in which elephants play an important role, but only very few from African filmmakers.

List of films mentioned in the essay:
Hatari!, Howard Hawks, USA 1962
Bal Ganesh, Pankaj Sharma, India 2007
Babar: The Movie, Alan Bunce, Canada/France 1989
African Queen, John Huston, UK 1951
White Hunter, Black Heart, Clint Eastwood, USA 1990
The Elephant Man, David Lynch, USA/UK 1980
Electrocuting an Elephant, Jacob Blair Smith or Edwin S. Porter, USA 1903
Kein Platz für wilde Tiere, Bernhard and Michael Grzimek, Germany 1956
Elephant People, Tsitsi Dangarembga, Zimbabwe 2002
Sisters of the Wilderness, Karin Slater, South Africa 2018

LEARNING WITH THE COLORFUL PATCHWORK **ELEPHANT ELMER** WHAT IT IS LIKE TO BE **DIFFERENT**

INTERVIEW WITH DAVID McKEE

GRIT KELLER

David McKee (born 1935) works as a freelance painter and book illustrator whose children's books are known internationally. Elmer, a colorful, patchwork elephant, is his best-known and most successful creation, and his adventures have been translated into more than 60 languages. Time and again, Elmer experiences what it is like to be different, namely multi-colored. McKee's books for children are considered to be especially useful in teaching, since they convey values like tolerance and the acceptance of otherness. The morals of his stories are subtly told and have influenced a whole generation of children.

One day the black elephants decided to kill all the white elephants,

and the white ones decided to kill all the black.

1 David McKee, *Tusk Tusk*, 1978.

2 David McKee, *Elmer and the Hippos*, 2003.

The stories are by no means innocuous. *Tusk Tusk* (1978) is about hatred and violence (Fig. 1). There are white elephants and there are black elephants, and they hate each other so much that they fight, the black elephants having decided to kill the white, and the white to kill the black. A few peace-loving elephants from both sides have fled into the jungle. For a long time no elephants are seen. But one day grandchildren of the peace-loving elephants emerge from the jungle. They have outwardly changed: their skin color is gray. In *Elmer and the Hippos* (2003), the elephants ask Elmer to get rid of the hippos that have recently appeared at the river (Fig. 2). After speaking with them, Elmer decides not to drive them away but instead to help them, for their river has dried up. Finally, the elephants all help to break up the dam of rubble that has blocked the hippos' river.

This interview with David McKee was conducted in July 2019 in Plymouth, England, on the occasion of the Patchwork Elephant's 30th birthday with Andersen Press. Elmer has become independent and strode in a parade through the city. More than 60 Elmer figures were painted for the festivities by artists and school children.

Elmer is celebrating his 30th birthday with the publisher Andersen Press. Congratulations! How and when did Elmer first make himself known to you?

Elmer was first published in 1968, or 51 years ago. I had probably already worked on him a couple of years before, in the mid 1960s. I frequently drew cartoons for newspapers and such. I liked drawing elephants, so I produced a great number of them. My paintings were influenced by Paul Klee at that time; they were divided into squares and colorful. One day I simply divided an elephant into squares and painted them, and the result was this remarkable patchwork elephant. Then came the name. It's an alliteration: *El*mer, *el*ephant. First the picture, then the name, and then the story simply followed. Today it is interesting, of course, how so many people, especially minority groups, have adopted Elmer as a kind of symbol. The LGBT movement considers him its symbol, and other groups as well. But he's simply Elmer. He's there for everybody.

"And everyone," said Elmer, "means everyone!"

3 David McKee,
Elmer's Special Day,
2009.

How do you feel about the fact that Elmer has become a symbol of inclusion and acceptance? I think it's fine. He's there for all who like him.

Children are growing up with Elmer and his stories. What was your favorite story as a child? We didn't have very many books. I grew up during the war. It was simply a small house without books. A few things and one or two dictionaries. But everyone at home was a storyteller. My mother told stories. My teacher told stories, various other people told stories. So it was only natural that I began telling stories, too. Everyone did. So I told myself stories. I was allowed to walk on Dartmoor alone, which would no longer be possible today. At least for small children, I feel. But when you're on the moor, there is only the sound of the moor. The insects, the wind, the birds. There are no other noises. This was before portable phones. Today people are constantly in contact with other voices from outside. But when you're on the moor, you have only the voice in your head, and I feel that that's very conducive to stories.

Also, I grew up not far from Plymouth, in Tavistock, a town that is quite haunted; there are a number of ghosts. People told stories about the ghosts and repeated these different stories again and again. Of the cities I have visited, New York is surely the most haunted one after Tavistock. The very first time I was there I found that there is no city as spiritually restless as New York, but I suspect that's another issue.

Do you have anything in common with Elmer? Probably quite a lot. People say, after all, that every kind of art is a reflection of one's own person. So I probably let Elmer say what I would often like to say myself, or things I think about or that trouble me. I shine through, as in my other books as well, but Elmer can probably handle that differently; it is often easier for him than for me.

Why did you choose an elephant? I didn't choose the elephant. The elephant chose me. The atmosphere is filled with stories. The space we're in is filled with all conceivable television programs if one has the proper receiver. From this space you can pick so much. It is also filled with all the radio broadcasts; if you have the proper radio, you can hear them. So all that is in the atmosphere. I also believe that it is filled with music and with stories and that musicians and storytellers are simply the receivers. Elmer sought me out so I might listen to him, so he could speak to me.

It's also all right to be the same. I find that it comes down to being who one is, feeling good about oneself, accepting who one is. At the moment we find ourselves in an era of "Look at me!" Driv-

In his first adventure, Elmer is somewhat depressed. Brightly colored, he stands out from the monotonous gray elephant herd, but after he has dyed himself gray he realizes that it is all right to be different. Why is it important to tell children that being different is all right?

ing with the car windows down, with deafeningly loud music, so that everyone notices that one is listening to loud music—that means nothing but "Look at me!" People embellish themselves, but Elmer is someone who would be careful with that, because he's so different. But all the other elephants are also different. At the end of the story *Elmer and the Lost Teddy*, Elmer's black-and-white-checked cousin Wilbur says to him: "Your Teddy looks completely different; he is something very special." And Elmer responds: "You don't have to be different to be something special." (Fig. 4) That's very important to me: we're all special, for somebody we're special. My father was simply a no-nonsense fellow who helped the neighbors when it was necessary. He was never very wealthy or famous. He was the finest type I have ever known. I believe we sometimes make things simply too difficult. Life is there to be relished, and there are all the little things, like little children, that are so important. And the moment is important, but nobody has time. Everything takes place as fast as possible. You really have to downshift—that, I believe, is precisely Elmer's pace.

I read *Elmer and the Hippos* with a Berlin grammar-school class, and the pupils had a few questions. One child thought that tigers and lions do not have the same habitat. That cannot be! Where exactly is Elmer at home?

He's at home in the picture book. It's Elmer's jungle. It's not the "proper, actual" jungle. You don't find a jungle with plants and the kind of people who live with each other, and you don't find any elephants like Elmer. If you can accept Elmer, then you can also accept this jungle.

Why don't the gray elephants talk with the hippos?

It's just like people who complain about migrants. They don't go to the migrants and complain. They make a fuss and complain to each other without solving the problem. Why are these people here? Naturally Elmer tried to find that out.

4 David McKee, *Elmer and the Lost Teddy*, 1999.

"Elmer," said Wilbur, "weren't you worried that Baby Elephant would want to keep your teddy? Your teddy is very different; it's special."

"But, Wilbur, didn't you know?" said Elmer in surprise. "You don't have to be different to be special. All teddies are special, especially your own."

...CRASH!
They didn't notice the stilts and bumped right into them.

The elephants fell off, but, instead of falling onto the hard ground, they fell onto the soft, round, fat hunters.

5 David McKee, *Elmer on Stilts*, 1993. People rarely appear in Elmer's world, but in *Elmer on Stilts* he encounters hunters. The colorful elephant notices that the hunters keep looking downward, searching for the herd's footprints. So Elmer takes inspiration from the giraffes and convinces his elephant friends to stand on stilts. Since the hunters with their pith helmets don't see the green stilts, they run right into them, whereupon the gray giants jump on the men and squash them.

If your grandchildren were to describe your profession, what would they say?

"He's a grandfather" [laughs].
And I get letters from children:
"I love your books, but do you really have…? And similar questions. In reality I'm a steeplejack or a blacksmith.

Why is Elmer checked and not, shall we say, striped? Is he Scottish?

No. I'm no Scot, although I have a Scottish name. My grandfather came from Scotland, but that's another story. Elmer is simply that way. He's just as much Scottish as Italian, German, or what have you. He's really everybody. He's a symbol.

You are not only a painter and illustrator, but also a true storyteller. How do you come up with your stories?

Usually, somebody gives me the idea. For example, I heard some parents say to their child "Not now, Bernard", and you hear that very often. "Not now, Peter, not now, Bryan, not now, Mary…" It's simply not the moment.

Only recently I got the idea for a story. It was a very sunny day in the south of France. A mother and her child were standing in front of me and I noticed that they cast very distinct shadows. And with that came the beginning of the story. The boy says: "Mama, a man just went into the shop, and he didn't have a shadow." The mother suggests: "Oh, let's wait a minute and see whether he comes back out." And then Peter's shadow says to the mother's shadow: "Out there are all manner of shadows." At this point I commanded myself to stop, and said: "David, you don't need another story just now." But such things are constantly happening. The pots talk to each other, the water taps talk to each other. You go into the bathroom and notice that the water taps and the wet spots are making faces, and you think: "Oh, hello bathroom, how's it going?" And the bathroom answers: "I'm doing fine,

David, thanks! And how about you?" And I say: "Wow, you can talk. You never talked before." That happens constantly. Each of us is a story. I find that interesting. You live a story, I live a story, for a moment we have a common story . . . and that's how it goes with things all the time. Incessantly. Stories simply come. They are there, but you have to be prepared to become aware of them, to be conscious of the beauty that's everywhere around us.

Elmer lives in peace with many other animals, but in the real world elephants, tigers, and lions are threatened species. Every 20 minutes an elephant is killed for his ivory. Elmer doesn't have tusks. Do people have an impact on Elmer's world?

I think they're responsible for his world. This world exists because of them. Because these stories can't be told with men, they're told with animals. I suppose that's the world I would wish for, this peaceful world in which we can live together, all the different species, and can wish each other a good morning, can go about our business and let the others go about their business as long as it doesn't harm us. That's another world that has nothing to do with the real world. Or perhaps it does have a great deal to do with the real world. Or perhaps it is a reaction against the violence that's becoming more and more popular in literature and films. I find it very sad that this additional excitement is necessary. I find it exciting to watch the raindrops running down the outside of the window, and to see which one wins. I don't need all this exaggerated violence.

Elmer doesn't have tusks, to be sure, but you wrote a story about black and white elephants called _Tusk Tusk_ that was first published in 1978 by Andersen Press (Fig. 1). Why do they fight each other, and how do they use their tusks?

Because the others are different. We don't like it when people are different. We want everybody to be just like us, but we also want to set ourselves apart from them because we're better. That's a ridiculous contradiction. I think on the first page it says "_Vive la différence!_" I simply find that differences are absolutely important. At the end of the book, they actually become the same color, but there are other differences, like their ears. I feel that extreme differences and all the little differences need to be accepted.

It is an excellent book with which to familiarize children with the subjects of racism, prejudices, and tolerance. How is diversity promoted through children's books?

I have no idea. I don't pretend to know too much. I'm only a storyteller. Sometimes stories express things, and for me they're important things that need to be said. But you know, some people listen, but most people don't listen. It's only a story after all.

At 30, Elmer has experienced any number of adventures, and he has readers throughout the world. What will have changed for Elmer at 40, and how much more is he likely to experience?

We shall see. I would guess that as long as I can I'll continue to write stories about him. I believe that we're now at a point where we will also make films about him. Previously he wasn't yet ready for that, so to speak. I often say that characters are like your own children. He can now live a life of his own; perhaps he does things that make me think "I don't know whether he ought to do that", just as I sometimes think about my children. But that's how it should be, it's his life and he has to live it.

6 David McKee

ELEPHANTS, BEES, AND SUSTAINABLE CO-EXISTENCE

FRITZ VOLLRATH

SUMMARY

Human-elephant coexistence is under threat for a number of reasons, but mainly because of human pressure on space coupled with changing climatic conditions in elephant-range states. Sustainable mitigation methods have to be developed. Fencing farms with beehives is one of them. In Africa, the elephant and the bee have a fascinating relationship. It appears that the aggressive African honeybee is able to protect not only single trees but also small-holdings against raiding elephants. Properly managed, the bee-fence system provides the farmer not only with protection but also with a sustainable income from sales of honey and wax. This combination of farming bees for both income and protection acts as a strong double incentive to maintain a good fence. And as we know: good fences make good neighbors. Thus in the armory of migration methods for human-elephant-coexistence, bee-fencing is gaining traction, though this system, too, has limitations.

INTRODUCTION

This essay addresses the complex issue of turning human-elephant conflict into human-elephant co-existence. Ivory, one way or another, is a product of human-elephant interactions. After all, more often than not tusks are the spoils of poaching, trophies of hunting, or compensation for animal control and farm defense. Very rarely are they accidental treasures found in the bush after an elephant's natural death. Because of this commercial interaction between humans and elephants, it is only logical that a book devoted to ivory—which is essentially the legacy of dead elephants—includes a chapter on the natural relationship of humans with living elephants. And this essay addresses this relationship and proposes a novel way to mitigate against ill will on both sides.

All relevant conservation efforts are attempts to protect and maintain elephants in their natural ecosystems. As such, these attempts interfere with the goals of traders and consumers, who see elephants not as sustainable assets for tourism but as end-of-line producers of a high value and yet diminishing export commodity, ivory. In this sense, we cannot view ivory independently of the elephant. Nor can we view the elephant independently of its wider ecosystem, which today features humans more prominently then anytime in the history of the pachyderm. This observation is most certainly true for Africa, though Asia might be a somewhat different proposition for a number of reasons. The main difference may well be found in the ancient custom widespread in Asia of using elephants (and sometimes ivory) prominently in culture and religion.

Whatever the differences between Asia and Africa concerning human-elephant interactions, we as sentient as well as ethical beings must find ways to protect our own human livelihoods while respecting the needs of the elephant. Please note that I shall talk about human-elephant co-existence, though conflict is, alas, the more common usage of the C in the acronym HEC.

Let me begin with a tale. Legend has it that once upon a time in East Africa, Ngai the creator of the universe and supreme god laughed twice in a row. First he laughed when, looking down from his mountain, he observed huge gray beasts suddenly stop pushing over mighty trees to turn tail and run away, trumpeting in distress. They were chased by small upright figures running on two legs and furiously waving their arms with pointed sticks in their hands. A little later Ngai laughed again when he now saw those very same stick-figures suddenly stop whatever they were doing to run away themselves, chased by tiny winged creatures. Ngai concluded that size is not might and that in the African savannah the natural order of things is this: elephants fear humans and humans fear bees. As with all tales, there is a deeper message in Ngai's laughter of *Schadenfreude*. If elephants fear us and we fear bees— is it not possible that bees frighten elephants, too? As it happens, yes, they do. And, as it also happens, we humans can use this fact to frighten elephants away from us by using bees as our guardians.

I will start my essay by discussing the original observations and experiments that established the fact that elephants do avoid bees. Following this I will present the experiments that explored the full complexity of the relationship between elephants and bees. Next, I will examine a range of measures that use this relationship to protect human farming endeavors against the raids of hungry elephants. Finally, I shall explore the various implications of using bees as biological control agents in crop protection.

1 A young Samburu bull encountering, for the first time, the sound of bees broadcast from a remote speaker hidden in a green canvas bag (left).

2 Elephant herd fleeing from the relayed sound of angry bees buzzing, Kenya.

THE ISSUE OF "FOOTPRINTS"

Before going into the details of elephant-bee interactions, let us explore the concept of ecological and geographic footprints. Footprints are the fundamental issue of any discussion concerning the management of the co-existence between elephants and humans, which happens to be competitive wherever and whenever it concerns land and water. Before the expansion of the human population, which was largely fueled by the introduction of American maize (*Zea mays*) by the Portuguese, the elephant ruled supreme in the African savannahs, bushlands and forests, with a footprint that was huge and all-pervading. Humans were thin on the ground and mostly concerned with herding livestock in a pastoralist lifestyle that does not really compete with elephant ecology or behavior. True, some humans hunted for food but very few farmed, fencing their vegetable smallholdings with thorn bushes to protect against raiders, human or animal.

In those days, the elephants had an enormous footprint both geographically and demographically, as well as ecologically, while humans had relatively small and scattered footprints in the savannah, bushland, and forest ecosystems. This ratio changed when human populations increased, at first tentatively but rapidly from the beginning of the 20th century, and nowadays near-exponentially. Today, humans take up most of the fertile land and have pushed elephants into marginal territories. Of course, hunting for ivory added to the elephant's troubles, at first only negligibly, when human weapons where short-range and inaccurate and elephants had space to hide out. But since the beginning of the last century hunting became increasingly effective, with better weapons and less wilderness for elephants to hide in.

As it happens, elephants also need to eat and drink a lot—and to meet these needs in their natural habitat they require ample space to roam. In the increasingly fierce competition for land and water between elephants and humans, the elephant has size and strength on its side. It also has highly adapted senses coupled with local knowledge acquired during the long period of learning in the family unit as a youngster, if a bull, and an indefinite period of learning as a cow, which seldom leaves her family for good.

Humans have technology on their side, such as poisoned arrows, pit-traps, thorn bush or wire fencing, spears, guns, and fire. In addition, humans, the ultimate hunters, are cunning and collaborative, both traits that are especially effective in conflict situations. Moreover, and this is the crux of the matter, humans tend to be enterprising, imaginative and inventive, and are ever expanding their requirements of land, water, and other resources. Once secured, such resources are hardly ever relinquished but give rise to permanent settlements and land tenures that tend to more or less ferociously exclude wildlife.

This human tendency to subsume their surroundings affects the elephant's use of any shared ecosystem. After all, efficient and effective farming is based on the exclusion of wildlife. Moreover, it leads to the compression of farming into one or two specific seasons a year when the harvest provides high quality forage for both man and beast. During those times, raiding elephants can destroy a year's work in one night by eating and trampling, rendering the farmer and his/her family destitute. No wonder that under these circumstances anger runs high and co-existence turns to conflict. To avoid any disputes dangerous to both, the two species are best kept separate before such critical situations can arise. As it turns out, bees might be a part of the solution.

DEFENSE BY BEE-FENCE: FIRST EXPERIMENTS

The African honeybee *Apis mellifera scutellata* occurs throughout the African elephant's range, with a "hive" naturally nesting in tree hollows or, when in swarming mode, hanging in big huddles from branches. This provides ample opportunities for elephants to experience the bees and their formidable hive defense, which uses a sharp sting coupled with an assembly pheromone that calls for murderous mass attacks.

One might think that elephants, being thick skinned, i.e. pachyderm, are physically protected against bee stinging. Alas (for them), the area around the eye and the tip of the trunk are soft targets. And it seems from our experiments that natural encounters in the wild are teaching elephants about bees and their stings, which can be very painful, though they are very seldom lethal to a grown elephant. This combination of pain without death makes for a perfect pattern for teaching the elephants to avoid bees—if at all possible. Learning from their elders teaches the youngsters through something called social facilitation, i.e. by observation and putting "two and two together". Simply by watching and following relatives who have been stung, all family members are taught to avoid an angry swarm or an alarm-buzzing hive even without first personally experiencing the pain of many stings. Indeed (and more about this later), in northern Kenya, and perhaps also elsewhere, elephants have developed a dedicated "bee-ware" alarm rumble.

This highly tuned natural alert-and-avoidance behavior of the African elephant makes for a perfect setting to develop bee-protection technology by positioning beehives in order to create no-go zones for elephants. Following this logic, we designed some first experiments to test the hypothesis and hopefully confirm the idea. As it happened, the story of the bee defense concept (bee-fence for short) started with a rather simple chance observation.

While studying elephants in Laikipia, northern Kenya, I was told by the manager of a ranch that he thought that trees with bees were not browsed or pushed over by the elephants roaming the land. Talks with other ranchers, farmers and also local beekeepers seemed to confirm this notion, though only one beekeeper had actually seen bees attacking elephants. However, the trainer of a tame bull elephant told me how Booper (the bull) was indeed attacked and very badly stung when he had run into a low-flying swarm of bees. So I "borrowed" that elephant for an experiment which confirmed my suspicion. Booper strenuously avoided going near a tree he normally favored for forage when a hidden speaker broadcast the buzz of a beehive, but he went happily to browse it when the speaker played a Bach violin concerto. Another experiment, now done with my friend and collaborator Iain Douglas-Hamilton, confirmed the conclusion: beehives hung low into trees deterred elephants from browsing on their branches or gouging their bark.

This suggested another simple experiment: denying access to a dense copse of delicious fever trees in the bend of a deep river by hanging a row of 24 traditional log hives from a long wire just over 2.3 meters high. This allowed most wildlife and also vehicles to pass under, while elephants would bump into the wires and swinging hives. This bee-fence worked and kept the elephants from crossing. Not surprisingly, occupied hives seemed a stronger deterrent than empty ones. Importantly, an interesting little experiment on one of the hives in the fence showed that even at night a hive can erupt when agitated: while I filmed (stupidly unprotected) my assistant John, dressed in a thick bee-keeper's suit, hit a sleeping hive a few times hard with his club. We were soon running away rapidly and for a few hundred meters before the bees gave up chasing us.

These simple pilot experiments convinced Iain and me that elephants actually did fear bees, and that the idea of using bees to fence out elephants might indeed work. This led us to embark on a long series of more detailed experiments. For these we teamed up with Lucy King, first as a Master's student and then as a PhD student at Oxford. In ever

3 A modern bee hive optimized for honey production with a roof to protect against the heat of the sun and sheeted poles to deter honey badgers.

expanding experiments, Lucy followed up on our initial work as project manager at Save the Elephants, the aptly named conservation charity founded by Iain in 1993.

FURTHER EXPERIMENTS ON THE ELEPHANT-BEE RELATIONSHIP

A particularly exciting experiment required the collaboration of Dr Joseph Soltis from the Disney Zoo in Orlando, where he was studying the calls and responses of the elephants in their substantial tame herd. Iain and I already knew from very simple pilot experiments that elephants reacted with alarm to bee buzz played from a speaker. The detailed studies with Joseph and Lucy allowed us to record, playback and analyze the response of known elephants to buzzing bees. Importantly, these studies in Samburu, northern Kenya, also showed that the local elephants make a special rumble to communicate the presence of bees. In effect, these elephants seem to have a dedicated call meaning "bee" which elicits alarm in the herd. Our studies on elephant language (if that is the right word) further showed that these

elephants can also distinguish the sound of, for example, the speech of harmless tourists from that of potentially harmful Samburu warriors. And react accordingly. Elephants never fail to surprise.

These experiments were interesting as well as important because they gave us a new window into the elephant's perception of its environment. They confirmed our conclusion that elephants and bees might have a very old and long-standing relationship. One so strong that it should be easy to co-opt it for our vision of using bees to protect crops against raiding elephants. This view was supported by another set of experiments demonstrating that it is indeed possible to protect crops against elephant depredations by placing a simple barrier of chest-high beehives suspended in a long row from a wire interlinked with another wire that would set them swinging when an elephant tried to sneak between them. In this case, Lucy decided to upgrade from the traditional log-hives to Kenyan box-hives because of better hive management and higher yield. And these more modern hives did indeed seem as effective as the log hives, if not more so.

Importantly, these early trials of bee-fence defense demonstrated not only that elephants do avoid crops thus protected, but also that the farmer appre-

4 A fence of hives designed to protect a farm from elephant raids by linking the hives with a wire that alerts the bees when disturbed.

5 A tempting field of maize near Voi in Kenya successfully bee-fenced.

ciated the help provided by bees a great deal more than we had anticipated. The farmers, when asked about the benefits of the bee-fence system listed not only the honey crop, but also the chance to sleep comfortably at home at night rather than sitting awake (and frightened) in their fields. In addition, and this really surprised us, the farmers also admitted that hearing an elephant trumpeting in distress gave them a warm feeling of personal power over what they see as thick-skinned and destructive giants. Indeed, destructive is the perfect description, because a herd of elephants, even quite a small herd, can easily destroy a whole field in a single night, and with that a year's sustenance and livelihood for a family. And that devastation can be caused as much by foraging for food as by walking over the growing crop and thus trampling it all into the ground beyond recovery.

The various outcomes of all these experiments further confirmed our vision of developing a farmer-driven, semi-commercial bee-fencing system to protect against elephant raids. The goal of Lucy King and her team envisioned the perfection of the bee-fence as part of a strategy to develop sustainable methodology and techniques/technologies that would allow us to turn human-elephant conflict into human-elephant coexistence. Sustainable, in this context, means both ecologically and environmentally friendly as well as self-financing.

Importantly, the presence of wild bees in the elephant's natural environment means that the elephants should constantly be on bee alert to avoid natural hives and attacks. This natural co-existence would suggest that elephants do not easily associate attacking bees with being assaulted by people, as would be the case if burned by firebrands or hit by bullets. This lack of a direct mental association between harm and humans should in the long run protect the local population from individual elephants gone rogue because of bad memories.

In addition to avoiding directly antagonizing elephants, the bee-fence, unlike an electric fence, provides a natural and eco-friendly fencing technology. Importantly, the financial aspect is covered by the sale of honey and wax, which are both cash crops with good markets even for small-scale producers with outputs that are variable in both quality and quantity.

IMPLEMENTATION, INSTITUTIONALIZATION, AND LIMITATIONS OF BEE-FENCING

Our original vision of expanding the bee-fence was both developed and implemented by Dr Lucy King in a most spectacular way. Lucy and her team tested the concept in hundreds of communities and farms in all African elephant-range states. The trials always had considerable success, though there were, of course, some issues with farmers having to suppress or shed their anxiety about being stung and having to learn about modern bee-keeping techniques. One also has to consider the additional infrastructure necessary for the production of quality honey that can be sold at a good price.

As well as convincing farmers that installing bee-fences is a good idea all round, Lucy's data also convinced the Kenya Wildlife Service (KWS) that bee-fencing would be a valuable addition to the techniques employed to mitigate human-elephant conflict. Indeed, the KWS featured the beehive fence on the cover of one of its wildlife management reports. What more could one want for the success of an innovation that started with some rumors and a simple observation followed by a few simple experiments?

The concept to the bee-fence has considerable relevance to the wider issue of ivory as a commodity that entails the killing of elephants. If elephants pose no big threat to lives and livelihoods, then the farmers will be more relaxed about elephants, which in turn would reduce the killing of so-called problem animals. In a country like Kenya, where the hunting of elephants is illegal, most of the legal ivory stored by the KWS comes from such problem animals, or from animals that have died of natural causes. Obviously, less ivory in the stores will lead to fewer incentives to vote for the sale of such ivory. Let us put this statement into perspective: a growing stockpile of $100 million will inevitably lead to calls by politicians and the public to sell the ivory to fund public works, be it schools, hospitals, or wildlife conservation. Some of the ivory in these stockpiles comes from intercepted poaching, but a not insubstantial amount comes from so-called problem animals, i.e. crop raiders or habitually angry elephants which tend to chase humans.

Bee-fences are helping to avoid the shooting and taunting of elephants. They do not directly affect poaching, but might do so indirectly by reducing antipathy to elephants in front-line localities. Importantly, coexistence rather than conflict will lessen local ill-will and reduce complaints to the government about elephants straying into farmed areas, which in turn generates a general feeling in the nation of elephants as pests rather than assets. Moreover, coexistence rather than conflict leads to a community viewing poachers not as protectors of people but as strippers of an asset, elephants, with implications for tourism as well as community cohesion.

There are, of course, other techniques to protect farms. Electric fencing is particularly effective all round but very costly to install and run, which places it outside the budget of a typical community. Moreover, such fencing tends to be governmental and large scale, often denying the elephants valuable foraging grounds and age-honored migration routes that might link unfenced areas. Walls and ditches may work for a while, but with time crumble or fill in. Fire and noise work on a case-by-case basis, but antagonize the elephants and could lead to both direct or delayed confrontations with humans hurt, maimed or killed, and with some elephants killed in retaliation.

Another interesting, biologically friendly agricultural product that is both crop and protectant in one is chili pepper. Loki Osborn discovered that elephants avoid chili peppers as forage and will run away if peppered with chili spray, smoke, or missiles. Peppers could even be used as protective strips around palatable crops. But as elephants have a fine sense of smell and are clever at figuring out such ruses, they are likely to power through the

6 Elephant near a homestead close to Lake Jipe, Kenya.

peppers (as they power through wire fencing) onto the edibles they seek to raid, i.e. maize, cabbages, or tomatoes.

WHAT ABOUT **ASIA?**

So far, this essay has focused on African elephants. What about elephants in Asia? The Asian elephant, *Elephas maximus*, while closely related to its African cousins, the savannah and forest elephants, *Loxodonta africana* and *Loxodonta cyclotis* respectively, is in fact more closely related to the extinct wooly mammoth. Nevertheless, it appears that the Asian elephant also fears bees. Just after our first experiments were reported in the press, a farmer in Nepal wrote to me that he had put a hive on an elephant track to his crop with the result that they avoided the hive, preferring to walk around it through the thick bush. Lucy King confirmed this observation in a series of controlled experiments in various Asian countries and found that here, too, the concept of a beehive fence worked for the farmers and against elephant raiders. This is especially interesting because the native Asian hive bee, *Apis cerana*, is rather less aggressive than the African honeybee, *Apis mellifera scutellata*.

So we have to ask: What in the wild teaches the Asian elephants to fear bees? Perhaps it is the native giant honeybee, *Apis dorsata*? This hangs from a tree branch or a rock overhang in a huge vertical comb densely covered in bees that attack aggressively when disturbed. Alas, this bee is not really suited to commercial farming in hives. So in Asia, a bee-fence would use either the local *Apis cerana* or the European/Italian bee *Apis mellifera* (*ligustica*), which are both widely used for commercial bee keeping. Neither is as aggressive as the African bee. Perhaps Asia provides us with a good testing ground for efficient bee-fencing? For example, how does bee-fencing work with the combination of a super-aggressive wild bee that teaches the elephants to respect bees, and a docile domesticated hive bee that allows hive-fencing without excessive danger to humans and livestock?

7 A group of bull elephants ready to raid and unafraid of the humans nearby.

However this may be, it remains to be seen whether bee-fencing can be used as efficiently in Asia as in Africa without other changes. For example, in India the farmers tend to store their grain in dedicated huts inside the village. Elephants learn about this and night-raid whole villages, pulling down houses in search of forage. It is questionable whether bees would be of any use in such circumstances. In any case, because of the long tradition of catching large tuskers for service in temples, a gene for tusklessness has pervaded many Asian elephant populations. Moreover, female Asian elephants do not have tusks, unlike their African cousins. Both facts suggest that in Asia the killing of problem elephants rarely leads to ivory stockpiling in governmental strong rooms, so that Asian range states are not pushing CITIES for the sale of ivory on the open market.

THE OUTLOOK

In summary, we can say that the bee-fence is a proven, ecologically sustainable elephant barrier. Of course, there would also be limitations with this

8 Zoologist Fritz Vollrath with the bull elephant Booper and his guide, Joseph, Kenya. Note the broken tusk.

technology. For example, if all farms were bee-protected, what would the elephants do? Would they respect all fences, or would they brave the stings and break into some farms? If, on the other hand, they always respected the fencing, would the elephants in time forget not only the taste but also the smell of the crops behind the fence and return to the natural forage diet of their ancestors in the times before humans started farming?

And if the draw of smell and taste overcame the fear of stings, how might the farmers respond? Should they try to select more aggressive bees, or bees with more toxic stings? This would, of course, have implications for other wildlife, as well as consequences for any humans coming near those bees. Actually, in my first trial bee-fence around a smallholding, the bees, aroused by an elephant that quickly ran away, attacked and killed all the farmer's chickens in their pens. In any case, selecting for more aggressive bees in Africa might not even be possible as these bees may already have been selected over millennia by honey badgers and other honey hunters for an optimized combination of aggression and toxicity.

Another hypothetical development for sustainable farm protection might, along the lines of the Asian scenario, select two distinct populations, a ferocious one in the wild and a docile one around the farms. But in that case, would the clever elephants not quickly learn to distinguish between the two? I believe that a most likely scenario for long-term management of both bee-fencing and elephant behavior would probably involve the establishment of a patchwork of farms with some being bee protected and others not, to allow elephants corridors to move through the farming community as well as forage en route on sacrificial crops.

CONCLUSIONS

We have seen that bees can protect trees and that the bee-fence can provide farmers in potential conflict areas with an effective and efficient eco-friendly defense system that more than pays for itself. Thus bee-fencing should help to reduce human-elephant conflict and thus encourage and support human elephant coexistence. Coexistence would lead to fewer so-called problem animals being shot, with implications for the ivory stock in government strong rooms. The issue of governmental ivory stock is, of course, at the very heart of a vicious circle of supply and demand. As these stores grow in volume, they grow in value and with that they raise public pressure for sales to fund a society's needs such as wildlife conservation, healthcare, or schools. Such unquestionably important national demands can and do lead to governments deciding to lobby CITIES for a sale of their ivory on the open market. And any sale of such legal ivory allows illegal ivory to sneak into the market because the two are near impossible to distinguish.

In conclusion, one can say that the conversion of human-elephant conflict to human-elephant co-existence could help to reduce both the production of and trade in ivory. And bee-fencing could be a stepping-stone to this ultimate goal.

Links and literature
Conforming with modern times, I will list a few key web links that provide relevant information and further reading:

Save the Elephants:
https://www.savetheelephants.org/
In particular within Save the Elephants:
https://www.savetheelephants.org/about-elephants-2-3-2/elephant-news/ (accessed March 24, 2021) and
http://elephantsandbees.com/ (research papers) (accessed March 23, 2021)

Connected Conservation:
https://connectedconservation.com (accessed March 23, 2021)

The International Union For Conservation Of Nature (IUCN):
https://www.iucn.org/ssc-groups/mammals/african-elephant-specialist-group/human-elephant-conflict (accessed March 23, 2021)

Ecoexist:
http://www.ecoexistproject.org/reporting-back/blog/building-elephant-economy/ (accessed March 23, 2021)

And the first and the latest publication on the bee-fence concept:

Fritz Vollrath and Iain Douglas-Hamilton, "African bees to control African elephants", *Naturwissenschaften* 89 (November 2002), pp. 508–511, online at: https://link.springer.com/article/10.1007%2Fs00114-002-0375-2 (accessed November 2019).

Lucy E. King, *Beehive Fence Construction Manual*, 4th ed., *Elephant and Bees Project*, Nairobi, 2019, available online at: http://elephantsandbees.com/wp-content/uploads/2019/07/LKING-2019-Beehive-Fence-Construction-Manual-4th-edition.pdf (accessed November 2019).
This is a step-by-step guide to building a protective beehive fence to deter crop-raiding elephants from farmland.

THE **AFRICAN ELEPHANT**
IMPORTANCE AND ENDANGERMENT

KATHARINA TRUMP

Humans have always been fascinated with and amazed by elephants. Many see the gray giants as gentle creatures who function in complex social systems and are endowed with remarkable memories. In Hinduism, as the god Ganesh, the elephant personifies wisdom; in other cultures, they are symbols of strength, intelligence, and docility.

1 An Asian elephant in Kui Buri National Park, Thailand.

Given how much they are admired and the immense importance they have for the ecosystem, it is paradoxical that elephants continue to be mercilessly hunted for their ivory. Once numbering in the millions, only a few hundred thousand survive today.

ELEPHANTS WORLDWIDE

Elephants are found in both Africa and Asia. The numbers of Asian elephants (*Elephas maximus*) (Fig. 1) are not fully known. Experts estimate that there are now from 45,600 to 49,000 animals.[1] The International Red List of the International Union for Conservation of Nature (IUCN) lists the species as "endangered". The animals suffer especially from shrinking habitat and conflicts with human interests in specific areas. They are currently distributed across 13 Asian countries, India being home to by far the greatest number.

Africa's elephants are considerably more widespread (Fig. 2). They are found in 37 countries, with a range of several million square kilometers. Nevertheless, in the last ten years deaths of elephants have outnumbered births, so that their number has shrunk by more than 100,000. Rampant poaching and a continuing loss of habitat are two of the main reasons for this. In view of the genetic, reproductive and ecological differences, experts today agree that we must speak of two species of African elephants:[2] the savannah elephant (*Loxodonta africana*), which primarily inhabits the grasslands of southern and eastern Africa, and the forest elephant (*Loxodonta cyclotis*), whose main distribution area is in the rainforest regions of the Congo Basin. With this new classification, the precarious situation of the forest elephants in particular, which have suffered massive population declines in recent years, will be better focused on in the future.

Official estimates from 2016 indicate that together there are 400,000–570,000 elephants in Africa, the trend being downwards. The forest elephant population has collapsed by around 86 percent within 30 years, that of the savannah elephant by 60 percent in 50 years.[3] In view of this dramatic development, the forest elephant is now considered to be critically endangered, and the savannah elephant is considered endangered. In east and central Africa in particular, the ongoing poaching in recent years has led to heavy losses. Regional elephant populations have in some cases significantly decreased or even completely disappeared. Given that it is thought that there were millions of elephants in Africa at the beginning of the 20th century, this is a devastating analysis.

2 An African elephant cow with calf in the Masai Mara nature reserve, Kenya. The larger ears of the African elephants are the most obvious distinguishing feature compared to the Asian species, which in turn has distinctive head humps.

GREAT STRENGTH AND SENSIBILITY IN ONE

African elephants are the largest land mammals on earth, larger than their Asian relatives. Their dimensions are truly impressive: adult males are on average a good three meters tall and can weigh six tons—as much as five small cars.

In addition to its body size, the elephant's distinguishing features are a long trunk and large tusks. The trunk is an elongation of the nose and upper lip, and is highly sensitive to pressure and temperature. With roughly 40,000 muscles, the elephant's trunk is considerably more richly furnished than

3 Group of Asian elephants taking a dust bath, Corbett National Park, Uttarakhand, India. The elephant's trunk is a remarkably sensitive tool.

the entire human body and can exhibit enormous strength. Working elephants in Asia are known to be able to lift logs weighing as much as 300 kilos with their trunks. At the same time, as a sensing and grasping tool, the trunk has amazing sensitivity (Fig. 3). Animals have been seen to pick up a single peanut, shell it, and place the contents in its mouth with their trunk. Moreover, the trunk is involved in many forms of social behavior, for example the "embrace" after separations, in which the trunk and tusks of a fellow creature are encircled by it, or a mother's reassurance of her calf when she places her trunk across its back. The trunk is also an extremely delicate sense organ: elephants have an outstanding sense of smell. In one experiment, animals were able to distinguish by smell alone between pails filled with different quantities of food.[4]

The elephant's striking tusks are formed from two of its upper incisors. They grow throughout the animal's lifetime and can attain a remarkable length and weight (Fig. 4). African elephants of both genders generally carry tusks, among Asian ones only the males. In all species and genders, however, a genetically determined absence of tusks is possible. In mature animals, from the base of the tooth at the jaw, roughly a third of the tusk is hollow, becoming solid only toward the tip. A delicate nerve canal runs through the entire tooth, thanks to which it is sensitive to pressure. Elephant ivory, traded at high prices, is thus nothing other than a normal, though greatly overgrown, tooth, just as that of other mammals, the hippopotamus or the narwhale, for example.

The tusks assist the elephant in its search for food, in digging for water, and in defending itself. Elephants are normally either "left- or right-toothed", preferring to use one tusk over the other, normally evident from its traces of use or shorter length.

IMPORTANCE FOR THE ECOSYSTEM

With their size and strength, elephants have a tremendous impact on their habitat. Their grazing, for example, keeps the vast grasslands of African savannahs open, preventing the unhindered growth

4 Group of African bull elephants, Tsavo, Kenya. The length of the elephant tusks depends on the age and genetic makeup of the animals.

5 An elephant calf a few days old, Chobe National Park, Botswana. Elephants are known for their distinctive social behavior and close family ties.

of shrubs and trees. At the same time, they often transport the seeds of fruits they have eaten for miles before egesting them and thereby helping to distribute their food plants. According to model calculations, seeds can even be carried up to 65 kilometers in the digestive tract of a savannah elephant.[5] As yet there is no known land vertebrate that disperses seeds over greater distances. In their role as landscape gardeners and sowers of seeds, elephants are of importance to the many other species with which they share Africa's savannahs and forests.

The elephant's influence on its habitat also has consequences for the climate: scientists were recently able to determine that even a single forest elephant per square kilometer can increase the above-ground biomass by 26 to 60 tons per hectare.[6] With their grazing and movements, the animals reduce plant density, which supports the growth of fewer but larger trees with greater biomass. Were forest elephants to become extinct, this volume in Central African rainforests would be reduced by around seven percent, together with important stores of carbon dioxide.

Elephants are strictly vegetarian; their diet consists of grass, leaves, branches, roots, and tree bark. To provide their massive bodies with sufficient energy, they spend up to 19 hours a day eating. The composition of their diet can vary greatly through the year depending on availability. Researchers have shown that their annual menu incorporates hundreds of different kinds of plants.[7] Depending on habitat and supply, savannah elephants can scour

6 African elephant, Serengeti, Tanzania. Elephant herds consist of several mostly related females and their young, which are led by a lead cow, the matriarch.

from 50 to 25,000 square kilometers in search of food and water, and in doing so cover distances of up to 60 kilometers in a day.[8]

CLOSE **FAMILY BONDS**

Elephants are highly social animals (Fig. 5). Their close family ties are legendary. It is said that they mourn their dead, comfort distraught fellow animals, and accept orphaned youngsters into the herd.

At the head of these social groups is the matriarch (Fig. 6), the herd's dominant cow. As an older female, she can draw on long years of experience. With the elephant's proverbial memory, she can, for example, recall the locations of remote water holes and food sources, an ability that in dry periods can mean life or death to a herd.

The group also includes several adult females with their calves. As a rule, the members of a given herd are related to each other, though unrelated animals can also join together into groups. A family group, in turn, can unite with larger herds, separat-

ing for days, weeks, or even months and later reuniting. Males tend to be more solitary, though lasting ties can even be observed among them—this, however, only outside the so-called musth period, a phase of heightened aggression and sexual activity.

To maintain their complex social relationships, elephants employ various forms of communication, some of which are visible and audible to humans—their body language, for example, or their typical trumpeting. Others lie outside the range of human senses. Elephants also communicate by way of chemical signals and infrasound. By means of these low-frequency sound waves, they can stay in touch with each other over several kilometers. Their audible and inaudible sounds have not as yet been fully decoded, but it is known that some of their messages are quite specific; they can, for example, communicate a warning against bees (see the contribution by Fritz Vollrath). Experiments also show that elephants are capable of identifying more than a hundred of their fellows on the basis of their vocalizations.[9]

Elephants are not only extremely social, they are also highly intelligent. They are among the small number of animals that can recognize themselves in

7 African elephants in the savannah, Amboseli National Park, Kenya. The rearing of the offspring is, as with many mammals, the responsibility of the mother. The females stay with their group for life, the males migrate when they reach sexual maturity.

a mirror[10]—an ability that attests to a consciousness of self. Aside from elephants, only a few other animals achieve such recognition, chimpanzees and dolphins among them. Moreover, researchers have observed elephants making use of tools, for example branches with which to scratch themselves or ward off flies.[11]

REPRODUCTION

African elephant cows have a gestation period of 22 months, and usually bear a single calf, which already weighs 220 pounds (100 kilos) at birth (Fig. 7). In other respects, the average reproduction cycle of savannah elephants is not unlike that of humans: females become sexually mature between 11 and 14 years of age. In the wild, however, most females become pregnant only at 30 or 40 years of age, and in their mid to late 50s many cows appear to undergo menopause. Incidentally, unlike many other female mammals, the female elephant's teats are found between her front legs.

Calves are already able to walk just an hour after birth. After roughly three months, they first sample solid food. Although at the age of two they mostly eat normally, they may not be completely weaned until their fourth year, which is usually forced by the birth of a sibling. Male calves appear to require more energy to be reared than females, as sons tend to be nursed more frequently than daughters. Moreover, intervals between births are longer if the elephant cow is nurturing a male calf. Such unequal commitment is explained by the genders' different growth rates, and is mainly evident in species in which a male animal's reproductive success depends largely on his size.

THE ELEPHANT'S **GREATEST ENEMY: POACHING**

Whereas young elephants can fall victim to big cats, a full-grown animal has only a single enemy to fear: man. And man is indeed a serious threat. In addition to ongoing competition with humans for habitat and resources, massive hunting for the sake of ivory is the greatest problem.

Ivory has fascinated humankind for millennia, and elephants have been hunted and killed for it since time immemorial. Even at the time of European colonialization, there were mass killings of elephants. However, the extent and the consequences for the populations moved into the focus of political action only a few decades ago and have been well documented since then. Between 1979 and 1989, the demand for ivory led to the number of African elephants being more than halved.[12] It is estimated that in a single decade the continent lost 700,000–800,000 of its 1.3 million elephants. Given this startling development, the international community determined to act, to put a stop to the unsustainable harvesting of elephant ivory. Thus in 1989 the Convention on International Trade in Endangered Species of Wild Fauna and Flora (CITES), which regulates international trade in protected animal and plant species, issued an international ban on commercial trade in ivory from African elephants. The Asian elephant and its ivory had already enjoyed the highest protection since the accord took effect in 1975. Since then, the sale of elephant ivory between countries of southern Africa, whose elephant populations were large and stable enough, and Asia have been permitted only twice.

Excessive trade was thus reduced. Yet a portion of the demand persists to this day—with fatal consequences. In order to meet the demand for "white gold", the animals are killed illegally and their tusks smuggled into consumer countries. The elephant has become a woeful symbol of poaching and the illegal wildlife trade.

Currently, up to 20,000 African elephants are killed for their ivory each year (Fig. 8). Individual animals are shot and entire herds poisoned at water holes. The tusks are cut off at the root with axes and power saws and smuggled, mainly to Asia, by way of worldwide criminal networks. Poaching in the past few years has meant that deaths of the animals have outnumbered births. Once again, in only ten years Africa has lost more than 100,000 of its elephants.

Most of the illegal killings in recent years have occurred on the once elephant-rich savannahs of East Africa and in the forests of the Congo Basin. Within less than eight years, between 2006 and 2013, elephant populations in the Tanzanian Selous ecosystem were reduced by more than 80 percent, their numbers shrinking from an original 70,400 animals to a mere 13,000.[13] All told, in these years some 87,000 elephants died in East Africa.[14] Recently, poaching in the region has lessened a little. Yet many experts suspect that this is only because of the reduced number of elephants. At the same time, an increasing trend toward poaching can be observed in southern Africa—a region that is home to 70 percent of the continent's elephants and that was previously a relatively safe refuge for them—unlike the Congo Basin in Central Africa, which has been under enormous and unceasing pressure from poachers. There, more than seven of every ten dead elephants discovered did not die from natural causes.[15] This is particularly disturbing inasmuch as studies have shown that the forest elephants of the Congo Basin reproduce more slowly than savannah elephants, and thus fail to recover as well from such massive depredations.[16]

Illegal trade in wildlife has become a branch of international organized crime worth billions. Professionally organized networks poach and smuggle millions of individuals of thousands of species across the globe. Not only elephant ivory, but also rhinoceros horn and such less well-known species as pangolins, abalone, rosewood, and seahorses are also highly sought-after. Live parrots are smuggled in

8 An elephant killed by poachers in Hwange National Park, Zimbabwe. Poaching for the illegal ivory trade is a cruel business. Across Africa, up to 20,000 elephants are currently victims of unscrupulous poachers every year.

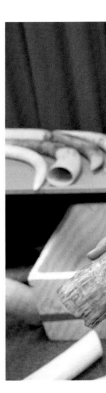

PET bottles, young chimpanzees sold as house pets, and sun bears captured in the wild for a woebegone life on bear-gall farms. The list of cruelties in this illegal trade is virtually endless.

Poaching and illegal trade have become far more than a mere problem in species conservation. Many of the species traded are of enormous importance to their countries of origin. To profit a few, countries are being robbed not only of their species diversity but also their ecological, economic, and culturally important natural capital. For the year 2016, for example, the gain poached elephants could have meant for the economies of their home countries from tourism revenues is estimated at roughly 25 million US dollars.[17] Thanks to poaching, people lose their incomes, and urgently needed opportunities for development are lost to the rural regions of Africa. In addition, professionally organized crime on such a scale goes hand in hand with the utilization and promotion of corrupt structures. There are also known connections between poaching, the illegal trade in ivory, and destabilizing groups and militias such as the Central African Séléka or Sudanese Janjaweed.[18] Like criminals trafficking drugs and weapons, poachers and traders in illegal wildlife products undermine the rule of law and are a threat to good governance in the affected countries.

HIGH DEMAND DESPITE THE **INTERNATIONAL TRADE BAN**

Despite the international trading ban adopted by CITES in 1989, demand for elephant ivory continues to be high. Two factors importantly contribute to this: for one, the trading ban only managed to stop trade *between* countries. Within a country's borders, it is up to the individual state's authorities to either shut down its legal ivory markets or continue to sell older inventories. Thus central trading hubs like China remained open for many years after the international ban, legitimizing the sale of ivory products and thus boosting demand. For another, smugglers increased the stockpiles of Asian traders with illegal African ivory, and illegal markets supply consumers in countries where trade in it is illegal.

The quantity of smuggled ivory seized worldwide underscores the fact that the problem of elephant poaching cannot be eliminated with a trading ban alone. The volume of illegal trade in ivory is too great: according to analyses by the Elephant Trade Information System (ETIS), between 2008 and 2017 more than 390 tons of elephant ivory were confiscated (Fig. 9).[19] That figure is all the more disturbing when one recognizes that only a small fraction of smuggled items is ever discovered. For example, it is calculated that roughly only 23 percent of smuggled rhinoceros horn can be intercepted.[20] This means that smugglers are successful 77 percent of the time, and the products captured by the authorities are only the tip of the iceberg (Fig. 10).

In the last few years China has been seen to be the largest market, having made possible the laundering of tons of illegal elephant ivory from Africa into its legal markets. In the period 2012–2014 roughly a third of the confiscations worldwide were destined for the People's Republic.[21] Ivory carving has a long tradition there, and since 2006 has been celebrated as a national cultural heritage. The precious material is sought primarily for decoration and as a status symbol. Whole tusks are carved into valuable works of art. But also small figurines and adornments like bracelets and pendants are fashioned from them (Fig. 11).

HOPE FOR A **BETTER FUTURE?**

Despite the immense cultural importance of ivory, in 2018 China took a major step. Since the country found no effective way to prevent the laundering of

9 Ivory confiscated by customs. Despite the international trade ban, the demand for ivory is high. Elephants are killed illegally and their tusks are smuggled. Very few of these events are exposed by the authorities.

illegal elephant ivory into its national markets and assumed partial responsibility for the precarious situation of elephants in Africa, the government determined to shut down the legal ivory markets. Welcomed worldwide, the decision was a clear signal that the consumption of ivory, despite the populace's traditional fondness for the material, could no longer be justified. It was an effective signal. A study of buying behavior before and after the trading ban was issued indicated that the number of purchases was reduced by more than half. Moreover, eight out of ten people indicated that since the ban they were no longer interested in buying ivory.[22]

Nonetheless, the ban on *legal* trade cannot prevent the fact that *illegal* trading continues to lead to the slaughter of thousands of elephants. The same study showed that for all the effect of the trading ban, some 14 percent of those interviewed continue to be interested in acquiring objects made of ivory, even though they know that they would be breaking the law. Sad proofs of this are the continuation of intensive poaching in Africa and the confiscation of tons of ivory shipments to or within China. Moreover, as a result of the trading ban, markets appear

to have simply moved to neighboring countries. According to analysis of illegal international ivory movements, Vietnam has recently become the primary destination for illegal elephant ivory and is competing with China for dubious supremacy.[23]

For elephants and for all other species threatened by illegal trade, it is a fact that as long as there is a demand there will be poaching.

For the future of African elephants as well as for all the other species threatened by human indifference, what is mainly required is a societal change. For the recent years of poaching and their consequences have made one thing clear: our planet's wealth of species is by no means a given. To ensure its survival we all need to respect it and do what we can to protect it (Fig. 12). We need to ask ourselves a simple question: Do we choose to imagine a world without such magical creatures as the African elephant, the black rhinoceros, and the Sumatran tiger? A world in which we are ultimately able to show these species to our children only in picture books because we were incapable of preventing their extinction? My answer to this question is clear. I am certain yours is, too.

10 The burning of stacks of confiscated ivory by the Kenya Wildlife Service (KWS) in Nairobi National Park. Many countries are destroying ivory stocks from seizures to prevent them from coming back into circulation.

1 UNEP/CMS/COP13/Doc. 27.1.1, online at: https://www.cms.int/sites/
   default/files/document/cms_cop13_doc.27.1.1_proposal-inclusion-asian-
   elephant_india_e.pdf (accessed September 10, 2019).
2 See John Hart and others, "African forest and savannah elephants
   treated as separate species", *Oryx* 55, 2, 2021, pp. 170–171, online at:
   https://doi.org/10.1017/S0030605320001386 (accessed March 25, 2021).
3 Kathleen S. Gobush and others, *Loxodonta africana. The IUCN Red List
   of Threatened Species 2021*, https://dx.doi.org/10.2305/IUCN.UK.2021-
   1.RLTS.T181008073A181022663.en. *And Loxodonta cyclotis. The
   IUCN Red List of Threatened Species* 2021, https://dx.doi.org/10.2305/
   IUCN.UK.2021-1.RLTS.T181007989A181019888.en (accessed
   March 25, 2021).
4 Joshua M. Plotnik et al., "Elephants have a nose for quantity", *Proceedings of the National Academy of Sciences* 166/25 (2019), pp. 12566–12571,
   online at: https://www.pnas.org/content/116/25/12566.short (accessed
   September 10, 2019).
5 Katherine Bunney and others, "Seed dispersal kernel of the largest
   suviving megaherbivore – the African savanna elephant", *Biotropica*
   49/3 (2017), online at: https://onlinelibrary.wiley.com/doi/abs/10.1111/
   btp.12423 (accessed September 10, 2019).
6 Fabio Berzaghi and others, "Carbon stocks in central African forests
   enhanced by elephant disturbance", *Nature Geoscience* (July 2019), online at: https://www.nature.com/articles/s41561-019-0395-6 (accessed
   September 10, 2019).
7 Don E. Wilson and Russell A. Mittermeier (eds), *Handbook of the Mammals
   of the World*, vol. 2, *Hoofed Mammals*, Barcelona: Lynx, 2011, p. 64.
8 Ibid., p. 72.
9 Ibid., p. 60.
10 Joshua M. Plotnik and others, "Self-recognition in an Asian elephant",
   Proceedings of the National Academy of Sciences 103/45 (November 2006),
   pp. 17053–17057, online at: https://www.ncbi.nlm.nih.gov/pubmed/
   17075063 (accessed September 10, 2019).
11 Benjamin L. Hart and others, "Cognitive behaviour in Asian elephants:
   use and modification of branches for fly switching", *Animal Behaviour*
   62/5 (2001), pp. 839–847, online at: https://www.sciencedirect.com/
   science/article/pii/S0003347201918159 (accessed September 10, 2019).
12 Wilson and Mittermeier 2011 (as note 7), p. 74.
13 Environmental Investigation Agency, "Vanishing Point – Criminality,
   Corruption and the Devastation of Tanzania's Elephants" (2014), online at: https://eia-international.org/report/vanishing-point-criminality-
   corruption-and-the-devastation-of-tanzanias-elephants/ (accessed
   September 10, 2019).
14 Christopher R. Thouless and others, "African Elephant Status Report
   2016: an update from the African Elephant Database", *Occasional
   Paper Series of the IUCN Species Survival Commission* 60 (2016), pp. 1–37,
   online at: https://portals.iucn.org/library/sites/library/files/documents/
   SSC-OP-060_A.pdf (accessed September 10, 2019).
15 CITES Secretariat, "Report on Monitoring the Illegal Killing of
   Elephants (MIKE)", CoP18, 69/2 (2019), online at: https://cites.org/
   sites/default/files/eng/cop/18/doc/E-CoP18-069-02.pdf (accessed
   September 10, 2019).
16 Andrea K. Turkalo and others, "Slow intrinsic growth rate in forest
   elephants indicates recovery from poaching will require decades",
   Journal of Applied Ecology 54/1 (2016), pp. 153–59, online at: https://
   besjournals.onlinelibrary.wiley.com/doi/full/10.1111/1365-2664.12764
   (accessed September 10, 2019).
17 Robin Naidoo and others, "Estimating economic losses to tourism in
   Africa from the illegal killing of elephants", *nature communications* 7
   (2016), online at: https://www.nature.com/articles/ncomms13379.pdf
   (accessed September 10, 2019).
18 Cathy Haenlein and M.L.R. Smith, *Poaching, Wildlife Trafficking and
   Security in Africa: Myth and Realities*, Abingdon: Routledge, 2016,
   chapters 2 and 3, online at: https://rusi.org/publication/whitehall-
   papers/poaching-wildlife-trafficking-and-security-africa-myths-and-
   realities (accessed September 10, 2019).
19 CITES Secretariat, "Report on the Elephant Trade Information
   System (ETIS)", CoP18, Doc. 69/3 (Rev. 1) (2019), online at: https://
   cites.org/sites/default/files/eng/cop/18/doc/E-CoP18-069-03-R1.pdf
   (accessed September 10, 2019).
20 IUCN Species Survival Commission, "African and Asian Rhinoceroses – Status, Conservation and Trade", CoP18, Doc. 83.1 (2019),
   online at: https://www.cites.org/sites/default/files/eng/cop/18/doc/
   E-CoP18-083-01.pdf (accessed September 10, 2019).
21 CITES Secretariat, "Report on the Elephant Trade Information System
   (ETIS)", CoP17, Doc. 57.6 (Rev. 1) (2016), online at: https://cites.org/
   sites/default/files/eng/cop/17/WorkingDocs/E-CoP17-57-06-R1.pdf
   (accessed September 10, 2019).
22 Wander Meijer and others, "Demand under the Ban – China Ivory
   Consumption Research Post-ban 2018", *TRAFFIC and WWF* (2018),
   online at: https://www.traffic.org/site/assets/files/11150/demand-under-
   the-ban-2018-1.pdf (accessed September 10, 2019).
23 CITES Secretariat 2019 (as note 19).

11 Ivory carvings confiscated by customs. Ivory is processed into pieces of jewelry and figures as well as filigree-carved works of art.

12 A herd of African elephants in the savannah, Amboseli National Park, Kenya. As the largest land mammal in the world, the elephant has no enemies when fully grown—apart from humans. Its continued existence is our responsibility.

VOICES OF **IVORY**

EBOA ITONDO

Why is ivory so popular as a material for craftwork? Can elephants and humans peacefully coexist in a given environment? Should museums continue to exhibit ivory objects at all, despite the increasingly endangered elephant population? These and other questions were discussed in separate interviews with IFAW (International Fund for Animal Welfare) campaigner Robert Kless, the veterinarian Khyne U Mar, and the artist Ai Weiwei.

What sparked your initial interest in animal welfare?

Ai Weiwei: My personal interest in animal welfare started around 2008, when I was in China. I got a phone call from an organization—a kind of NGO [Non-Governmental Organization]. Volunteers contacting me, telling me that they spotted a trunk full of cats. I asked: "How many?", they said: "About 400 or 500." Those cats were supposed to be delivered to Guangzhou in south China for cooking. People there eat cats. So I immediately joined the campaigners. All those cats were left in a big warehouse, they were scared and treated badly. You could see that some of them must have been stolen from their homes, since they were still wearing their collar. Those were beloved pets. We had to take care of these pets. I took 40 of them home to my place in Beijing. That was the starting point.

There was another incident in China that sparked my interest: at some point they had to kill 40,000 dogs in a small Chinese province because they seemed to transmit diseases. The way they went about it was problematic because it was so cruel.

I wrote articles about both incidents and the relationship between humans and animals. During our travels over the past years, we saw massive refugee problems. We went to Africa and Asia. You can see many different animals running around the streets in our footage. Animals are always the first casualties in human crises. So that's how I got here. For me animal welfare is directly linked to human dignity. This is part of my longtime struggle with humanity, human rights, and the dignity of life.

Khyne U Mar: When I graduated high school at the age of 15 or 16, my final score wasn't quite high enough to study human medicine, but it was high enough to study veterinary medicine. At that time, students in Myanmar chose the subjects to study at university based on the grades they received in tenth-grade or matriculation examinations. I was interested in science and I've always liked animals and wanted to work with them, so I decided to become a vet. It took six years to finish the veterinarian course. After graduation in 1973, I worked on the teaching staff at my university in Yangon, the University of Veterinarian Medicine. While teaching there, I was invited to become a consultant vet for Yangon Zoo. Among the animals in zoos, the elephant is not only the largest but also the most tamed. I was instantly intrigued by that and it sparked my interest in elephants. In 1994 I was invited to work for the Ministry of Forestry as the Head of Veterinary Research in the Elephant Division of the Myanmar Timber Enterprise (the department that is responsible for logging in Myanmar). I was not only the first veterinarian, but also the first woman to set up elephant research in Myanmar; I later became known as the "Elephant Lady of Burma". My job in the Myanmar Timber Enterprise was to reduce elephant mortality and to boost captive breeding so that the department did not need to capture wild elephants. This task automatically made me aware of the importance of the welfare of the elephants under our care.

Ai Weiwei

Robert Kless

Robert Kless: I grew up in a small village in the southern Black Forest, so I always felt very close to nature. During my school years and later at university I joined local conservation and environmental groups and had the good fortune to be able to make my honorary post a career. Fifteen years ago I came to the International Fund for Animal Welfare (IFAW). The organization's aim is the protection of individual animals and entire populations and species, as well as their habitats, and always with the involvement of local communities. This approach reflects my own feeling about nature and animal protection very well.

I have always been fascinated by elephants: because of their size, for one thing, but also their gentleness. In addition to the destruction of habitat and human-wildlife conflicts, ivory poaching is the greatest threat to elephants. As I am a campaigner in the realm of the trade in wild animals, the elephant and the problems relating to it today are an important and fascinating focus of my work.

What is it about this animal that fascinates people?

Khyne U Mar: Elephants represent a variety of things. In Buddhist countries, for example, our god is Lord Buddha and he appears in the form of an elephant in his past lives. So when you see elephants, you equate the animal with a religious icon. In ancient times, elephants also used to be important in warfare. Kings' armies would rely on them in the frontline. Because elephants can be used in different weather conditions and in various types of terrain, they are more reliable than horses. People might be fascinated by elephants because they look gigantic in size, but they are really delicate in touch and silent in movement. Those might be some general reasons, I think. Personally, I am always enthused to see how animals respond to their trainer. I have met a bull elephant whose intelligence level is unparalleled. I was on a field trip with other foresters and officers. I was the only female in the group and I was very tired of the heat and the long walk. One of the bulls of the group brought me water from the nearby river. I was surprised, because the water was very clean. Normally, if the water was taken from the bank of a river, it would be muddy because the elephant had to wade or swim in the river. But his mahout apparently asked for "fresh, clean" water. So the bull swam into the middle of the river, where the running water is clean, he dipped the bucket into the river, held the water-filled container on top of his head and brought it back to me. How did he know the water was for me? Because his mahout told him to give it "to the lady". That's when I realized that this bull could also differentiate between male and female.

Khyne U Mar

Ai Weiwei: Elephants are so smart. If they have a bond with a human, it takes them only a few months to learn commands. They will listen to you and do what you want them to do. They are reliable and get the job done. In Myanmar, they have many employed elephants who pull timber logs out of the forest. Those trees are very expensive, and no other machine can access these areas. But a new law forbids the foresting of timber, which left 6,000 elephants unemployed. Those elephants are being abandoned because they lost their jobs and now they are objects of trophy hunting.

China is the biggest marketplace for these kinds of "treasures", including teeth, bones or other body parts. China has this old tradition with the material of ivory, which was okay in ancient times, I guess, but is no longer so. It was a tradition for men to show their power by killing animals. Women would wear jewelry they got from loved ones, who killed animals to create it. There is a picture of Trump's son Donald holding the tail of an elephant to show how brave he is. This comes from an insecure heart trying to display power and superiority. It would be amazing, though, if he killed with his own bare hands. But, of course, he had to use "dirty tricks". That's just human.

Ai Weiwei: Yes ... one of the earliest ivory findings dates back to the Shang Dynasty, around 3,000 years ago. I think they found some kind of wine cup in a tomb in China. It was very beautifully made out of gemstones and ivory. It must have been very hard to work with this material, really difficult. China had great economic strength and significant power during the Tang Dynasty (618–907). Many people from Persia came to the Chinese capital and they often brought luxurious gifts for the emperor to honor him. Ivory has always been related to the court of the emperor. This material has always been associated with status. It wasn't used by ordinary people, though personal seals might have been the exception.

Khyne U Mar: In Buddhism, elephants, known for their superior power and wisdom, epitomize the boundless powers of the Buddha. Elephants are widely regarded as sacred animals, so we in Myanmar generally value all elephant body parts. Since they belong to the most precious parts of an already sacred animal, their use is commonly related to the Buddha or religious causes. Very fine carvings, prayer beads or Buddha-related figurines are made out of ivory. There is a traditional belief that God gave the elephant an additional tooth intentionally. Using this material for other causes is frowned upon and not accepted in Buddhism.

The German word for ivory, "Elfenbein", could be misunderstood as literally meaning "fairy leg". I feel this creates a detachment from the origin of the material and the cruelty that is often linked to it. Since it has this representational value, I was wondering if there were different, similarly poetic words for ivory?

Khyne U Mar: Ivory or tusk is a type of dentin—a hard, dense bony tissue that forms most of a tooth. Some consider it an additional tooth—in Burmese tusk is called "a-swae".

Ai Weiwei: It's a scientific name in Chinese, which translates as "elephant's tooth". We are not as romantic as the Germans. That's a little problem Germans have. By romanticizing something, you are putting a moral judgement into a physical existence. You distort the truth and thereby adjust yourself into another position. I think German culture does that often. People avoid talking about problems and prefer talking about anything else. I often found it that way. For me that is a weakness. Not being able to face reality causes anxiety. I don't know the German language, so I cannot judge it. But in my personal life I know many cases where this observation seems to apply.

How can museums bring this important issue to visitors, especially since the display of ivory—artwork or stored elephant tusks—is highly controversial?

Robert Kless: In Europe we are currently working to implement an ivory trade ban that is as far-reaching as possible. Under certain conditions, museums should be exempted from this ban. As long as elephants are poached and ivory is sought-after, existing stores of ivory must be well secured or destroyed, as they repeatedly have been, for example in Kenya. Ivory must not find its way back onto the market, or otherwise the demand for "white gold" will be further stimulated. To impressively illustrate this problem, a few years ago our colleagues in our British office started a public appeal, asking that ivory objects in private possession be turned over to IFAW for a public educational action. They commissioned an artist to fit together these many small carvings and ornaments into a single large elephant tusk. This was then shredded, ground up, and the powdered ivory placed in an oversized hourglass. This appeal was presented under the title "Time is Running out for Elephants". In this case, ivory that had already been processed was used to draw attention to the fatal situation of the elephants: each year some 20,000 elephants are poached for their ivory!

IFAW aid for orphaned elephants in Zimbabwe. A keeper takes care of an elephant.

From the museum's point of view, the presentation of confiscated and warehoused tusks would be about making clear to visitors the great number of victims of elephant poaching. This would encourage direct appreciation of the consequences of human consumer behavior. As opposed to a display text, a graphic, or a poster, the visitor would then be confronted with the actual, unworked remains of an elephant. Don't you think that such a presentation achieves more than letting tusks "rot" in warehouses?

Robert Kless: That's an interesting idea, and I can well imagine it. But perhaps we are here simply bumping up against the limits of practicability. A few years ago, there was a regular raid on German museums of natural history, in Berlin as well as elsewhere. The raiders were after rhinoceros horns. A kilo of horn can be worth roughly tens of thousands of euros. Since then, such horns in museum displays are made of plaster. This shows that there is a great danger that even displayed ivory could be stolen and misused.

Khyne U Mar: Personally, I think it is acceptable to show artworks made from ivory. At the same time, however, museums should make it clear that the works in question are ancient and that the ivory came from elephant populations that at the time thrived and were not then endangered. Today, there are very few elephants left, both in the wild and in captivity, and so it is now widely accepted that we should not kill them for ivory and other body parts. It's necessary to make the public aware of this and so museums need to educate people on the need to protect elephants. But I think museums should still display ivory artworks, or else people will not know how the craft of ivory carving evolved globally over the course of time; we could not honor their creators and their techniques if such works were not displayed. Because of the material's rarity, sculptures, ornaments, and decorative or utilitarian articles made of ivory are regarded as masterpieces; flourishing from at least the second millennium BCE, ivory carving is one of the oldest arts in Asia. Museums can provide visitors with both an appreciation of the holistic value of the artworks *and* a keen awareness of today's brutal and illegal trade in the body parts of wild elephants.

How did ivory become such a popular material globally for arts and crafts?

Ai Weiwei: I think it's because of the demand—the market creates its value. The ivory trade used to be very difficult but it started getting easier and gaining popularity in colonial times, when the English, Belgians and Germans went to Africa and brought back ivory pieces to venerate powerful people and to glamourize their colonial victory. They made enslaved Africans carry these tusks through remote areas. If you look at old photographs from that period, you can see that very often they would take pictures of "their history" showing huge, heavy tusks carried by Africans.

Ivory became a popular decoration, it was put into precious music instruments and everyday objects. This unreasonable use of the ivory has been a crime from the very beginning—it has just been wrapped up in glamour. After the industrial revolution, transport became so easy, killing became so efficient, the market grew and the demand for ivory increased. At least that's how I imagine it becoming popular.

Khyne U Mar: Especially in Buddhist countries it's linked with culture and religion. For the majority of people today, ivory represents a highly valuable natural product and so ivory objects are perceived as precious objects. Looking at an ivory object, everyone instantly knows that this piece must be a valuable object.

Robert Kless: I think it has to do with man's cultural history. Perhaps ivory is so interesting to people because a long history links us with the material, or with the elephant and related species, as for example the mammoth. Also, it is a natural product; formerly one "had" to resort to it. In our modern society, there is once again a special interest in natural products. But what's tragic is that one can use the tusks only after the animal is dead. Generally, the elephant is poached so as to get at the coveted material immediately.

Unfortunately, in our society the tusks and the products derived from them are highly valued. In South East Asian countries like China, where the situation is currently changing, in part thanks to our educational efforts, ivory is a status symbol. It is this "owner's mindset" or "status-symbol mindset" that has to be changed. This slightly contradicts the treatment of artworks in ivory, which of course have an art-historical value. But that has to be seen separately: today ivory is very clearly associated with poaching.

IFAW aid for orphaned elephants in Zimbabwe.

Mr. Kless, you just spoke about enlightenment work in China. What does that involve?

Robert Kless: First it has to be explained that ivory comes only from dead elephants. The Chinese word for "tusk" is the same as for "tooth", and it has been found that many people believe that elephants simply lose their tusks the way we lose teeth. So our work has to make it clear that tusks can only be removed from a dead animal. We have spread this message in a highly emotional way through poster campaigns, videos, and with the support of opinion makers from economics, pop stars, and influencers. It comes down to changing behavior, and that can be accomplished in this way, as we have determined.

Organizations and activists often use pictures depicting the misconduct of people towards animals to raise awareness and funds for their welfare projects. It's not that I approve of their behavior, but I feel that these people are somewhat misrepresented as the "villains" by such organizations, though they are just a symptom of animal cruelty and not the cause. It creates a stereotype and a specific narrative that seem elitist and shifts responsibility. Do you think activists and organizations need cruel images or need to shock people to raise awareness in order to do their job?

Khyne U Mar: We live in a time when "only bad news is good news". As the pay of mahouts is low, their job is often regarded as menial. But this is not the case. Mahoutship is a profession and requires a long period of training. In Myanmar, all elephant calves born in captivity, as well as sub-adult elephants measuring 1.40 m (4.6 ft) at the shoulder or aged four years, are weaned and tamed/trained during the cool season (November to January). After they are tamed, elephants between five and seventeen years old are used as baggage elephants, their training continuing until they become used to the verbal cues, as well as to the logging or baggage harnesses and fettering chains. Elephants are considered adult at the age of seventeen. Two mahouts generally handle each elephant in the workforce. At fifty-five, working elephants retire and spend most of their time roaming and foraging with a mahout who is assigned to take care of their well-being. At night, working elephants may forage unsupervised in the adjacent forests in their family groups, where they encounter other tame and wild elephants. Working elephants are maintained as mixed herds consisting of adult males and females and calves of various ages, thus mimicking the social structure of wild elephant herds.

The main characteristic of traditional elephant management in Asia, including Myanmar, is close contact between people and elephants, similar to contact in zoos. Ideally, the mahout should stay with and train the elephant for its entire life. The longer he stays, the greater the benefit to their relationship.

Ai Weiwei: I wouldn't put it that way: I don't think that those are shocking images. If it reflects reality, it isn't more shocking than stripping meat from a chicken or putting it in the oven. It's not different only because we are concerned with the decrease of elephant populations right now.

But using these images without understanding their impact is bad. Very often there is a feeling of moral superiority, which is indicative of a certain perception of the world. The thought that "we are better than others because we are different, and that what they do and the way they do it is bad" is prevalent in society. I think that we are all the same and we should all be ashamed. Not only the people who hunt or harm elephants, but also we ourselves. We just found a "more civilized" way to do it. We don't see it directly in our surroundings because we are so far removed from it.

So it should be of interest to animal welfare organizations to involve the people living in regions nearby in their projects?

Ai Weiwei: Yes. There is no way you can just protect the elephants. Let's say you had a son or daughter and they are going to school, so you need to provide for them. A tusk is guaranteed financial security. It could change their lives completely. I would kill in that situation, to be honest. I would do it. Because it is directly related to my family. Those crimes are such a clear reflection of the human condition.

We have to be realistic. We can't just say "They are born as criminals" when they are being trained as criminals. Well, who trained them? [laughs].

Let's say an elephant needs three people to take care of it. The care of the animal could create jobs for humans. But if the simple answer is to kill this animal, three people now have nothing to do. If you don't solve the human condition, you cannot stop the crime.

Khyne U Mar: In our case we badly need well-trained mahouts or keepers in our workforce and in elephant management. Because of years of logging in South East Asia, there are far fewer wild elephants living in the forests than there were two or three decades ago. Most working elephants in South East Asia are born in captivity, and the capture of wild elephant is now illegal. So all countries in the region have a duty to conserve their elephants in the wild. And those elephants that are in captivity need to be trained how to live in harmony with human beings.

Historically, most elephants were captured from the wild then tamed and used as draft animals for various purposes. Then, the only way to tame a newly caught animal was to break its spirit so that it was submissive. Elephants caught in the wild take more time to tame than those born in captivity, which is thought to be because of prior negative experience of humans. The procedure of breaking an animal's spirit undoubtedly caused stress and compromised the welfare of the animal, especially during the first few days of taming. Today, elephants are valued as flagship species with the highest level of international legal protection.

Advances in the science of animal welfare, along with a deeper understanding of the basic needs of elephants in captivity, have enabled methods for taming elephants to be fine-tuned over the past decades.

Unfortunately, because these methods rarely reach this grassroots level, some mahouts or people from the range states don't know or sometimes don't understand them. So people continue to believe that the traumatized elephant with a broken spirit is more likely to perform well.

This is why I support the idea of "capacity building workshops" at a grassroots level to help mahouts and people in the range states to develop skills in elephant behavior, welfare, and basic elephant management. Well-trained mahouts are an ultimate requirement, for elephants living in captivity or in a human-dominated environment.

Who do you think could change the situation?

Khyne U Mar: It's a complex issue. As about half of the captive elephants in Myanmar are under the management of the government, a lack of financial and professional resources are the main problems. Those who are concerned with the future of Asian elephants should encourage the governments in the region to undertake positive initiatives. International NGOs [Non-Governmental Organizations], major funding agencies, and wealthier governments in the Western hemisphere should support the governments of those South Asian countries that have a good record on the conservation of elephants. This also means investing in infrastructure; there is weak governance in some of the range states when it comes to investing in their own infrastructure.

Ai Weiwei: I think there are two important factors: the first is the culture. There needs to be an understanding and an awareness of the human condition, and that it is going to be measured by the way humans treat other species. Whether a society is a civilized or a barbarian society can easily be measured by the way it treats animals. By that measurement, we can say we've truly become a barbarian state. It isn't scientific development or money and wealth that makes for a civilized society. I feel that Asian cultures were more civilized when people ceremonially killed the animals they lost. There used to be a kind of spiritual respect. Every part of that animal was used or repurposed and treated respectfully. Today, animals are just seen as meat. Meat we put in the oven, and don't even think about the life of this creature and what it must have been like. Animals are fed for capitalistic mass production. The way they are fed is horrifying and tragic. Everybody knows it, but no one cares. I think it's an education problem. That's why I would say that consciousness is really important.

The second thing: if you call yourself a democratic society, you not only have to elect politicians, but also to measure their policies by the quality of their application and enforcement. Ask: Did they really do a good job with this? And are these laws and legislations that protect and respect life?

Robert Kless: There needs to be collaboration between the local populace, officials, and politicians. We believe that this is the most effective approach. In our work, it's often a matter of improving and consistently implementing existing animal and environment protection laws, not their actual execution. That is a task for the state or sovereign, to be carried out by the appropriate authorities. We help to ensure that law enforcement staff have sufficient capacity for their work by providing equipment such as vehicles or radios, or through training programs. We consider it equally important to work together with the local communities. Ultimately, they usually know best what is happening on the spot.

Our ammunition is information. Preventing poaching is like averting acts of terrorism: using information from various sources, for example villagers, community rangers, and state game wardens, or from air and satellite pictures, we can draw conclusions and gain a sense of where and when something could happen. With this knowledge, enforcement figures can be on the spot before the poachers strike.

For example, alarm bells ring if in an area near a reserve, sugar, tea, and water are stolen or purchased, and then a few kilometers farther on a car is rented and larger quantities of gasoline are acquired, and so on. Poachers in the bush for ten days need these things. Knowing things like this, governmental agencies or state institutions can respond quickly.

In many regions, states do not necessarily conform to our notion of democracy. Often corruption is a problem. And here it is a matter of degree. On the one hand, we must and would like to work with the state officials, but on the other hand it may be a regime that was not democratically elected or whose democratic processes are open to criticism. How far do you then go? At what point do you say "No, cooperation with these partners is no longer possible"? To what extent do we accept the situation as it is, since we need this collaboration in order to be able to change anything? If we come to the conclusion that processes are under way that we cannot reconcile with our philosophy and our ethical standards, it is perfectly clear that the cooperation or a project is ended.

Rangers training to combat elephant poaching in Kenya.

To be honest, I'm not always sure if Western animal welfare organizations are changing the situation in other countries for the better. Especially because some organizations tolerate trophy hunting, for example. How do you feel about this?

Robert Kless: A number of organizations or governments, for example in southern Africa, argue in favor of trophy hunting as the profit can be used for species protection. Otherwise, at some point there would no longer be any "trophies" at all. This would be a way of creating economic value in order to preserve species populations. But IFAW is convinced that all too often this does not work in practice, the money does not actually reach the people on the ground, and is not used for sustainable species protection. Moreover, this takes place in a manner that is morally indefensible. In our opinion, killing animals merely for trophies is not acceptable.

Khyne U Mar: In general, I do not agree with trophy hunting. But since elephants are migrating animals, they travel long distances. Overpopulation in one country doesn't necessarily reflect their global reproduction rates. It's a really complex issue, that's why we don't speak of the "abundance" of an elephant population until we know the socio-economic impact it has on the resident elephant population.

In general hunting, if done scientifically, is a means of population control. The number of elephants killed by hunters should be based on the populations' reproduction rate and the supporting capacity of their natural habitat. If the fertility rate is higher than the mortality rate, we risk overpopulation.

To conserve elephants for future generations to enjoy, wildlife management needs to establish systematic hunting regulations. For example, hunting laws need to set out safety guidelines that protect both hunters and non-hunter, and to establish specific hunting periods that limit harvesting and avoid hunting during mating and calving seasons. Also, the use of loud guns should be avoided, for they scare the overall population and causes great stress both to elephants and other wildlife populations. Scientifically based and regulated hunting protects threatened or endangered wildlife populations.

Ai Weiwei: Animal welfare is like human rights. People have to realize that there is only one human right and it does not depend on location or social development. Anyone being hurt is being hurt and any problem happening anywhere can relate to here, relate to me. Very often people either forget about that, or purposely ignore it. They try to pinpoint the problem, saying "it's this" or "it's that", as if there were only one species—in this case the elephant—threatened with extinction. It's not just that one species. The value of an elephant's life is no different from that of a chicken. It shouldn't be regarded as more crucial or viewed differently because of its size.

Do you think that the development of wildlife or eco parks reinforces the seeming dependence between Western countries and countries with an elephant population? Does this kind of "nature tourism" feed into Western stereotype images of "Africa" or "Asia"?

Robert Kless: Our goal is to preserve this natural heritage not only for tourists from "rich Western countries" but for all. That means for the local people as well. I don't believe that nature tourism ought to be a privilege for the Western world that thinks of Africa as "one great zoo". The goal would be to make species diversity and natural beauty available to all people. Ultimately, it is about protecting Creation and preserving species diversity and the basis of life for humans.

The elephant is a so-called "key species", one that is ecologically important. If you protect the elephant and its habitat, you protect its entire living environment: all the animals and plants that share the elephant's habitat. For example, there are many savannah grasses and even trees whose seeds can germinate only if they have passed through an elephant's digestive tract. In the elephants' footprints rainwater collects that is used as a source of water by insects. Where there are insects, there are more birds, and so on. The existence of each species has consequences for countless others. They are all intertwined. For us it is thus a matter of biodiversity and species preservation, the conservation of habitats for people and animals.

One thing is very important: we always work together with the local people. It would be a false approach were we to pronounce from Germany that "we now have to help the Kenyans protect their elephants" and point our fingers at others, especially since we have many problems of our own in animal and species protection.

Khyne U Mar: We are well aware of this kind of wildlife tourism. Some countries generate part of their income through wildlife parks. But bear in mind that only countries with sound infrastructure benefit from wildlife tourism. Countries like India, Myanmar or Malaysia, with many beautiful remote regions, do not have good infrastructure and can't make money from wildlife tourism. In fact, very few countries are able to make money out of it, because they can't offer the infrastructure needed by tourists looking to experience "real" wildlife. Many "wildlife" experiences are based on entertainment: they use elephants, ride them, and make them do tricks. This is not "wildlife tourism", this is an abuse of the animals. To stop this, we want professionals from the Western world or rich countries, who themselves may not have a diverse wildlife, to support the range states in South East Asia by providing insight on ecotourism through "capacity building" workshops: helping them to increase and update the knowledge of their staff so they can take care of their own resources and the development of their wildlife.

After everything we have just discussed, for you what message does ivory as a material convey today?

Khyne U Mar: Ivory is just dentin—a very hard white material. It grows very slowly and like all slowly growing things it's rare. Rarities are often viewed as highly valuable and people like to possess valuable things. The appeal lies in the look of ivory and its sparseness.

For a veterinarian like me, ivory is nothing more than dentin if you carve it into little statuettes. I cannot find any value in it.

Ai Weiwei: Depends … do you mean an evaluation based on the material or on moral aspects?

A herd of wild elephants in Amboseli National Park, Kenya.

Both.

Ai Weiwei: Material wise, we are looking at something created by God, which can never be replaced. A man-made material could never be the same. Ivory comes from life. We should respect life and the mystery of being.

Regarding morals, people appreciate the finest miracles either unconsciously by mistake or because they are ignorant. They are insulting these lost lives by not being aware about what it took to obtain this material.

Robert Kless: For me, ivory now stands for the poaching and extermination of elephants. As for the creation of craft objects, I feel that there are alternative materials, tagua nuts, for example. Crafts are subject to social changes. If a majority says "no" to ivory, in my view there is no reason to cling obsessively to this material.

Half Remembered Past

ASHER JAY

When I was ten, I read a haiku that impacted me immensely and has stayed with me ever since.
"Tiger, eyes dark,
with half remembered forest night,
stalks an empty cage."

As I traveled through Thailand and encountered the current plight of indentured Asian elephants, I could not help but experience the void evident in their eyes. It seemed as though I could peer through dark windows into these deserted souls that had been hollowed out by human apathy, avarice, and aggression. A gradual evisceration of self and spirit due to subjugation had systematically shattered and replaced the indomitable wild essence that once fueled their being. This series of layered elephant portraits were created through a unique process. I shot the subjects at an intimate range but enhanced a shallow depth of field by placing a monochromatic, paint-obscured translucent filter between the lens and the final composition. This intentionally distorted the framing of each still by projecting pre-existing myopia onto the landscape in the form of a conceptual bias. I wanted to bring into focus how any splintered predisposition or colored understandings of the world are only capable of perceiving the parts, often at the cost of the whole.

When a viewer navigates this pictorial narrative arc, they will perceive the parts that make the whole, but seldom encounter the whole in its regal, dynamic, magical, persuasive, singular countenance. This is because wild has become the compromised subset of anthropocentric progress. Each print constrains slivers of the overall story into curated measures of space, and controlled tears in time, arresting the flow of life in the same manner that the shackles restrict the movement, growth and wellbeing of the elephants. These stolen pauses show us the truth between the folds of their skin, and within the vacant stare of their heartbroken eyes. Their future is in our hands, and it is my hope, that in coming to know of their predicament, we will be inspired to take more informed actions to ameliorate their lives. For instance, do not buy ivory products, support the use of pachyderms in the logging industry or ride elephants on your travels to the Far East.

As a consumer you have the choice to not support the exploitation, slaughter or tortured oppression of other living creatures for the purposes of entertainment, vanity, trophies, trinkets, cosmetics or snake-oil cures. The fate and future of nature rests on you. You get to shape the world we live in with every action you take, every word you utter. You determine whether wild has a place in our collective timeline, so choose wisely, as though every decision matters, because it does. Countless lives are affected by and depend on your every choice. The trade in ivory alone claims 96 elephants a day, or one every 15 minutes, and it also endangers and ends countless human lives. You can elect to be an active part of the solution instead of a passive part of the problem.

The "Half Remembered Past" photographic chronicle coaxes viewers into the quiet of being "elephant", instead of underscoring the heart-wrenching suffering imposed upon their lives when we use them as a means to our ends. It asks us to contemplate how this external narrative is expressed within our own selves, because who we are and how we are comes to color and shape the world around us. We are all born into prisons of expectations and limited human understanding, but we can always elect to break free of these shackles and re-wild ourselves. When we do so, we help animals like these elephants re-wild their selves as well. I strongly maintain that it is the extent to which you are connected to nature and wild that each of us extends as a commitment to protect the wild nature we perceive around us. Wild is the indomitable, free, quality of belonging and presence that I assiduously effort to evoke in my compositions, it is a sense of wonder and surrender to something greater than the parts we isolate our understanding to. Wild, accounts for the whole, and as a whole it is all about wonder; its tapestry is rich in magic and awe. The question that ought to be intensely considered by the viewer is, "What is such inimitable, fragile, untamed, unrehearsed wonder worth to you?" We will only protect what we deem an extension and expression of our own selves; my work consequently strives to catalyze connections over separations intrinsically and extrinsically. The only way the next generation will have direct contact with the priceless quality of wonder that wild imbues our biosphere with, along with a plethora of expensive ecosystem services it implicitly bestows upon us, is if we choose to preserve it today. We need to stop taking our natural world for granted. We need to spend more time reflecting on its current state of depletion and deterioration, which is a direct product of our gross negligence. In introspecting and assuming responsibility, we can hold ourselves accountable to transforming our present paradigm.

I have used art, photography, illustrations, installations and other sensorially immersive experiences to hold people accountable toward the treasure trove of biological diversity that sustains us daily. I rely on creativity, because it inspires emotion over reason, it has the power to make you feel instead of think about your role in the whole. People often feel repelled by graphically expressive photographic captures of animals being slaughtered for the illicit trade in contraband such as ivory, rhino horn, pangolin scales or shark fins, and this immediate repulsion disengages them from both the problem and their consequent participation in the solutions. My campaigns thus strive to accomplish engagement. My illustrations and animations condense complex visual data and hard science into captivating juxtapositions between positive and negative space,

in an effort to contrast life that has been lost forever against death that can be prevented. My color palettes are intentionally minimal to avoid visual clutter, which garners stark focus on the core premise of an ecological concern. Each campaign I coin targets consumer demographics in nations that form the primary market base for the trade in wildlife contraband, such as China, Vietnam, Thailand, Cambodia, and Japan. The image titled "Blood Ivory" was captioned in Chinese, as it was run as informative billboards in areas with heavy foot traffic, "Every tusk costs a life. When the Buying Stops the Killing Will too". An additional insight into this concept was the notion that the trade in bloody ivory bolsters the one in arms trafficking, resulting in the destabilization of various African nations in the process. The campaign entitled "Family Values", portraying two calves fleeing from their disintegrating mother, deliberates rampant poaching as the propelling reason for the scientifically unenlightened undoing of the very social structure of elephant families. Young elephants across Africa are now at a loss for the intergenerational knowledge that the murdered matriarchs would have been in a position to teach them, such as ancient migratory routes, how to survive droughts, where to find their favorite morsels each season and other topographical and ethological insights. Yet it is important to present content in a manner that transports viewers from what is previously known to wisdom that eludes them, hence the "Pandas of Africa" image which portrays elephants as treasured national assets in African countries, just like pandas are synonymous with China, African megafauna like elephants and rhinos are analogous with Africa. The Chinese Government reserves the death penalty or life imprisonment for any individual who kills a panda, yet don't mind taking the lives of countless iconic species from other nations, this is what I aimed to subversively highlight in this image. The most controversial image I wound up releasing in a traditional Chinese medicine conference was the one entitled "Yellow Stars Shed Light" as the two Chinese motifs that compose the body of the elephant embody the *Zhōngguó*, which is a historical appellation for China. I questioned tradition, and its unquestioned embodiment in an ignorant consumer culture through this work, and that hit home in a way that no other data visualization or statistics did at that forum.

Pictorial representations of wild have always been a part of how we handed wild onto the next generation, from cave paintings to contemporary sculptures, so I always saw the relationship between the two as significant. I am careful to choose my mediums wisely, as they can either send a responsible or irresponsible message. Ivory, or other animal substrates and by-products being used to create art when there are plenty of far more responsible mediums available to innovative minds and dexterous hands globally, is unforgivably reckless. I highlight this dire need in the age of communications; to discontinue taking for granted the precious little that remains despite our ruinous actions under the name of progress and parochial bottom-lines.

Wild is where we come from, wild is who we are, and wild is what we need to rediscover during the Anthropocene, the Age of Man. Wild is the wonderstruck child within us that we stand to lose forever, when we fail to preserve it with passionate conviction. If there is one take-away I can leave you with today, it is this, let the wild within you relate intimately with the wild beyond, not just in this moment through these images but in every instant through all your words and actions. Thank you.

Page 147: *Quiet Reflection.* A tusker languishes in silence, resigned to his boredom and confined movement. There is grace and elegance to his regal poise, an implicit beauty to his presence. Even in that sullen space, a shackled soul retreats to within, where there is the solace of wild memories.

Pages 148/149: *Unseen.* Photograph of the eye of an indentured elephant as it glimpses the forest over the horizon. Its context remains unseen by the person it is coerced to serve.

Pages 150/151: *Body Language.* Elephants communicate to one another in numerous subtle ways, from the swishing of their tail, and the swaying of their frame, to the flapping of their ears, and the way they land their feet on the ground beneath them. We may not understand their complex communication, but that does not mean they are silent.

Pages 152/153: *Here For You.* Elephants mourn, recall conflicts, connect intimately, nurture deep interpersonal relationships, and make sentient judgment calls on impending threats. They not only possess the ability to emote extensively but intuit and empathize with one another, and are able to extend that to other species as well.

Pages 154/155: *Between the Fold.* Contrary to misguided human understanding, elephant skin, albeit coarse to us, contains numerous nerve endings and is deeply sensitive to external stimuli. This makes the use of bull-hooks or any violent means of suppressing or culling them deeply painful for these expressive giants to endure.

Pages 156/157: *Resilience is Learned.* Hurt and fear were assimilated by her as a child, taught to her by ropes, chains, guns, sticks, bull hooks, and loud antagonizing commands. She has found a way to age trauma into resilience.

Page 158: *Family Values.* This work was created for Elephant Voices in Nairobi to raise public awareness about the impacts of poaching on elephant families. The loss of the larger, older members of the herd implies a loss of inter-generational knowledge and the inability for an extant younger elephant to find the resources and insights it needs to survive its intra-generational challenges.

Page 159: *Yellow Stars Shed Light.* Created for Elephant Voices, this utilizes the motif of the *Zhōngguó*, a historical Chinese appellation for China that I have strategically employed to challenge the unquestioned tradition-based status bestowed upon gifts made out of ivory. The image holds China's unquestioned cultural mores accountable for the loss of elephants and the destabilizing of African national economies through this illicit blood trade.

Page 160: *Pandas of Africa.* When the buying stops, the killing will too. China is immensely proud of its conservation success with its nationally emblematic species, the Panda, but they do not evidence the same empathy for the national heritage of African countries. Elephants, rhinos, lions etc. are the Pandas of Africa. China must objectively examine its hypocritical position on preserving a singular living legacy in their nation while having no qualms about pillaging and slaughtering every other living legacy in its own as well as in other nations. Why conserve only the Panda? What of the countless other essentially iconic species? Why did they let the Baiji Dolphin die out in their Yangtze River? It isn't well considered and thus needs to be scrutinized.

Page 161: *At Arms Length.* The ivory trade is closely linked to arms trafficking, as poachers often need military-grade equipment, including helicopters, to execute, retrieve and transport ivory contraband. The other narrative this image explores is that an elephant is worth "76 times more alive than dead. Ivory from a poached elephant sells on the illegal market for about $21,000. A living elephant, on the other hand, is worth more than $1.6 million in ecotourism opportunities." Data disclosed in *Scientific American*.

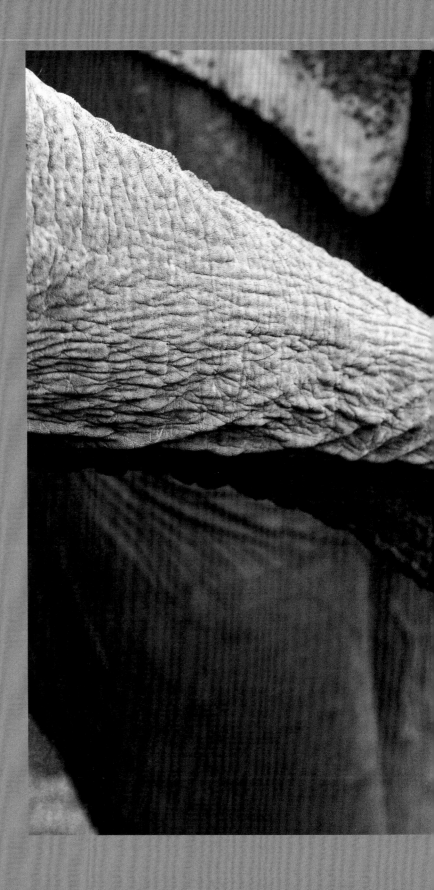

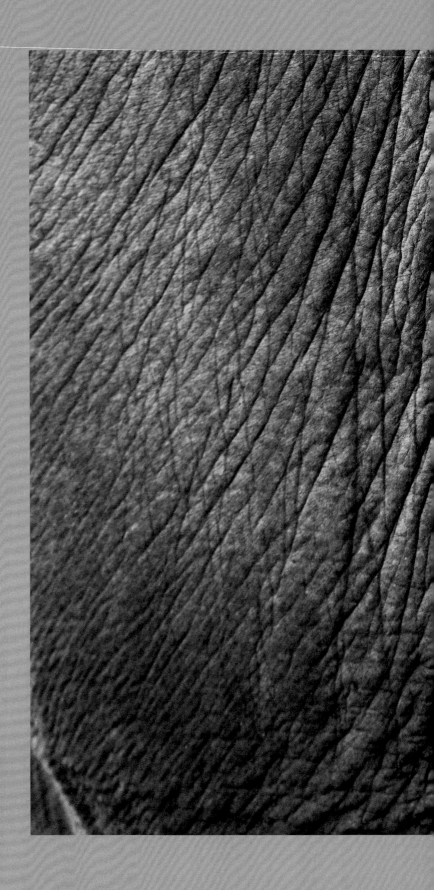

Aim for their future.
End the Trade.

ASHERJAY

MUSEUMS
& IVORY

FACING THE CHALLENGE OF IVORY IN MUSEUMS

THE NATIONAL MUSEUMS OF KENYA

LYDIA KITUNGULU

1 Nairobi National Museum:
main entrance with contemporary sculpture.

Exhibiting ivory at the turn of the 21st century in post-colonial museums in Europe and Africa is a contentious practice. And all the more so when it is linked to the various purposes of storing or exhibiting ivory, its intrinsic values, and the interpretation strategies employed in developing an exhibition. These aspects are often guided by the key messages of exhibitions and by curatorial dilemmas that attempt to address the concerns about the ban on ivory and the conservation of elephants. It is also about the impact the exposure to exhibitions on ivory could have on diverse audiences.[1]

The curatorial dilemma is rooted in the correlation between what most exhibition messages convey versus international fears regarding elephant conservation. The issue here is that the elephant is the main source of ivory, hence the ever-diminishing elephant populations, and the efforts made to curb poaching and trafficking, should ideally be the motivations behind exhibition messages. The educative role of museums in this respect gives them a singular authority. Regardless of the probable security risks posed by having ivory in their custody, museums have become a critical preference for audiences. As custodians of heritage, museums play a key role in the practice of exhibiting ivory.

In this essay I want to contribute to the debates on exhibiting ivory in museums in the two geographic extremes of Europe and Africa, the focus here being on the National Museums of Kenya (NMK), and in particular on the Nairobi National Museum (NNM, Fig. 1), as seen in a wider international context. Among several other stations across the country, the NNM is the NMK's national flagship museum. The NMK and the Humboldt Forum (HUF) in Berlin are key players in this discourse on exhibiting ivory, and the two institutions have been working together to plan for the exhibition *Terrible Beauty: Elephant–Human–Ivory.*

The essay first discusses the value of ivory in relation to the custodial role of museums; then considers the role of museums and provides an account of how ivory is represented in exhibitions at the NNM; and finally suggests ways of enhancing museums' opportunities for interpretative collaborations, and their changing role in safeguarding both ivory and elephants for posterity.

The focal points are an interrogation of what the key message of an exhibition of ivory should be in relation to its value and its historical background, as well as its role as both part of a shared heritage and as an illicit trade commodity. A curatorial assumption is that the conservation messages in an exhibition of ivory should be accessible and impactful to diverse target audiences. This could include non-visitors in the source community or consumer markets for ivory, who are often relatively far removed from the cognitive or geographical reach of an exhibition. This interrogation looks at the responsiveness and transformation of the institutional frameworks of the museum and ultimately at its role in creating a desirable re-population of the elephant.

The essay therefore questions the role of museums in conservation education and how this could bring about societal transformation through its impact on both the visiting and the non-visiting public. On impactful museum exhibitions, Rhiannon Mason, in her scholarly study of the theoretical frameworks of museums and cultural heritage, notes that practices that target visitors and non-visitors are often overlooked, or visitors' responses oversimplified.[2] This recognizes that the purposed impact of an exhibition on the visitor is a complex matter, but also that transformation in social and institutional practices can be achieved.[3]

A questionnaire I sent to targeted professionals in museums in Africa was aimed at gaining first-hand knowledge of the situation regarding ivory in

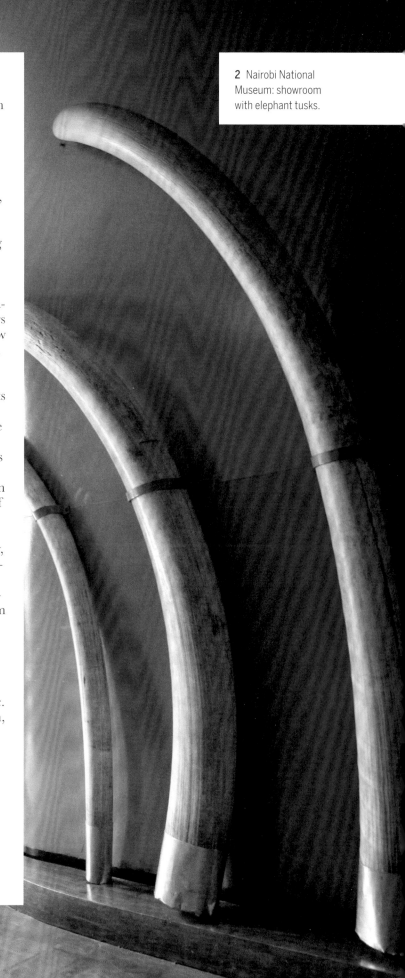

their respective museums. The ten museums sampled were in Mauritius, South Africa, Seychelles, Uganda, Tanzania, Zambia, Egypt, Ghana, Zimbabwe, and Kenya, all museums that emerged during the same colonial period as did the NMK and that have similar institutional roles to those of the NMK.

THE VALUE OF IVORY: THE MUSEUM AS CUSTODIAN

The custodial and educational roles of museums may be left wanting when little attention is paid to the impact of an exhibition's message.[4] And all the more so when museums are faced with conserving the ivory in their custody, as seen against its presence elsewhere, including private collections. Ivory is exhibited in diverse ways in museums, with themes ranging from its materiality, processing and usage, aesthetics and artistry, to ivory as an object in the history in colonial trade and slavery, its socio-economic and political significance, as well as species protection, illicit trafficking, the relationships between elephants and humans (including human-wildlife conflicts), its role in medicine and as a religious and ceremonial adornment, the use of isotopes in the analysis of ivory, and measures to protect the environment. It can be presumed that ivory is exhibited in larger quantities, and more variedly, in museums in Europe than in museums in Africa.

3 Ivory trade, probably in Mombasa, Kenya: weighing the ivory before shipping.

Especially in Europe, museums are also finding themselves faced with the custodial dilemma of holding and displaying collections from diverse communities across Africa. Most museums of natural, cultural, political or art history hold ivory artifacts in storage or on display. The provenance of many of these objects is controversial, as most are believed to have been plundered during the colonial era. Due to the present restrictions on the movement of ivory because of illicit trafficking, in some instances it has been destroyed, for example in Kenya, the USA, and recently China. In an article published in 2014, Jonathan Jones argues that while ivory is now dead as an art material, he regards calls to destroy ancient ivory artworks barbaric.[5]

Historically, most museums of mixed heritage, whether their focus is natural, cultural, national or artistic history, have their origins in the desire to classify nature and so satisfy scientific curiosity. Ivory too found its place in this *systema naturae* in museum collections.[6] Before it was banned, ivory was traded widely from ancient times, used, for example, as an adornment in temples and palaces, as in the biblical era. During the 19th century, ivory became a very lucrative trading commodity for colonial hunters.[7] Such was the case with the notorious English adventurer Arthur Henry Neumann, who not only earned a fortune from ivory, hunting elephants in Kenya between 1893 and 1896 (Fig. 3), but who also worked as a collector of specimens for the British Museum.[8] In total, it is estimated that over 30,000 tonnes of ivory were shipped to the UK alone from Africa in the 18th and 19th centuries.[9] This translates to around at least half a million elephants, if not more.

One security concern for museums is that wildlife trafficking is a part of organized crime and is suspected to be funding terrorism, with Kenya being a key transit country in the illicit trade.[10] This raises fears over the security of the ivory in museum collections and government stockpiles. Even though recent isotope analyses of seized ivory indicate that the illicit trade thrives primarily on poached elephants, curators are keenly aware that the illegal market is turning with increased regularity to museum collections, and not only for elephant ivory and rhinoceros horn, but also for gemstones, African rosewood, and cultural artifacts.[11] For instance, in recent years 67 rhino horns have been stolen from museums in countries as diverse as South Africa, Kenya, Ireland, Germany, Portugal, Spain, Italy, England, Belgium, Austria, France, Sweden, and the Netherlands.[12] In the mid-1990s, a rhino horn was cut off a taxidermy exhibit at the former Nairobi

Museum (now the Nairobi National Museum). This threat calls for alternative ways of safeguarding and using the ivory collections in museums while at the same time using innovative interpretive strategies aimed at promoting elephant conservation.

Conservationists estimate that there are approximately 350,000 savannah elephants remaining, spread over 18 African countries. About 10,000 to 15,000 are killed each year for their ivory, making the fear of rapidly diminishing populations very real.[13] Indeed, the African savannah elephant, *Loxodonta africana*, is close to extinction. Unfortunately, those who carry out the mass killings seem not to relate their actions to the harsh reality that elephants, the very source of the ivory they want, are rapidly disappearing precisely because of the mass killings. They may also fail to relate the killing of elephants to the ivory and ivory products displayed in museums.[14]

Nevertheless, international efforts to curb the illicit trade in ivory are continually being promoted by like-minded multi-sector agencies. Kenya is one of the leading proponents of these conservation efforts; as one of the principal countries through which illegal African ivory passes, it cannot afford to ignore this growing reality.

The destruction of ivory obtained mainly through illicit trafficking has been witnessed in Kenya on several national occasions, spearheaded by the Kenya Wildlife Service (KWS), which is based at the Nairobi National Park. One such event occurred in 1989 and another in 2016 (Fig. 4). At the 2016 national effort to end the trade in ivory, Kenya's President Uhuru Kenyatta stated that ivory is "worthless unless it is on an elephant". Kenya's action in 1989 accompanied the international call for the protection of threatened species, including the African elephant, that led to the banning of the ivory trade by the Convention on International Trade in Endangered Species of Wild Flora and Fauna (CITES).[15]

A common approach taken by most museums, as well as by collaborators such as the KWS, is to preserve and use ivory as a tool for research and conservation education. So museums of mixed heritage which hold ivory in their custody are taking on the challenge and responsibility of using their collections to impart powerful conservation messages.[16]

It is debatable how the key message of an exhibition impacts on an array of audiences and non-audiences. Some may never get to interact with the exhibition; for instance, the poacher, the private art collector, the police or customs official, or the sculptor. Other potential audiences include a worshipper who uses a rosary made from ivory, the musician with a piano whose keyboard is made from ivory, or the game warden whose life is often at risk from both poachers and elephants. And what of the local farmer who may be in constant conflict with elephants, or rangers in a national park whose lives are often threatened by both illegal hunters and elephants?

IVORY AT THE NMK

The heritage value of ivory correlates historically with the institutional authority of the museum. Ivory presents itself as being an integral part of the birth and growth of museums as the custodians of heritage. It is estimated that worldwide in natural-history museums relatively similar to the NMK there are around three billion objects of natural heritage.[17] The NMK itself has a collection of more than ten million items (of which ivory forms a key part), housed mainly within the Directorate of Research and National Repository (DNRR) and the Directorate of Antiquities, Sites and Monuments (DASM).

In relation to ivory, the NMK is no exception in its historical placement, evolving as it did from a colonial museum to a futuristic strategic institution. It began with collections of cabinets of curiosities from the years preceding 1910, when the museum was established and when collecting was carried out by various natural-history enthusiasts, including Sir Robert Thorne Coryndon. He was a colonial governor of Kenya, hence the name the Coryndon Museum at that time; the museum later came to be managed by the then East Africa Natural History Society. Ivory thus forms an integral and valuable part of the NMK's national historical collections. The NMK became a state-owned institution when Kenya became an independent republic in 1964. It has since grown with the vision to be a "global leader in heritage research and management",[18] its institutional mission being "to sustainably manage national heritage resources through innovative research and knowledge sharing for the benefit of humanity".[19]

The NMK carries out its mandate through various activities, with exhibitions being a mainstay in its interpretive approach to public programs. In carrying out its mandate, the core values of NMK are driven by "the imperative of inclusivity in the processes of carrying out its obligations in promoting and advancing research collaboration, conservation and management".[20]

The NMK's value of inclusivity is set out in its annual strategic commitments. The commitment is engrained in the institutional Performance Contract with the Government of Kenya through the Ministry of Sports, Culture and Heritage, and overseen by the museum's Board of Management. From its humble beginnings in collecting, the NMK now plays a specialized critical role in dispensing and sharing expert in-depth conservation information and knowledge, and not only on elephants, but also on diverse other areas of concern. To this end, the institution is increasingly involved in various collaborative initiatives with several consultancies, including community-based projects at various levels of need.

The NMK's strategic approaches to interpretation are achieved through varied activities, including research, public programs, exhibitions, and education. The institutional structure provides for an integrated approach that creates synergies between the research and public programs departments. The key role of the DNRR, in liaison with DASM, is in the management of collections, conservation, preservation, documentation, and dissemination. In relation to research, the NMK offers technical support in forensic analysis, for example in determining whether a sample is in fact elephant ivory, especially during judicial investigations.[21] Guided by the core value of inclusivity, the NMK also collaborates with the KWS in research on the conservation of elephants.

REPRESENTING IVORY
AT THE NNM

At the NNM, and the NMK at large, ivory has over the years featured in a variety of ways that speak of its colonial origins in collecting. The significance of ivory at the NMK is exemplified by its integrated presence in all the four main conceptual pillars of its exhibition development, that is, in Nature, Culture, History, and Contemporary Art. The NNM, as well as the NMK at large, has ivory in its major permanent and temporary exhibitions, and in the storage facilities that fall under the research sections of the DNRR comprising, but not limited to, Osteology, Mammalogy, Paleontology, and Cultural Heritage. There are notable and identifiable collections of ivory and ivory products on exhibition at the NNM and a few other stations under the ambit of the NMK, including the Lamu Museum on Kenya's coast, and the Nairobi Gallery.

Previously at the NNM, when it was named the Nairobi Museum, visitors came face to face with a set of large tusks that adorned the main entrance (Fig. 2). They were removed in 2006 to safeguard

6 The skeleton of the elephant Ahmet and other animal specimens in the Mammal Radiation Gallery in the Nairobi National Museum.

5 A model of the elephant Ahmet in the outdoor area of the Nairobi National Museum.

them during a major multi-million Kenya Shilling refurbishment project dubbed the National Museums of Kenya Structural Programme (NMKSP). The ivory collections at the NNM are unique as they span millions of years, from the oldest prehistoric forms of fossilized ivory to very recent items.

In the conceptual pillar of the NMK's natural heritage, ivory features in storage as preserved artifacts and on display, both outdoors and indoors, in the galleries of both permanent and temporary exhibitions. Two outdoor exhibits displayed at separate locations are Ahmed the elephant and the Baringo elephant fossil. The forms in which ivory is represented in these two instances do not depart much from the conventional scientific ordering of a natural-history museum.

The remains of Ahmed the elephant were acquired by the NMK from Marsabit in northern Kenya. Ahmed is of such national significance that, following a Presidential decree, it was accorded 24-hour security, due, among other factors, to the enormous size of its body and tusks (Fig. 5). It has since been preserved in two display forms: its skeleton, and a life-size outdoor model. The model of Ahmed was

based on the skeleton in the mammal radiation gallery (Fig. 6), and on a taxidermy of an elephant called Abdul, another display where the visitor can encounter ivory on the model of an elephant. Ahmed can now be seen displaying its long tusks in the main courtyard of the NNM, which has become a popular spot for corporate events and for visitors who want to take photo mementos of their museum visit. Overlooking the museum's visitor center, the model of Ahmed is a centerpiece, and visitors can also enjoy a spectacular view of him from the gallery of contemporary art on the upper floor. Given that elephants with tusks of Ahmed's size are now rare, the museum's mammal hall and courtyard exhibits can be used to promote elephant conservation education, highlighting the effects of the ivory trade on the elephant population and on ecology.

The NMK continues to expand its ivory collections. A recent addition to the elephant and ivory story at the NMK are the remains of Tim, a renowned elephant from the Amboseli National Park in Kenya (Fig. 7). Aged 50, Tim died in 2020 of natural causes and was brought to the NMK in collaboration with the KWS so that the remains could

7 Conservators from the Nairobi National Museum preparing the elephant Tim, who died of natural causes in March 2020.

be prepared for exhibition. It may well be displayed in the way Ahmed and Abdul are. Several specialists from the NMK were involved in this exercise to ensure its proper documentation, skinning, preserving, and sampling, and so to safeguard it for further research. It is hoped that the display of five life-size models of elephants in both real and cast forms will initiate debates on conservation and so promote collaborative efforts. It is a given that all the animals on display died of natural causes, in contrast to the majority of elephants, which die through poaching and hunting. The multi-agency efforts to protect elephants are well documented in these collections, as are the effects of poaching.

IVORY AS CULTURAL AND NATIONAL HERITAGE

Ivory is also well represented in another two of the NMK's conceptual pillars, cultural heritage and national heritage, in other words the history of Kenya. Various notable exhibits feature in permanent exhibitions represent these pillars: the *siwa* in the Hall of Kenya gallery; a fine fiberglass cast of a tusk in the Historia ya Kenya gallery; the *kiti cha enzi* in the Cycles of Life gallery; and an elephant tusk in the numismatic exhibition, a collaborative project with the Central Bank of Kenya.

The *siwa*, a ceremonial horn, is one of the six iconic centerpieces exhibited in the Hall of Kenya; as a gazetted Kenyan monument, it is of national significance (Fig. 8). Intricately carved out of ivory, it has been described as an outstanding piece of craftsmanship. This particular *siwa* on display at the NNM (Fig. 9) is the original of a copy that is on display at the Lamu Museum. The *siwa* in the Hall of Kenya, with its varying provenance of cultural interest, is a historical document. Historical sources and traditions suggest that its inspiration can be traced to the Pate Chronicle, an account of oral traditions, which records that the Sultan of Pate wished to hold a circumcision ceremony at which the royal *siwa* was to be blown. This inspired the crafting of a copy of the *siwa* by princess Mwana Darini that is now on display at the NNM as an original work of craftsmanship from coastal Kenya.

The text on the display label describes it in both Kiswahili, Kenya's national language, and English: "Huu ni upembe wa sherehe unaopuliziwa upande. Upembe huu ulitengenezwa kwa pembe ya ndovu mwaka wa 1688 na umetoka kisiwa cha Pate. Siwa ilitambulika kama ishara ya umoja na viongozi wa waswahili walikuwa waangalizi wa kipekee wa siwa. Waangalizi hawa waliaminika kuwa na nguvu za kipekee na kimiujiza."

The English text reads:
"The *Siwa*, the ceremonial side-blown horn, is one of the most distinctive items of regalia from sub-Saharan Africa. This one made of ivory in 1688 is from Pate Island. Among the Swahili people, the *Siwa* was perceived as a symbol of unity, and Swahili rulers served as its sole guardians. The *Siwa* was also believed to have supernatural and magical powers."

According to the text, in Kiswahili the word for the tusk of an elephant relates to horn, like that of a cow, rather than to teeth. A questionnaire response from an exhibition designer based at Lamu Museum who hails from a local coastal Kiswahili-speaking community indicates that a tusk is commonly known as *pembe ya ndovu*, meaning "the horn of an elephant",[22] which corresponds to the description of ivory as horn found at the Uganda National Museum. Similarly, in the local dialects of the Akan-speaking people of Ghana, ivory is referred to as *osono aben*, and the Gaa-speaking people call it *shuo klonto*, both of which literally mean "elephant horn".[23]

Another unifying factor can be seen in the use of the elephant, the largest territorial mammal, as a symbol of might and power, to which are attributed African personal names that are associated with the elephant, such as *Ndlovu* (Zulu, South Africa), *Enzogu* (Maragoli, Kenya), *Njogu* (Kikuyu, Kenya), and *Oliech* (Luo, Kenya).

IVORY IN THE HISTORY OF KENYA

Ivory occupies prominent places in two other permanent displays at the NNM that focus on the history of Kenya and on currency in Kenya respectively. In the Historia ya Kenya gallery, ivory is presented in the form of an interactive dummy tusk at the entry to the exhibition, which has as its theme the external trade influences featuring the slave trade/ human trafficking (Fig. 10). Visitors are allowed to interact with the realistic cast of the tusk by trying to lift it, an experiential approach to appreciating what the enslaved persons might have gone through. Ivory is also contextualized in a mural that forms the backdrop of this interactive exhibit. The display resonates with the concept of ivory in historical trade relations that is also the basis of a display at the Dar es Salaam National Museum in Tanzania, in which mannequins depict enslaved persons carrying ivory (Fig. 11). Ivory takes on a similar historical

value in the exhibition on the history of currency in the Numismatic and Currency gallery at the NNM (Fig. 12), where tusks are displayed as a key commodity in the fostering of external trade during the colonial period.

Yet another permanent exhibition at the NNM, in the Cycles of Life gallery, which focuses on the various cultures in Kenya, has on display its *kiti cha enzi* (Fig. 13), a ceremonial leadership seat from the Kenyan coast that has an intricate pattern of ivory inlays on its backrest. A similar seat is on display at the Lamu Museum.

These exhibitions—at the NNM in the Hall of Kenya gallery, the Historia ya Kenya gallery, the Cycles of Life gallery, with its *kiti cha enzi*, and the Numismatic and Currency gallery, together with the exhibition on slavery at the Dar es Salaam National Museum in Tanzania—all present ivory as a key commodity in fostering colonial trade, external relations, and exchange between East Africa and other parts of the world.[24] The value of ivory at the NMK can be traced back to the historical beginnings of the institution. This is evidenced by the presence of ivory in previous permanent displays that adorned what was the main entrance of the museum and that gave ivory such deserved prominence. These exhibitions convey the message that ivory was a key trading commodity that in colonial times became the object of an insatiable lust.

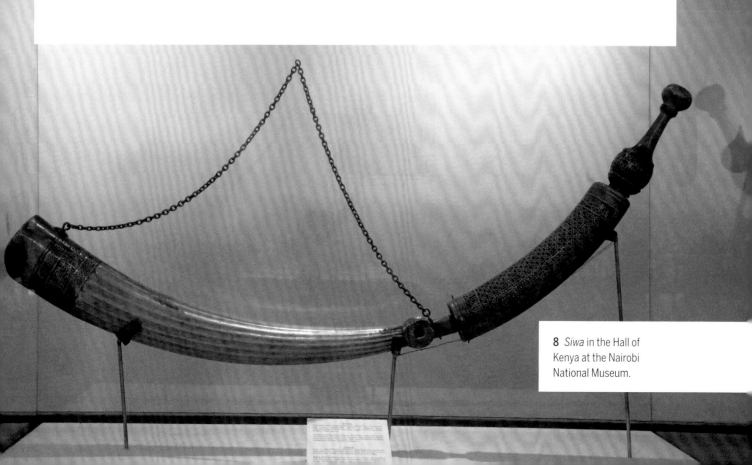

8 *Siwa* in the Hall of Kenya at the Nairobi National Museum.

IVORY AS ART: AESTHETICS FOR CONSERVATION

A different, more creative, mode of representing ivory at the NNM can be found in the temporary gallery of contemporary art. The regularly changing displays feature a variety of modern and diverse art forms, including paintings, sculptures, and installations. Such exhibitions embracing a range of visual expressions can be an effective way of confronting the issue of conservation, as seen in the 2019 exhibition *Nearly Extinct: Elephants and Rhinos*,[25] which focused on two of Kenya's most endangered species. On show were 96 sculptures, each displayed in glass-cased pedestals arranged in rows. The exhibition was the product of a keen interest in the natural world on the part of Kenyan art aficionado Mutuma Marangu. He believes that there is a need to bridge artistic and cultural sectors on the one hand with wildlife and conservation on the other, in this case by engaging the renowned wood and stone sculptors Charles Duke Kombo, Peter Kenyanya Oendo, Robin Okeyo Mbera, and Gerard Motondi Oroo.[26] Some of the sculptures were elephant or rhino figurines carved from an array of rare precious stones

sourced from Kenya, including Kisii soapstone, mud stone, blue lace agate, and pumice magma. Using precious stones rather than ivory conveyed the message that the elephant and the rhino can be conserved through the use of alternative rare and precious materials. The use of contemporary art provides an avenue for exploring alternative materials to ivory in art. Perhaps it can also promote ideas for finding alternatives to ivory in other fields, such as medicine, as well as for religious, cultural and royalty adornment, as seen in the case of the *siwa* and the *kiti cha enzi*.

BROADER COLLABORATIVE OPPORTUNITIES

The story of ivory at the NMK shows an evolution from the museum's early colonial practice of collecting, storing, and exhibiting, to its present commitment to the development of more opportunities for inclusivity and institutional commitment.

The emphasis on broader collaborative opportunities require a reorientation of the functions of the museum based on multiculturalism and a new museology.[27] The emergence of the new museology is attributed to the British art historian Peter Vergo and the Dutch scholar Pieter van Mensch, and was a response to a widespread dissatisfaction with the old museology, which was seen as too much about museum methods and too little about the purposes of museums. This I suggest would further embrace trans-geographic co-curating as a collaborative approach. As a way of enlivening and celebrating their collections, co-curating allows museums, in the development of exhibitions, to share curatorial authority, ideas, skills and knowledge with members of source communities across geographic divides.[28]

The NMK embraces co-curating with a cross-team approach, with members comprising both internal and external experts. This is carried out at various levels in the development of an exhibition, often through stakeholder workshops and field research. The internal teams are skilled in providing advisors, including exhibition designers and researchers. Based on resources, timeframes, venues, and financial obligations, the team develop an exhibition from the concept, storyline, and research to interpretation scripts.

In so doing, the NMK fulfils its mandate by offering consultancies to institutions both locally and internationally. Four illustrations that relate to ivory are provided here. The first is the establishment of the Judiciary Museum of Kenya (JMK), an initiative in which the NMK took the lead role; the second is the Kipepeo Butterfly Project; the third consists of initiatives on a trans-geographic sharing of heritage that is in favor of the repatriation and restitution of heritage to source communities; and the fourth, most importantly, is the upcoming exhibition on ivory developed in collaboration with the HUF, *Terrible Beauty: Elephant–Human–Ivory,* a project central to the present discussion. There are, in fact, ever more opportunities at the NMK, and these serve merely as highlights.

At the JMK, ivory is featured in one of the sections of the newly established museum. The highlight is a display of ivory on the theme of Justice, Science and the Arts, a display that seeks to illustrate both the JMK's and the NMK's research and technical roles

10 A visitor to the Nairobi National Museum lifts a replica of a tusk on an interactive display on the ivory trade.

11 A model of enslaved people carrying tusks, on display at Dar es Salaam National Museum, Tanzania.

12 An elephant tusk on exhibition at the Nairobi National Museum.

in forensic investigations. A graphic depiction of the ways of differentiating between elephant ivory and hippo tusks is provided, with a cross-section detailing Schreger lines, one of the typical characteristics used to identify of ivory.

The second illustration is the Kipepeo Butterfly project, which provides another diversified museological approach that could also be explored in exhibiting ivory beyond the museum walls. The project is a community-based enterprise located in Gedi on the Kenyan coast. It is a unique initiative which aims to conserve the Arabuko Sokoke forest, flora and fauna, while at the same time benefitting the local communities by supporting their day-to-day livelihoods. Members of the community are directly involved in the project through several activities, such as the rearing of butterfly pupae for export, and in turn the proceeds help in the development of community facilities, such as schools. A collaboration with the local community, the Kipepeo Butterfly initiative exemplifies the role of museums both in conservation education and in the encouragement of societal transformation through addressing the needs of community development.

The third collaborative and relational approach to sharing heritage is a trans-geographic museology which favors the repatriation and restitution of heritage materials. According to the policy of ICOM (International Council of Museums) regarding

repatriation, museums should be prepared to initiate dialogues for the return of cultural property to a country or people of origin. Various source communities are increasingly demanding that their heritage held by museums in other parts of the world, above all Europe, should be repatriated, and some artifacts have already been returned to Africa.[29] As part of this, the NMK is currently actively involved in the International Inventories Programme (IIP), a research and database project investigating the collections of Kenyan objects held in cultural institutions around the world. It is funded by the Munich-based Goethe Institute and hosted by the NMK. There have already been success stories of repatriation, such as the return in 2007 of *vigango*, wooden memorial grave figurines belonging to the Mijikenda, a community from coastal Kenya, that were held in museums in the USA.

The fourth illustration, uniquely trans-geographic, is the cooperation between the Humboldt Forum in Berlin and the NMK, motivated by the historical commonalities and mandates of the two institutions. It was established by a familiarization visit to the NMK by an exhibition management team from the HUF. Prior to the visit, an international workshop was held in Berlin in June 2018, with representation from the NMK, to plan preparations for the temporary exhibition at the HUF *Terrible Beauty: Elephant–Human–Ivory* (Fig. 14). Establishing what the two institutions hold in common forms a basis for inter-institutional collaborations that fulfill their respective mandates in heritage management. This valuable initiative is guided by top management—the Director General of the NMK and the Director of the HUF—with various consultations being undertaken with the relevant experts in the partnership. Opportunities created by the collaboration will include the exchange of exhibitions, the loaning of artifacts, the sharing of research information for the inclusion of local voices on ivory and elephant conservation, the building up of skill sets and knowledge, the expansion of collections, and other related aspects of corporate development.

The key messages of such a cooperation is similar in most museums, especially in Africa. Kenya's story of coming to terms with the challenges raised by holding and exhibiting ivory provides a basis for understanding the diversities and commonalities involved. A common theme, as illustrated by the mannequins on display at the Dar es Salaam National Museum, is that of the slave trade and other forms of external trade. The use of ivory in royal ceremony and as a symbol of national significance is encapsulated in the *siwa* and *kiti cha enzi*, while the message

13 Swahili *kiti cha enzi* (grand chair), 19th century, Lamu, Kenya, wood, ivory inlay, and cotton fiber. Art Institute of Chicago.

14 Participants in a workshop preparing for the exhibition *Terrible Beauty: Elephant–Human–Ivory* on the construction site of the Humboldt Forum, Berlin, June 2018.

with ICOM's call for museums to facilitate societal development.[31]

The benefits of co-curatorship are as generic as the opportunities to be explored in addressing curatorial dilemmas and the ever-growing needs of diverse target audiences. The key message for the museums that store or exhibit ivory is the need to review their inter-institutional curatorial strategies and related policies. There is also a need to develop interpretive strategies that bring out the diverse values of ivory without ignoring the museum's responsiveness to transformative conservation education. As illustrated by the close cooperation between the NMK and HUF, there is a need for a trans-geographic collaborative curatorship that shifts from the traditional museology of mono curating to the new museology[32] and to co-curating with source communities.[33] Together with other like-minded multi-sector agencies, museums have a futuristic and dynamic educative role beyond their custodial role—one that promotes, to quote Tony Bennet, "civic seeing".[34] There is potential for a more inclusive, multi-vocal, relational, and constructive representation of the ivory in their custody. Indeed, the issue of ivory in museums is inexhaustible.

of elephant conservation is conveyed by the display of the Baringo fossil, Ahmed, Abdul and Tim, and the art exhibition *Nearly Extinct: Elephants and Rhinos*.

FACING THE CHALLENGES OF IVORY COLLABORATIVELY

In general, this essay attests to the continual yet contested practice of exhibiting ivory in post-colonial museums in Europe and in Africa as seen through the eyes of the NMK. Ivory at the NMK is stored and exhibited in line with the institution's roles as both custodian and educator. As in most other museums of its kind, exhibiting ivory at the NMK is a historical practice that is now attracting emerging interpretive approaches through exhibition exchange and other trans-geographic collaborations. These includes new curatorial ways of interpreting ivory through the development of multi-vocal exhibitions created through co-curating.[30] Museums the world over are embracing co-curating with source communities with the aim of including once-marginalized voices in order to renew their relevance to the societies and economies in which they operate. This accords well

1 Caroline Good, Peter Tyrrell, Zhaomin Zhou, and David W. Macdonald, "Elephants never forget, should art museums remember too? Historic ivory collections as ambassadors for conservation education", *Biodiversity and Conservation* 28 (2019), pp. 1331–1342, online at: https://doi.org/10.1007/s10531-019-01735-6 (accessed June 13, 2020).
2 Rhiannon Mason, "Cultural Theory and Museum Studies", in: Sharon Macdonald (ed.), *A Companion to Museum Studies*, Malden, MA/Oxford (UK): Blackwell Publishing, 2006.
3 Lydia Kitungulu, *In Co-curating with source communities: Politics of Liberating Museum Practices*, Master's thesis, Amsterdam, 2008.
4 Mason 2006 (as note 2).
5 Jonathan Jones, "Ivory: the elephant in the art gallery", *The Guardian*, May 15, 2014, online at: https://www.theguardian.com/artanddesign/jonathanjonesblog/2014/may/15/ivory-elephant-artworks-banned-cultural-legacy (accessed June 13, 2019).
6 Information text in the exhibit in the cabinet of curiosities at the Tropenmuseum in Amsterdam, February 2008. See Kitungulu 2008 (as note 3).
7 Kiprop Lagat and Julie Hudson, *Hazina: Traditions, Trade, Traditions, Eastern Africa*, National Museums of Kenya, Nairobi, 2006.
8 Arthur H. Neumann, *Elephant Hunting in East Equatorial Africa (1893–1896)*, London 1898.
9 Eric J. Dorfman, "Elephants and Ivory Coordinating Natural History Museum Action to Address Wildlife Crime", *Curator: The Museum Journal*, vol. 61, no. 1, 26 January 2018; online at: https://onlinelibrary.wiley.com/doi/abs/10.1111/cura.12243 (accessed 14 April 2019).
10 Sam Weru, *Wildlife protection and trafficking assessment in Kenya: Drivers and trends of transnational wildlife crime in Kenya and its role as a transit point for trafficked species in East Africa*, Traffic Report, May 2016, online at: https://www.traffic.org/site/assets/files/2410/kenya-wildlife-trafficking-report.pdf (accessed May 15, 2019); and *Enhancing the Detection, Investigation and Disruption of Illicit Financial Flows from Wildlife Crime*, Research Report, UNODC, 2017, online at: https://www.unodc.org/documents/southeastasiaandpacific/Publications/2017/FINAL_-_UNODC_APG_Wildlife_Crime_report.pdf (accessed May 15, 2019)
11 Dorfman 2018 (as note 9).
12 Ibid.

13 Fiesta Warinwa, Erustus Kanga, and William Kiprono, "Fighting Wildlife Trade in Kenya", UN Chronicles 51 (2), September 2014, online
   at: https://unchronicle.un.org/article/fighting-wildlife-trade-kenya
   (accessed October 26, 2019); and Thure E. Cerling, Janet E. Barnette,
   Lesley A. Chesson, Iain Douglas-Hamilton, Kathleen S. Gobush,
   Kevin T. Uno, Samuel W. Wasser, and Xiaomei Xu, "Radiocarbon
   dating of seized ivory confirms rapid decline in African Elephant
   populations and provides insight into illegal trade", PNAS 113 (47),
   November 7, 2016, online at: https://www.ncbi.nlm.nih.gov/pmc/
   articles/PMC5127328/ (accessed October 26, 2019).
14 Jones 2014 (as note 5).
15 Convention on International Trade in Endangered Species of Wild
   Fauna and Flora, online at: https://www.cites.org/eng/disc/text.php
   (accessed March 23, 2021)
16 Good 2019 (as note 1).
17 Dorfman 2018 (as note 9).
18 National Museums of Kenya, *2017–2019 Biennial Report*, p. 8, online
   at: https://www.museums.or.ke/wp-content/uploads/2020/05/NMK-
   Annual-Report-2017-2018-2019.pdf (accessed December 2020).
19 Ibid., p. 42.
20 Ibid., p. 27.
21 Communication with Dr Ogeto Mwebi, Osteology Section, National
   Museums of Kenya, 2019.
22 Questionnaire correspondence with Zein Mohammed, Exhibition
   Designer, Lamu Museum, National Museums of Kenya, 2020.
23 Questionnaire correspondence with Mr Francis Ayi, Ghana Museums
   and Monuments Board, Accra, Ghana, 2020.
24 Lagat and Hudson 2006 (as note 7).
25 For a review, see Kari Mutu, "ART: Endangered wildlife carved
   in unique stone", *The East African*, 30 August 2019, online at:
   https://www.theeastafrican.co.ke/tea/magazine/art-endangered-
   wildlife-carved-in-unique-stone-1426066 (accessed February 13,
   2019); and Margaretta wa Gacheru, "Indigenous Stone Sculptures
   Speak For Endangered Wildlife", *Kenyan Arts Review*, Sunday August
   25, 2019, online at: http://kenyanartsreview.blogspot.com/2019/08/
   stones.html (accessed September 6, 2019).
26 Anjellah Owino, "Together for the tusk ahead", *The Standard* [Nairobi],
   September 6, 2019.
27 Peter Vergo (ed.), *The New Museology*, London: Reaktion Books, 1989.
28 Lydia Kitungulu, "Collaborating to Enliven Museum Collections",
   Museum International, vol. 65, 2013, pp. 257–260, online at: https://
   www.tandfonline.com/doi/abs/10.1111/muse.12043 (accessed October 23, 2019).
29 *ICOM Code of Ethics for Museums*, 2004, online at: https://www.ecsite.eu/
   activities-and-services/resources/icom-code-ethics-museums (accessed
   October 23, 2019).
30 Kitungulu 2008 (as note 3).
31 *ICOM Code of Ethics for Museums*, 2004 (as note 29).
32 Vergo 1989 (as note 27).
33 Kitungulu 2008 (as note 3). Tim Boon, "Co-Curation and the Public
   History of Science and Technology", *Curator: The Museum Journal*,
   vol. 54, no. 4, 6 October 2011, online at: https://doi.org/10.1111/j.2151-
   6952.2011.00102.x (accessed March 15, 2021).
34 Tony Bennett, "Civic Seeing in Museums and the Organisation of
   Vision", in: Macdonald 2006 (as note 2).

LIVING MATERIAL
HUMAN SUPREMACY IN IVORY EXHIBITIONS

S. MAREK MULLER

In this special exhibition, the Humboldt Forum describes ivory as a "living material" with a complex history. In my essay, I emphasize the "living" aspect of ivory in two ways: first, I explicate the sentient animal bodies slaughtered for their tusks to create genteel products and pristine artwork during colonial times; second, I reiterate that ivory may come from a dead animal, but its tooth lives on through the immortal, ever-changing nature of the (post)colonial museum and its displays. This special exhibition on ivory is representative of how the animal's tusk is indeed a living material rendered from a once-living sentient pachyderm subject (Fig. 1), a non-human animal that, despite its species status, was just as intertwined in the histories of especially European colonialism as the human colonizers and colonized. Museums—and that includes the Humboldt Forum—house this living material in what is essentially a living locale that is capable of telling and retelling these fateful colonial histories through the collection and display of ivory artifacts. Thus, if a metaphorical or literal "decolonization" of museums such as Germany's Humboldt Forum, Belgium's Royal Museum for Central Africa, or Britain's British Museum is even possible, these institutions must

grapple not only with the ecological devastation wrought by the historical and ongoing collection of ivory, but also the historical and ongoing racist-speciesist intersections of the history of ivory collection and display.

To "decolonize" ivory collections and displays is to engage in a critical emancipatory process that grapples with the legacy of European colonialism and its effects on both the colonizers and the colonized. This process must not involve merely taking down or hiding those statues or collections deemed offensive. It must not involve some abstract "honoring" of the animal shot and killed to make a billiard ball from its tooth. And it must not involve an erroneous nature/culture divide wherein the history of the animal is relegated to an "environmental" display while its ivory tusks and the products created from it are displayed as something "cultural". Curators of and visitors to ivory displays and collections must take the time to grapple with difficult, perhaps unsolvable, questions of displaying acts of murder as artwork, of creating veritable menageries of death for guiltless public consumption. Both parties must acknowledge how anti-African racism, European exceptionalism, and anthropocentric speciesism played integral parts in allowing such displays to exist at all—much less exist as objects of beauty, not of mourning. Ivory, then, is not so much a product as it is a literal and metaphorical severing—literally an animal's severed tooth, and metaphorically a severing of the product from its violent history. To summarize, the (post)colonial museum cannot possibly decolonize itself without acknowledging, mourning, and quite literally providing reparative penance to those human and non-human animal subjects dominated, exploited, enslaved, and slaughtered in the service of the museum's own creation.

To this effect, I offer my readers a lens through which to understand and critically analyze the Humboldt Forum's current display (as well as any museographic depiction of animals and ivory): postcolonial critical animal studies. To some extent, the term is redundant. Critical animal studies is both an academic theory and an approach to critical inquiry that acknowledges the interweavings, not separation, of human domination of non-human animals and human domination of other humans.[1] Central to its tenets is the deconstruction of "speciesism"[2]—an unnecessary "-ism", much like racism or sexism, that elevates *Homo sapiens* to the realm of moral superiority at the expense of other species (and that defends such elevation through constantly shifting constructions such as human "logic", "intelligence", "consciousness", etc.). In other words, racism, sexism, heterosexism, ableism, classism, and speciesism are not separate manifestations. Bolstered by the desire of the powerful for more power, these systems of domination create and recreate one another. The history of ivory collection and display in European museums is representative of this uncomfortable fact.

Such is the reason that the word "postcolonial" must be emphasized. Europe's museographic history of ivory collection and display cannot be separated from the history of European colonialism. And, even though countries such as Germany, France, Belgium, and Britain have since "pulled out" of their "scramble for Africa", the devastating legacy of colonization is still manifest both in colonized countries and in the museums claiming not to celebrate that colonization.[3] This is why the "post" in postcolonial must be taken with *many* grains of salt. Postcolonial studies condemn the notion that colonialism is over and done. Extending postcolonial approaches to speciesism, as a pointedly postcolonial critical animal studies does,[4] is a fruitful tool through which to view and critique how Euro-

1 A mounted elephant in the "Landscapes and Biodiversity" gallery of the Royal Museum for Central Africa, Tervuren, Belgium.

pean museums have changed (or not changed) their collections and displays of colonial artifacts in response to increasing calls for restorative justice. Restorative justice, however, remains incomplete without a large-scale acknowledgement of how racism and speciesism were intertwined in the colonization of Africa(ns) and the subsequent collection and display of colonial artifacts (and body parts) in European museums.

2 Thomas Vinçotte (1850–1925), *Bust of King Leopold II*, 1900, ivory. Royal Museum for Central Africa, Tervuren, Belgium.

IVORY BUSTS:
THE GAZE OF A KING

One of the most distinctive examples of the rhetorical power of museographic ivory displays can be seen in the Royal Museum for Central Africa's (RMCA) famed bust of King Leopold II (Fig. 2), the dreaded ruler of the Congo Free State (1885-1908). After years of public outcry, the RMCA has now hidden this haunting bust from view. But for decades and decades, Leopold II's bust gazed stoically upon museum patrons. While this depiction of the Congo Free State's cruel king was merely one of many ivory carvings littered throughout the RMCA, it has been the focus of many writers critical of the museum's warped sense of public memory. Prior to the RMCA's reconstruction project, nearly every room contained a statue or at least a callback to a "regal Leopold",[5] but only one bust was carved entirely from ivory. Designed by Thomas Vinçotte at the dawn of the 20th century, the statue has from 1897 to the present day been frequently moved by the museum. At times it was located at the midpoint of the RMCA's central rotunda.

Leopold II's ivory bust, be it on display or hidden away, serves as a continuing reminder of the origins of the gorgeous neoclassical art littering the RMCA, and the lack of reparations paid to its colonized subjects—both human and animal. Ivory played a pivotal role in the colonization of the Congo, and in Africa as a whole. Indeed, early European settlers utilized elephant ivory to finance African explorations and settlements, i.e. the colonization of African spaces, engaging in a multicultural "ivory network" employing indigenous peoples and caravans of enslaved Africans. As the age of imperialism progressed, the harvest and trade of elephant ivory did too. Elephant populations declined in the process. Because of its exoticism and its ease of carving, the product could be sold at great expense in Europe and in the USA to make luxury items: billiard balls, piano keys, chess pieces, snuff boxes, and other cachet items. At the peak of the trade, between 800 and 1,000 tons of ivory were exported from Africa to Europe alone each year.[6]

When Belgium's dreaded King Leopold II first colonized the Congo, he did so primarily to extract and profit from its plentiful stock of ivory. African elephants were known to have extremely large tusks compared to Asian pachyderms, the tusks of a single African elephant being capable of producing hundreds of piano keys. Ivory exports from the "Congo Free State" quickly filled Leopold II's coffers. In 1888, the Congo Free State exported 54,812 kilos of ivory. In response to lowered elephant populations and increased interest in ivory, the colony instituted an elephant-protection measure in 1892. That same year, Belgium, France, and Portugal signed and ratified an agreement at the Congo Basin Convention seeking to create uniform duties on elephant tusks. Such agreements did little to stop the mass slaughter of elephants for their tusks, and in 1899 Congolese ivory exports peaked at a massive 291,731 kilos. By the end of the Congo Free State's existence, ivory exports were still holding strong at 243,823 kilos.[7]

The Congo Free State's ballooning ivory trade of the 1890s did not harm Congolese elephants alone. Despite scholarship's emphasis on the brutal "red rubber" trade of the Belgian Congo, which originated in 1908 when King Leopold sold his privately owned Congo Free State to the Belgian state, Congolese civilians were massively abused in the hunt for ivory. Some Congolese were driven into poverty, as they were forbidden to sell ivory to anyone other than an agent of King Leopold II. Leopold's agents, however, profited from a commission structure that gave them a cut of the ivory's European market value, thus giving them "a powerful incentive to force Africans—if necessary, at gunpoint—to accept extremely low prices".[8] Indeed, the indigenous ivory trade had been dismantled in favor of a "command economy" that specifically created low-paid porters.

Congolese ivory porters endured gruesome working conditions, with tasks ranging from carrying the ivory agents' food and drink to dismantling entire steamboats and moving them from one section of a river to another—a task which consisted of some 3,000 porter loads. Some were paid, usually in just enough food to keep them alive, but most were conscripts. Anyone who complained was beaten with a chicotte whip. The death toll was high, and those who trekked long distances often never returned. King Leopold II insisted that such extreme "employment" methods were in fact benevolent, stating that "in dealing with a race composed of cannibals for thousands of years it is necessary to use methods which will shake their idleness and make them realize the sanctity of work".[9]

Certain colonists believed that elephants were just as valuable as draught animals as they were sources of ivory. To advance this theory, they engaged in projects intended to "domesticate" the African elephant. In the 1908 newsletter for the International Society for the Preservation of the Wild Fauna of the Empire, writers P.L. Sclater and Monsieur Nibueld commended the work of the "much-abused Congo Free State" for its domestication project on the Kiver Welle, and advised other colonists to "take a lesson from the Free State authorities on the capture and taming of the African elephant".[10] What they referred to was a colonial project started in 1899 by Belgian Commandant Laplume to try such an "experiment". By 1905, the Congo Free State had captured 13 elephants, and by 1908 the number had doubled. These numbers did not, however, include the 22 that had to be released or the

86 that died during the domestication process, which would have put the number captured since the beginning of the domestication experiments at 132.

The advent of the Congo Free State transformed the way history was written and interpreted in Belgium, and this reinterpretation "broke the mold" of royal art museums.[11] The RMCA became "a tool of propaganda" that justified imperialism and extolled the virtues of "colonial heroes" and Leopold II.[12] From the 1897 exhibition through the official 1910 opening of the RMCA, curators displayed collections of a range of abject objects that celebrate the slaughter of the colonized animal in an attempt to prove Belgian superiority over the Congolese. This superiority was particularly poignant in the form of ivory artwork. The unveiling of colonial museums was an attempt to educate the Belgian people as to "who they really were" in contrast to the "uncivilized Congolese 'tribes' […] the black savage Africans" far off in the Congo.[13] In 1904 Leopold enlisted the help of famous architect Charles Girault to build a permanent museum structure funded through the very ivory and rubber profits that the temporary museum had displayed, and this was officially opened in 1910. Along with stuffed taxidermy and mounted skeletons, chryselephantines (sculptures composed of gold and ivory) were littered through the museum. The entryway rotunda highlighted the imposing ivory bust of Leopold II, a set of ivory statuettes encircling it.[14]

In terms of artistry, Leopold II's bust is hardly a "creative" piece. Much as in any monarchial bust, the king is depicted starting intently at an unknown subject, bereft of empathy or even a hint of a smile. At times protected behind glass walls and at others placed upon a slab of Congolese wood, Leopold II appears to his subjects dressed in formal militaristic garb. He is the gray-white color of elephant ivory, as it appears no attempt has been made to cloak the sculpture's material origins in expensive elephant tusk.

The rhetorical force of the bust, wherever it is at the current moment, is difficult to overstate. Wherever it is placed in the museum, Leopold II's pervasive gaze ensures that "the museum has remained frozen in time".[15] Leopold II's unblinking stare ensures that the museum remains haunted by the poltergeist of the brutal Congo Free State. In his corporeal absence, Leopold II is still very much present. When the statue is on display, gazing coldly at its subjects, museum goers are inundated with the memory of a monarchy swollen with capitalist greed—at least until the museographic narrative provided to patrons attempts to correct this unseemly memory. When the bust is hidden away, media narratives critical of the RMCA have continued to remind patrons of its existence in the bowels of the museum, symbolically representing the museum's desire to stow away bad memories of the Congo Free State without dealing with the colony's angry ghosts. A nation's specters, after all, do not vanish by sheer force of national will.

But the bust's potential to haunt its subjects comes not solely from Leopold II's gaze. The ghostly king is not the only specter that emerges from the statue. Rather, a discerning patron might feel the uneasy presence of the elephant sacrificed for the construction of the elegant bust. The absent referent is not so absent when reconstructed into the shape of the human who ordered its death. As is typical of an ivory sculpture, cracks and crevices can be seen throughout, depicting the areas where a new ivory slab had to be used to accommodate the sheer size of the bust. In this way, a close glance at the bust of Leopold II shows a king unsubtly reconstructed from severed teeth, a king whose colony would, like the statue itself, have come apart at the seams were it not for the destruction of profitable elephant bodies.

In constructing Leopold II's likeness from the corpse of an elephant, the sculpture reifies the concept of co-colonization. Specifically, it exemplifies the binding together of human and non-human animal bodies in the construction and maintenance of the Congo Free State. Looking at ivory work as a form of rhetorical taxidermy reveals how museographic displays are not merely representations of an artist's or curator's skill, but also exhibitions of a white-supremacist, speciesist, and thoroughly colonial system of domination. Leopold II's bust is one such example of this phenomenon.

BENEVOLENT GIFT OR BRUTAL TROPHY?

In the summer of 2018, the British Museum faced an ethical dilemma: should it or should it not accept the donation of over 500 "exquisite" ivory figures from a private donor. The ivory collection was from Chinese sculptors, not European aristocrats. It was acquired initially by Shanghai-based businessman and hotelier Sir Victor Sassoon in the early 20th century (the height of British imperialism in China), and included carved brush-washers, water-droppers, and figurines of Chinese deities (Fig. 3). The British Museum was and is known for having

one of the largest ivory collections in the world, including the Lewis Chessmen and Nimrud Ivories. Accepting this private gift, said the head of the Museum's Asia department, was one step further in making the British Museum a "global centre for the study of ivories".[16] Ultimately, the museum opted to accept the gift, with museum director Hartwig Fischer explaining that the ivory artworks were "of the greatest significance, they are documents of a vast culture and are therefore of the highest cultural value".[17]

The decision to accept the ivory donation caused an uproar amongst museum stakeholders and the broader British public. After all, given the brutality of the contemporary ivory trade and the ongoing threat of extinction to elephants and other tusked megafauna, taking the ivory could send the wrong message about Britain's stance on the ivory trade. At that same moment, the government had been passing a parliamentary ban on ivory sales. Among the only exceptions to the rule would be for museums acquiring ivory objects of, as Fischer strategically said, "cultural value". The British Museum, said Fischer, "fully and unreservedly" condemned the ivory trade, but noted that the gifted collection would exist whether the contemporary trade ended or not: "They exist [...] and they do not save any elephant's life today."[18]

To some extent, Fischer was correct. Ivory is always and already a symbol of death. Hating the ivory, refusing to glance at the ivory, and condemning museum displays of ivory will never bring the elephant back to life. And the ivory figurines are, indeed, figures of immense cultural value. However, what the British Museum overlooks is how accepting and displaying ivory collections—particularly those collections gathered during the height of colonial conquest and imperialist ideology—is in and of itself a manifestation of a cultural *value*. That is to say, regardless of whether the British Museum supports the ivory trade today, it values the ivory trade of *yesterday*. And, as the previous sections have demonstrated, clinging to the aesthetic beauty of a corpse does not stop the corpse from retelling its violent story. To accept, display, and ultimately to celebrate colonial ivory, no matter *where* it is from (China, India, Africa, or Europe) or *who* did the killing (the colonizer or the colonized), may not bring an animal back to life, but it brings forth the poltergeists of those human and non-human animals abused, exploited, and slaughtered as a form of the racist-speciesist practice of imperialism. In 2018, the British Museum engaged in a similar mode of discourse, albeit one with a "post" colonial mentality. To accept gifts from a private donor was to metaphorically sever the museum from the ivory's history, to negate the impact of European imperialism's role in acquiring the Chinese ivory in the first place via a Shanghai-based businessman, and to approve of the historical trade in ivory. To summarize, accepting ivory from a private donor, originally collected from a private businessman, a businessman only in business through colonial politics, cannot possibly absolve the British Museum of guilt.

One absolutely can claim to support conservationism and simultaneously accept colonial ivory. However, the conservationism being supported is one steeped in colonial history and values, a conservation ethic dependent upon hunting and killing for sport, an environmentalism best called a "colonial hunting privilege".

According to Achille Mbembe, hunting and colonizing are synonymous enterprises wherein "what holds for the animal holds for the colonized, and what holds for the act of colonizing holds for the act of hunting".[19] Such is the case because discourse on colonized publics "is almost always deployed in the framework (or on the fringes) of a meta-text about the animal".[20] For in both discourse and practice, "to *exist,* the colonizer constantly needs the native as that animal that serves as the support for the colonizer's self-consciousness".[21] A quick glimpse at the history of European "conservationism" in colonial nations exemplifies Mbembe's argument.

European colonial conservation societies engaged in a proto-conservationist rhetoric that, far from advocating for the conservation of fauna on the basis of heartfelt empathy, glorified trophy-hunting as an act of compassion, the single most authentic mode of nature appreciation. Indeed, "it was an animal rights ideology that separated the sport of hunting from subsistence hunting and hunting as a means to protect property. As the elite movement grew, so, too, did the romanticized image of nature."[22] Edward North Buxton, co-founder of the British-based Society for the Preservation of the Wild Fauna of the Empire (SPWFE), believed that African game should be viewed as "a precious inheritance of the empire, something to be guarded like a unique picture […] something which may easily be lost, but cannot be replaced".[23] An ardent hunter, he maintained that hunting "must not be done in such a way to endanger the existence or seriously diminish the stock of game" available to him and his compatriots.[24]

In the SPWFE's 1908 newsletter, a member named Sir Seton-Karr brushed off criticisms that

3 One of the figures donated to the British Museum from the collection of Sir Victor Sassoon: Guanyin, China, 16th–17th century, ivory, 34 cm. The British Museum, London.

called members mere "penitent butchers", men who "having in earlier days taken their fill of big-game slaughter […] now, being smitten with remorse, and having reached a less strenuous term of life, think to condone our earlier bloodthirstiness by advocating the preservation of what we formerly chased and killed".[25] Nothing could be further from the truth, he claimed, for true sportsmen were among the most authentic nature-lovers: "He kills, it is true, but only in sweet reasonableness and moderation, for food if necessary, but mainly for trophies. Wholesale and unnecessary slaughter is abhorrent to him."[26] By Seton-Karr's logic, trophy hunting ought to be considered a necessary enterprise, a morally justified killing. Sportsmen exuded compassion by leaving "severely alone all immature, and particularly all female-of-their-kind-producing wild animals".[27] Although he acknowledged that "amateur" ivory hunters and "certain" sportsmen were not altogether clear of guilt, the "real depredators […] in all wild countries have been natives […]."[28]

Colonial, proto-conservationist mentalities neatly fused classist conceptions of big-game hunting with racist depictions of savage colonial subjects. For instance, colonizers in Africa strategically specified who should be allowed to hunt and who should not. Colonial hunting privilege sought to curtail traditional forms of African hunting—more specifically, hunting without the use of firearms. At the same time, however, they banned native "savages" from purchasing or using guns at all, reclassifying those who did use them as "poachers".[29] They sanctioned colonial gun licenses and enforced restrictions on big-game hunting, making it nearly impossible for African subjects to kill animals for food or profit while white colonizers enjoyed the privilege of hunting game for trophies. Advocates of colonial hunting privilege justified these policies by contrasting their "noble respect" for the hunt as opposed to the careless, barbarous, and wholly unsympathetic killings instituted by natives. European-style, firearm-based hunting was, in more contemporary terms, more "humane" than its spear-, arrow-, snare-, and trap-based African counterparts.[30] In 1902, Buxton pinpointed the real problem facing Africa's game animals: the "reckless shooting" of an excessive number of animals, particularly by money-hungry entrepreneurs and savage Africans with access to firearms.[31] Colonial conservationism perpetuated the racist, speciesist ideologies that would later be put on display in the anthropological, zoological, and artistic displays of European museums. Ergo, without supremely careful exhibit planning *coupled with* a genuine commitment to restorative justice

for humans and non-humans alike, European natural-history displays risk perpetuating these pervasive ideologies.

CONCLUDING REMARKS

The history of ivory is not merely a history of humanity. It is a history of a more-than-human world[32] inter- and intra-acting with human manifestations of colonialism. To study ivories that originate from a colonial context is to study murder—the murder of the animal for its tusk, the murder of the colonized in the service of collecting those tusks, and the metaphorical murder of both of those histories in the service of genteel, artistic displays in individual households or public cultural institutions. Ivory collection and displays in postcolonial European museums are veritable menageries of death, corpse-ridden rooms haunted by the unsatisfied poltergeists of those harmed to transform the ivory from tusk to bust.

Viewed through the lens of postcolonial critical animal studies, museum curators and patrons alike can see how speciesism and racism manifested and intersected in the collection and display of ivory in European museums. If indeed cultural institutions like the Humboldt Forum, or the Royal Museum for Central Africa, or the British Museum, truly wish to "decolonize" themselves from the atrocities of "the past", then they must grapple with how the past still manifests in the present. A postcolonial globe is still colonized, albeit in a different fashion than before. Museum collections often represent a microcosm of such colonization, displaying the remnants of an exploited Other instead of offering reparations for the past in the service of a better future. Ivory collections are one such opportunity to atone for colonial histories and their racist-speciesist intersections.

Does this mean that to display ivory is in and of itself an act of violence? Or that merely certain ivory creations, like the bust of a violent king, should be hidden from view? Or, most simply, that ivory collections should only be accepted from donors as disconnected from a colonial past as possible? These questions do not yet have a consensus. But perhaps critical interrogations such as this special exhibit will bring museums slightly closer to answers.

1   Steve Best, Anthony J. Nocella, Richard Kahn, Carol Gigliotti, and Lisa Kemmerer, "Introducing Critical Animal Studies", *Journal for Critical Animal Studies* 5, 1 (2007), pp. 4–5.
2   Peter Singer, *Animal Liberation*, New York: New York Review, 1975.
3   Kwame Anthony Appiah, "Is the Post- in Postmodernism the Post- in Postcolonial?", *Critical inquiry* 17, 2 (1991), pp. 336–357.
4   Neel Ahuja, "Postcolonial Critique in a Multispecies World", *pmla* 124, 2 (2009), pp. 556–563; Billy-Ray Belcourt, "Animal Bodies, Colonial Subjects: (Re)locating Animality in Decolonial Thought", *Societies* 5, 1 (2015), pp. 1–11.
5   Charlotte McDonald-Gibson, "Forget King Leopold's Ghost. There are Still Skeletons in His Closet", *Time*, on-line at: https://world.time.com/2013/09/18/skeletons-in-king-leopolds-closet-colonial-era-belgian-museum-grapples-with-bloody-past/ (accessed March 15, 2021).
6   Keith Lindsay, "Trading Elephants for Ivory", *New Scientist* 112, 1533 (1986), pp. 48–52.
7   See Mark Cioc, *The Game of Conservation: International Treaties to Protect the World's Migratory Animals*, Athens, OH: Ohio University Press, 2009; David K. Prendergast and William M. Adams, "Colonial Wildlife Conservation and the Origins of the Society for the Preservation of the Wild Fauna of the Empire (1903–1914)", *Oryx* 37, 2 (2003), pp. 251–260.
8   Adam Hochschild, *King Leopold's Ghost: A Story of Greed, Terror, and Heroism in Colonial Africa*, Boston, MA: Houghton Mifflin, p. 118.
9   Ibid., p. 118.
10 Ibid., p. 46.
11 Debora L. Silverman, "Diasporas of Art: History, the Tervuren Royal Museum for Central Africa, and the Politics of Memory in Belgium, 1885–2014", *The Journal of Modern History* 87, 3 (2015), p. 619.
12 Matthew Stanard, *Selling the Congo: A History of European Pro-Empire Propaganda and the Making of Belgian Imperialism*, Kearney, NE: University of Nebraska Press, 2011, pp. 91–92.
13 Jean Muteba Rahier, "The Ghost of Leopold II: The Belgian Royal Museum of Central Africa and its Dusty Colonialist Exhibition", *Research in African Literatures* 34, 1 (2003), p. 61.
14 Silverman 2015 (as note 11), p. 641.
15 McDonald-Gibson 2013 (as note 5).
16 Quoted in Mark Brown, "British Museum Given more than 500 'Exquisite' Ivory Figures", *The Guardian*, June 27, 2018, on-line at: https://www.theguardian.com/culture/2018/jun/27/british-museum-ivory-figures-sir-victor-sassoon (accessed June 27, 2018).
17 Ibid.
18 Quoted in ibid.
19 Achille Mbembe, *On the Postcolony*, Berkeley, CL: University of California Press, 2001, p. 166.
20 Ibid., p. 1.
21 Ibid., p. 188.
22 Regina Capoccia, "The Impact of Animal Rights on Wildlife Conservation and Management in Kenya", PhD dissertation, Rutgers University, 2013, p. 9.
23 Quoted in Prendergast and Adams 2003 (as note 7), p. 252.
24 Ibid.
25 Sir Henry Seton-Karr, "The Preservation of Big Game", *Journal for the Society for the Preservation of the Wild Fauna of the Empire*, 4, 1 (1908), p. 27.
26 Ibid.
27 Ibid.
28 Ibid.
29 Lindsay 1986 (as note 6), pp. 48–52.
30 Capoccia 2013 (as note 22), p. 9.
31 Prendergast and Adams 2003 (as note 7), p. 252.
32 David Abram, *The Spell of the Sensuous: Perception and Language in a More-than-Human World*, New York: Random House, 1996.

IVORY OBJECTS IN AN IVORY TOWER

NANETTE SNOEP

Addressed from the point of view of the history of so-called ethnographic collections, ivory objects will appear very differently in this essay from how they appear in the other contributions to this volume. Here we will show how such artifacts today pose a problem that goes beyond ecological issues arising from the protection of an endangered species: namely, the place afforded in ethnographic museums to the historicity of the societies from which their collections originate. Due to the extraordinarily valuable nature of "white gold"—at once scarce yet relatively easy to work with—dealing with these types of objects, more that for other objects made of more commonplace materials, obliges museums to rethink a fundamental tenet of their practice. Rather than telling a story of cultural specificity, it will have to tell the story of the encounter of societies.

Before addressing the questions raised by ivory in ethnographic collections proper and the links between this typology of objects and the so-called "crisis" of the ethnological museum, we must go back in time to the origin of the fascination for a raw material that has proved such an inspiration to so many European artists and courts.

The famous portrait (Fig. 1) showing a servant of an emissary from the kingdom of Kongo carrying a precious unworked ivory tusk in his arms, painted by Jaspar Beckx (active 1627–1647) or Albert Eckhout (ca. 1610–1665) for the Count of Nassau with the title *Pedro Sunda, Servant of Don Miguel de Castro*, bears witness to this. Another portrait from the same series (Fig. 2) presents another servant holding a finely woven raffia box from the same kingdom. The tusk and the box held by these two boys represent the first so-called ethnographic objects from the African continent collected as early as the Renaissance: from the outset, this iconography links the issue of ivory to the history of ethnographic collecting and the foundation of the ethnographic museum. Among the immense variety of ivory objects in ethnographic holdings today, our focus will be on what are known as Afro-Portuguese ivories from the African coast, rarities and trophies in European ethnographic museums.

A contentious subject today in the context of the decline in African elephant populations, due in large part to their being hunted for their tusks as well as to the gradual degradation of their environment, the centuries-long trade in raw ivory and in the arts and

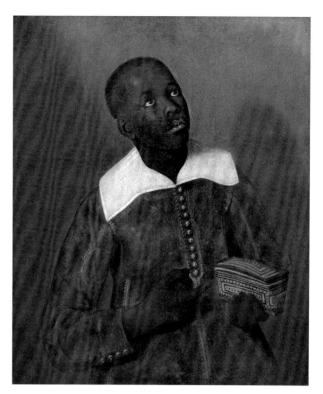

1 and 2 Albert Eckhout or Jaspar Beckx, *Pedro Sunda, a Servant of Don Miguel de Castro* (left), and *Diego Bemba, a Servant of Don Miguel de Castro* (right), before 1643, oil on wood, both 75 x 62 cm. Statens Museum for Kunst, Copenhagen.

crafts that make use of it flourished to the extent that nearly all the elephant population disappeared. It should be remembered that during the colonization of Africa at the height of the ivory trade, between 800 and 1,000 tons of ivory were shipped to Europe every year. In the second half of the 19th century, as ethnographic museums were being established all over Europe, colonial violence, forced labor, and the harvesting of ivory became inextricably linked. The colonial history of the Congo is a tragic example of this.

"IMPURE" OBJECTS

Although the artists of ancient Egypt were the ones who gave ivory statuary its letters of nobility, it was during the Renaissance that it developed considerably. Its flourishing accompanied European expansion and reflects some of its most notable forms. Ivory objects are not only artifacts that reveal the transformations affecting various societies at that time; their history equates to that of the emergence of a new world which was also a consequence of its production. In their fusion of artistic skills and the market value of an increasingly rare and costly raw material, ivory objects played their part in the making of modernity. Their biography parallels the general and overall encounter of societies, of which they are at once witnesses and agents: they produce a new world more than they bear witness to a given culture. They are "world objects" whose manufacture transformed all those involved in it.

The history of the ivory trade and its metamorphoses makes it easier to grasp some of the geopolitical economics at stake: the name Côte d'Ivoire (Ivory Coast) is the French translation of the Portuguese name Costa do Marfim given by merchant sailors on their way to India that appears in late 17th-century Portuguese portolans. It is constituted by the entire coastline of what is today Côte d'Ivoire and a small part of that of Ghana, flanked to the west by the "Pepper Coast" (today Liberia) and to the east by the "Gold Coast" and the "Slave Coast" (Bight of Benin).

3 School of Raphael, *Hanno the Elephant*, after 1516, pen and brownish-black ink over traces of black chalk, with white highlights, on grayish-brown paper, 27.9 x 28.5 cm. Staatliche Museen zu Berlin, Kupferstichkabinett.

From the 15th century onwards, Portuguese mariners searching for a sea route to India landed for the first time in Africa in the region of Sierra Leone, the kingdom of Benin in present-day Nigeria, and the coasts of the kingdom of Kongo. One of the most important relationships forged by the Portu-guese was with the Edo people of the kingdom of Benin, with whom they exchanged the so-called manillas or copper bracelets, brass, cloth, and cowry shells for spices, enslaved people, and later ivory. Soon setting up trading-posts, the Portuguese were merchants rather than military men during these early explorations, gradually becoming part of everyday life at the courts of the West African kings. Observed by local artists, their daily life and customs were depicted in ivory carvings which in a sense themselves amount to ethnographic descriptions,[1] the fruit of an original local knowledge production system.

The in-depth study of the Afro-Portuguese ivories produced in regions of present-day Sierra Leone and Benin in the 16th and 17th centuries has improved our understanding of the social organization of these extraordinary coastal kingdoms, which, before collapsing in the wake of the transatlantic slave trade, flourished for a long time in the Gulf of Guinea.

As in any art work (and why would those created in Africa be any different?), there are pieces that result from a complex interplay of allusions, references, and influences. One prime example is the Sapi-Portuguese olifant (horn) (Fig. 4) carved with various scenes, now in the Musée du quai Branly in Paris. One scene is of a lion turning on a dragon, which must clearly reproduce a detail from a 15th- or 16th-century Florentine engraving, while another represents an elephant led on a chain and mounted by a mahout, the implication being that this is a working animal, though elephants have never been

domesticated in Africa. According to Ezio Bassani, the African artist was inspired by a drawing by Raphael or one of his followers in the Kupferstich-kabinett, Berlin (Fig. 3).[2] The author also contends that the Raphael drawing had been copied in Portugal for the specific purpose of serving as a model for the African ivory carver.

Terminating in a carved crocodile's head, another astonishing 16th-century Edo ivory from the kingdom of Benin, now in the collections of the Rautenstrauch-Joest-Museum in Cologne, depicts men dressed in the fashion of the 16th century, an astronomical instrument, and the coat-of-arms of the House of Aviz—the "Joanine Dynasty" of the kingdom of Portugal (1385–1580)—albeit with a number of errors in interpretation (Fig. 5).

These can then be considered as "historiated" objects: narrative vehicles whose carvings represent the history of the societies in which they originated. As can be seen on the more modern sculpture reproduced here (Fig. 6), the scenes depicted function analytically. These pictures were not copied from models: they describe situations. They simultaneously document and recount history—rather like the narrative brass or copper alloy plaques from the kingdom of Benin or the history appliques from

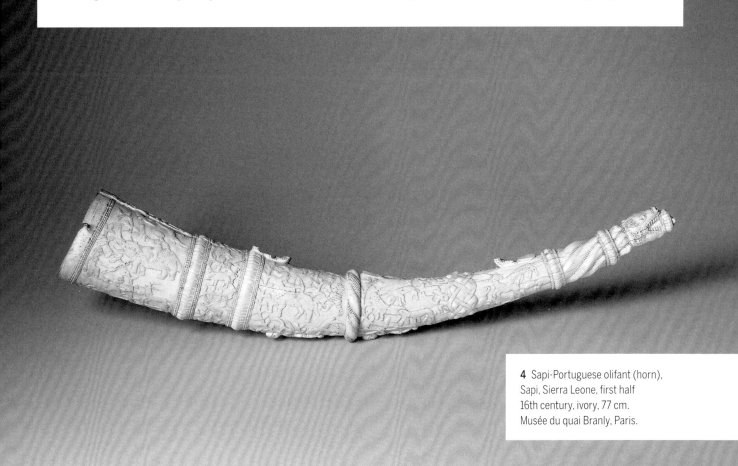

4 Sapi-Portuguese olifant (horn), Sapi, Sierra Leone, first half 16th century, ivory, 77 cm. Musée du quai Branly, Paris.

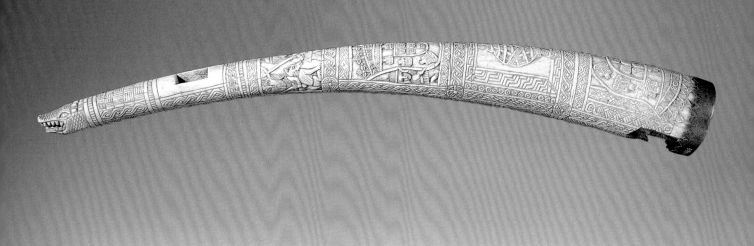

5 Ahoken olifant, Edo, Benin, Nigeria, 16th century, ivory with silver mount, 57 cm. Rauten-strauch-Joest Museum, Cologne.

the Dahome (Dahomey) court, and a host of other "texts" composed by societies that employ pictograms rather than letters.

The scenes on this late-19th-century artifact compose a picture of a society through images resulting from a critical analysis of the social context of the Loango region in the Kongo whence the artist who carved it may have come. Its sequences depict features of colonial trade in a specific area and demonstrate just how closely Europeans were observed by local carvers. Next to enslaved people, and what is surely a scene of forced labor, Western traders are represented reaching an agreement, smoking a pipe, or lighting a cigarette. It is interesting to note how, by the end of the 19th century, these Kongo ivory carvings were once again prized by European colonial agents, soldiers, and travelers. It was no longer the European aristocracy that ordered and/or collected them, but the colonial apparatus. They were already what came to be known as "souvenirs".

Today such objects present a quandary to ethnographic museums, which consider them unclassifiable, ethnically "mixed" and unauthentic. Seen as "impure", they are categorized as "tourist wares". Though fleetingly rescued from oblivion by Julius Lips in *The Savage Hits Back, or the White Man Through Native Eyes*,[3] they have since returned to obscurity. Though common in museum storerooms, to this day such objects remain little studied and infrequently exhibited.

A "MULTI-LOCAL" PRODUCTION

As early as the 16th century, these ivory objects were already being viewed as hybrid or impure, since they were the result of a collaboration and a market—part of a global history of exchange, they were contrasted with pure cultural expressions and "ethnographic objects".

The difficulties specialists encounter in assigning a place for these complex objects in their taxonomies determined how they are displayed in museums. Given that the set of taxonomies applied in ethnographic museums is based on the idea that there is an immediate correspondence between geographical space and cultural belonging, it becomes inapplicable when it comes to classifying an object that belongs to several places at the same time and whose production is due to an interaction inherent to changing societies, and not to cultural entities supposedly fixed and emerging from the "dawn of time", from the "untouched" and "authentic" world.

It thus appears that the history of the ivory trade and of the collection of non-European objects in ivory is that of a typical global object: its manufacture results from market forces, i.e. a field of interactions designed to relate supply to demand. In workshops set up for the purpose as early as the 15th century, craftsmen in Africa produced objects to satisfy orders from Europe, such as the famous salt shakers and spoons commissioned by merchants to be dispatched to European patrons, a number of which can be seen in the ethnological collections in the Ethnologisches Museum in Berlin, among the objects in the Grünes Gewölbe in Dresden, and in the Musée du quai Branly in Paris. Once in Europe, they were treated as luxury items and decorated aristocratic tables or adorned princes' "cabinets of curiosities", in the company of other natural or handmade "wonders". An overnight success among collectors of the nobility, these objects gave rise to a market for non-European objects that were "ethnographic" before the term was coined. Their trace can already be found, for instance, in the 1553 inventory of the Medici collection. With the intensification of the slave trade, however, Afro-Portuguese ivories ceased to be collector's items and vanished from princely banquets and collections of curios. Returning to prominence in the ethnographic market of the late 19th century, they once more disappear from view with the development in France, Germany, and Britain of museum collection guidelines, and, more generally, of an ethnology that favored what were seen as "pure" and authentic artifacts and subject matter.

ETHNOGRAPHY AND THE PROBLEM OF HISTORY

As the French anthropologist Alban Bensa has written: "The human sciences have always striven to address the historical situation in which we have our being. For its part, however, anthropology has gradually developed a knowledge based on timeless synchrony. This trend culminated in Lévi-Strauss's structural anthropology, at the cost of denying reality."[4] One may sometimes wonder whether the function of ethnographic museums designed to reflect anthropological methods of collection and analysis has ever been to display objects representative of a world that actually exists. The problems encountered by this type of museum in the present day have arisen because it reflects a world that never existed or no longer exists: emerging in a period of colonial expansion when Europe started encountering the "other" (to admire, subdue, or exterminate it), the ethnographic museum now needs to reinvent itself. For today this famous "other" is no longer somewhere else but in the city, and no longer an alien but a citizen, enjoying the same rights and participating in social life in the same way, by and large, as the European. Exactly the same problem arises with respect to the ivory objects with which we are concerned here: they render porous the partition between "us" and "them". Made, literally, by several hands of different color, Afro-Portuguese ivory objects were a joint effort. They are collaborative objects, the result of an interaction that shows that ancient African societies are historical societies that are part of a common history.

This global dimension has proved uncomfortable for museums of ethnography, so that, conceptually at a loss, they all too often skirt round its complexities. Preoccupied with the encyclopedic representation of a range of cultures—supposedly as numerous and distinct from each other as so many species of plants—ethnographic museums find it hard to come to terms with this type of hybrid object, which, though never less than fascinating, does not appear to them to be "authentic". The question, therefore, is whether most objects in such collections—gathered together at a time when societies were already in extensive contact with each other—can document the history of these relationships instead of some assumed cultural specificity of which they would be an artistic expression.

In the light of some specific examples, the focus turns to the responsibility of museums. It primarily consists in telling the complex history of "mixed" objects that resemble what have been termed "*sémiophores*",[5] as well as in bringing out strata of narrative that the objects convey above and beyond their material nature. The goal is to demonstrate how an object characterized as ethnographic translates (and this may equally be through what it conceals) the nature of the relationship between one society and others—the crucial question on which the museum of ethnography is based. The object expresses a form of hierarchy between societies by making *visible* a temporal order in which the present cannot be divorced from the past, so that instead they inform one other, fixing for all eternity a situation that was, in truth, contingent.

As has been seen above, accounting for the importance of the historical dimension of the social facts that produce objects means reconfiguring the time-honored structures of ethnographic museums accustomed to extracting objects from their time-frame rather than situating them in their historical complexity. The result of a co-production among various agents, Afro-Portuguese ivories, by showing that there has long been an "us" within the "other", also force museums to redefine, or even jettison, their definition of "authenticity". As they are not the product of some "untouched" society—a notion that persists despite attempts at inclusivity—they run counter to the guiding principle of the ethnographic museum, whose structure is still based on the affirmation of cultural difference, for which objects act as witnesses or even as evidence. Now, if the exotic has become Georges Perec's *endotic* (the "everyday", the "ordinary"), the precept of the supposedly cultural nature of the difference between people loses all meaning, since the self is the other and vice versa. This minor conceptual shift has sparked the wholesale revision of the display policy of museums, to the point of challenging their very existence in their present form. The treatment of this type of object, together with objects of similar nature, should usher in a new paradigm for museums, transforming them from encyclopedic projects whose aim is to exhibit cultural variation in a sort of three-dimensional catalogue of objects into a dynamic perspective on change materialized by objects of exchange such as these Afro-Portuguese ivory carvings. Destined to replace the storehouse of "cultural species" on the model of epistemological precedents in biology, museums would thus treat of the history of exchange and diversification. "World-objects" are not just pure expressions of a form of cultural alterity, but at the same time agents and the results of exchange relationships, peaceful or violent. So the Afro-Portuguese ivories confront us starkly with a problem posed by most objects in ethnographic collections, a problem prompting museums to rethink their approaches and emerge from their ivory towers. Museums are therefore called upon to become something more than ivory towers in which objects are preserved, and instead theaters in which objects converse with each other and with us. The museum is thus to be a place not only of conservation but also of conversation. A place whose mission is to create stories, narratives, and testimonials inspired by "crossroad objects": a forum for storytelling, for the unusual and the singular. No longer a locus of scientific order, museums could then bear witness to the cacophony of our world, allowing narrative strata to rise up in a chorus of innumerable voices. Within this amazing concert of world-objects, the ivory carvings at the heart of the present essay would be sure to occupy a place of honor.

1   Suzanne Preston Blier, "Imaging Otherness in Ivory: African Portrayals of the Portuguese ca. 1492", *The Art Bulletin,* vol. 75, no. 3 (Sept. 1993), pp. 375–396.
2   Ezio Bassani, "Un dessin de Raphaël copié par un sculpteur africain", in idem, *Ivoires d'Afrique dans les anciennes collections françaises,* Arles: Actes Sud, 2008, pp. 71–75.
3   Julius Lips, *The Savage Hits Back,* New Haven: Yale University Press, 1937.
4   Alban Bensa, *Pour une anthropologie à taille humaine – Entretien mené par Bertrand Richard,* Paris: Les éditions Textuel, 2010.
5   Krzysztof Pomian, *Collectionneurs, amateurs et curieux. Paris, Venise: xvie-xviiie siècle,* Paris: Gallimard, 1987.

6 Carved vessel, Loango region, Congo, ca. 1880–1890, ivory, 17 cm. The Metropolitan Museum of Art, New York.

Contributors

NICHOLAS J. CONARD is a professor of early pre-history and Quaternary ecology at Eberhard Karls University Tübingen and scientific director of the Urgeschichtliches Museum Blaubeuren. In addition, he is the director of the Senckenberg Centre for Human Evolution and Paleoenvironment. The mammoth-ivory figurines from his excavations in caves in the Swabian Jura number among the oldest works of art in the world.

KATHY CURNOW currently works at the Department of Art and Design, Cleveland State University. She does research in Cultural History, History of Art, and Cultural Anthropology. Her current projects include the art history of the Benin Kingdom, as well as the art of the Igala, Nupe, and Itsekiri. The 15th-/16th-century Afro-Portuguese ivories were her dissertation focus and continue as an area of research.

HARTMUT DORGERLOH has been the General Director and Chairman of the Board of the Humboldt Forum Foundation in the Berlin Palace since 2018. From 2002 to 2018 he was general director of the Stiftung Preussische Schlösser und Gärten Berlin-Brandenburg (Prussian Palaces and Gardens Foundation). An art historian and cultural manager, he has also taught at the Humboldt-Universität zu Berlin as an honorary professor since 2004.

HARALD FLOSS is a prehistorian at Eberhard Karls University Tübingen. His specialty is the earliest human history and the origins of art and culture. Ivory is an important material for him, as he has studied the roughly 40,000-year-old figurines from caves in the Swabian Jura. He is also interested in the relationship between man and animal in the Ice Age.

LAURA GOLDENBAUM studied art history and visual cultures as well as archeology in Berlin and Rome. She earned her doctorate in Florence and Berlin, and since 2016 has worked at Berlin's Humboldt Forum as an academic consultant in the General Director's office. She is currently working on issues of visual anthropology and media history, as well as on the aesthetic impact and history of reception in global art history.

SARAH M. GUÉRIN is Assistant Professor of Medieval Art at the University of Pennsylvania, and an expert on the production and use of medieval ivory carvings, as well as the long-distance, interregional trade routes traversed by elephant tusks. Her book, *French Gothic Ivories: Material Theologies and the Sculptor's Craft*, is forthcoming with Cambridge University Press.

EBOA ITONDO is a cultural historian and curator. In her scholarly work she devotes herself to material culture and the interrelationship between design, craftsmanship, and popular art. As a Black German, she is familiar with the challenges of intercultural communication. At the Humboldt Forum, she engages with these themes in the context of ethnological exhibition practice.

ASHER JAY is a *National Geographic* explorer turned entrepreneur and key advisor to a venture capital growth fund focused on SaaS, AI, renewables, smart farming, and eco aquaculture, as well as an international adventurer and public figure whose career arc has taken her from fashion designing to campaigning against blood ivory. Her multimedia work pursues a singular purpose: to solve for a sustainable, holistic future that fosters tangible coexistence between humanity and wild.

GRIT KELLER has studied history and French philology. At Humboldt Forum she is the curator of education and mediation and part of the curatorial team for *Terrible Beauty: Elephant–Human–Ivory*. She has created projects on political-history education, exhibitions, and publications at the Jewish Museum Berlin, the Haus der Geschichte Baden-Württemberg in Stuttgart, the Gedenkstätte Berlin-Hohenschön-hausen, and elsewhere.

LYDIA KITUNGULU has been employed as Senior Exhibitions Designer at the National Museums of Kenya (NMK) since 1994. She has been actively involved as lead designer, exhibitions developer, researcher, content developer, and text editor for several museum exhibitions both nationally and internationally. In her essay for this publication, she seeks to reveal the contestations in the display and storage of ivory at the NMK using the Nairobi National Museum as a highlight.

ROBERT KLESS is the country director for IFAW (International Fund for Animal Welfare) in Germany. He is responsible for national and international partnerships and projects. His primarily focuses are on trade in wild animals and the protection of elephants and their habitats in cooperation with the local populace. For him, ivory today stands for the poaching and extermination of elephants.

LARS-CHRISTIAN KOCH is Director of the Ethnological Museum and of the Museum for Asian Art Berlin and Head of Collections at the Humboldt Forum Berlin. He is Professor for Ethnomusicology at the University of Cologne and at the University of the Arts in Berlin. His research focuses among other topics on North Indian Raga music, organology with a special focus on instrument manufacturing, Buddhist music, and popular music.

KHYNE U MAR is a veterinarian who set up elephant research in Myanmar where she did groundbreaking research on captive timber elephants. Currently she is a guest lecturer for Wild Animal Health and Wild Animal Biology courses (jointly organized by the Zoological Society of London and the Royal Veterinary College of London). She is also a consultant veterinarian for Veterinarian International (USA).

DAVID McKEE was born in Devon and studied at Plymouth Art College. He has written and illustrated over 200 picture books and has penned a number of children's classics including *King Rollo*, *Mr Benn*, *Not Now Bernard*, and *Elmer the Patchwork Elephant*. Elmer remains one of the most iconic and widely read children's book series of all time, selling over 10 million copies worldwide since it was first published in 1989.

S. MAREK MULLER is an Assistant Professor of Rhetoric at Florida Atlantic University. She is interested in the intersections of human and animal oppression, particularly in institutional contexts such as "post"-colonial museums. She hopes that readers will be left feeling somewhat uncomfortable at her essay's morbid conclusion about imperialism, ivory collection, and the visual politics of the macabre.

ALBERTO SAVIELLO has a doctorate in art history and is an assistant lecturer at Goethe University in Frankfurt am Main. As a freelance collaborator, he was part of the curatorial team for the exhibition *Terrible Beauty: Elephant–Human–Ivory*. Among his research interests are the origin and function of ivory artefacts in transcultural and transreligious negotiations.

NANETTE SNOEP is an ethnologist and has been director of the Rautenstrauch-Joest-Museum - Kulturen der Welt in Cologne since 2019. Previously, she was head of the historical collection of the Musée du quai Branly in Paris (1998–2014) and director of the State Ethnographic Collections of Saxony (2015–2018). In addition to teaching African art history at the École du Louvre and the Université Nanterre in Paris, she has curated several international exhibitions.

KATHARINA TRUMP is a biologist and expert on poaching and illegal wildlife trade at (WWF) World Wide Fund for Nature Germany. In her work she specializes in the reduction of poaching and especially demand, consideration of underlying social and cultural factors, and international political discourse. Her chief specialisms are African elephants and rhinoceroses.

FRITZ VOLLRATH is an evolutionary biologist who specializes in spiders and silks in his research lab in Oxford; he also works with the charity Save the Elephants on the management, protection, and preservation of elephants, with fieldwork primarily in Laikipia and Samburu, Kenya.

AI WEIWEI is a Chinese artist renowned for making strong aesthetic statements that resonate with timely issues across today's geopolitical world. He uses a wide range of media as expressions of new ways for his audiences to examine society and its values. He is the recipient of the 2015 Ambassador of Conscience Award from Amnesty International, and the 2012 Václav Havel Prize for Creative Dissent from the Human Rights Foundation.

DOROTHEE WENNER is a freelance filmmaker, writer, and curator at Berlin's International Film Festival and elsewhere, as well as a member of the African Movie Academy Awards, Lagos, Nigeria. For Humboldt Forum she curated the film program for the special exhibition *Terrible Beauty: Elephant–Human–Ivory*.

SIBYLLE WOLF is a scientific member and coordinator at the Senckenberg Centre for Human Evolution and Palaeoenvironment at Eberhard Karls University Tübingen. She works with archaeological artifacts made from mammoth ivory and studies the production sequence of ivory objects and tools of the Upper Palaeolithic. Her main specialism are personal ornaments and their meaning, as well as the analysis of female statuettes of the Upper Palaeolithic.

Photo credits

Imprint

Published by the Stiftung Humboldt Forum im Berliner Schloss

This book is appearing in connection with the exhibition

Terrible Beauty:
Elephant–Human–Ivory

at the Humboldt Forum Berlin, 2021

An exhibition by the Stiftung Humboldt Forum im Berliner Schloss in cooperation with the Staatliche Museen zu Berlin and the Museum für Naturkunde Berlin, curated by Grit Keller, Alberto Saviello, and Daniel Tyradellis, with the collaboration of Anika Winge, after a concept by Raffael Dedo Gadebusch. In collaboration with the National Museums of Kenya.

Exhibition project team:
Antje Brörmann, Lydia Gulan Czelisch, Anke Daemgen, Katharina Flachs, Noelle von Galen, Cora Hegewald, Eboa Itondo, Johanna Kapp, Nathalie Küchen, Julia Kull, Friedrun Portele-Anyangbe, Leonie Seitz, Wolfger Stumpfe, Maike Voelkel, Constanze Wicke, Anika Winge

Publication project management:
Alberto Saviello

Concept:
Albia Consul, Raffael Dedo Gadebusch, Eboa Itondo, Grit Keller, Alberto Saviello, Wolfger Stumpfe

Editing:
Alberto Saviello, Susanne Müller-Wolff

Picture editing:
Barbara Martinkat

The Stiftung Humboldt Forum sincerely thanks for their professional assistance and support:
The authors, the lenders, City-Grundschule, the Bund für Naturschutz (BfN), the IFAW – International Fund for Animal Welfare, Save the Elephants, the WWF Deutschland (World Wide Fund for Nature), the Zollamt Flughafen Berlin Brandenburg, and Susan Arndt, Gregor-Donatus Bader, Mima F. Batalovic, Edda Behringer-Rosswinkel, Jens Burk, David Butcher, Nicholas J. Conard, Eva Doilezalek, Eva Dolezel, Harald Floss, Thomas Friedländer, Grace Ge Gabriel, Andreas Haesler, Ulrich Halder (†), Godfrey Harris, Nadja Haumberger, Wulf Hein, Holzer Kobler Architectures, Nadine Huber, Anika Janas, Asher Jay, Lydia Kitungulu, Patrick Krüger, Beate Kunst, Purity Lakara, Martina Lindemeier and the pupils of 3b, Cheryl Lo, Jochen Mannhart, Khyne U Mar, Gerd Mevissen, Anahita Mittertrainer, Agostino Moru, Patson Nkhata, Juliane Noth, Osman Örs, Martina Papiro, Werner Pich, Bernhard Röck, Avionam Shalem, Bernd Spachmann, Ian Stephen, Ulrich Struck, Bartek Szostakowski, Katharina Trump, Albrecht Wiedman, Roland Wilson, Sibylle Wolf, Inserk Yang, Stefan Ziegler, Jürgen Zimmerer.

We are also grateful to the staff of the Stiftung Humboldt Forum im Berliner Schloss and all those not named here who contributed to the success of this project.

www.humboldtforum.org

Project direction, Hirmer Verlag:
Kerstin Ludolph

Project management:
Silke Körber, Berlin

Copy editing:
Chris Murray

Translation from the German:
Russell Stockman

Layout and typesetting:
Sabine Frohmader

Lithography:
Reproline mediateam, Unterföhring

Paper:
Magno Volume 150 g/qm

Type:
Baskerville URW, Benton Sans

Printing and binding:
Appl aprinta druck, Wemding

Printed in Germany

The Deutsche Nationalbibliothek lists this publication in the Deutsche National-bibliografie, detailed bibliographical data are available at www.dnb.de

ISBN 978-3-7774-3363-9

www.hirmerpublishers.com